West Side Story

Cultural Perspectives on an American Musical

ELIZABETH A. WELLS

THE SCARECROW PRESS, INC.
Lanham • Toronto • Plymouth, UK
2011

Published by Scarecrow Press, Inc.
A wholly owned subsidiary of The Rowman & Littlefield Publishing Group, Inc.
4501 Forbes Boulevard, Suite 200, Lanham, Maryland 20706
http://www.scarecrowpress.com

Estover Road, Plymouth PL6 7PY, United Kingdom

British Library Cataloguing in Publication Information Available

Library of Congress Cataloging-in-Publication Data

Wells, Elizabeth Anne, 1964–
  West side story : cultural perspectives on an American musical / Elizabeth A. Wells.
    p. cm.
  Includes bibliographical references, discography, and index.
  ISBN 978-0-8108-7666-8 (cloth : alk. paper)
  1. Bernstein, Leonard, 1918–1990. West Side story. 2. Musicals—United States—
History and criticism. 3. Popular culture—New York (State)—New York. I. Title.
  ML410.B566W45 2011
    782.1'4—dc22   2010020727

Printed in the United States of America

To my family

Contents

Illustrations

Acknowledgments

As I finish this manuscript shortly after *West Side Story* returned triumphantly to Broadway, I realize how similar the completion of a book is to putting the final touches on the production of a musical. It also is a work of collaboration, and no one link is more or less important than any other, even if the finished product appears to be the work of only a few, not many. In particular, this research would not have been possible without the help of a number of libraries, archives, and special collections. I would like to thank first and foremost the staff at the Sibley Music Library of the Eastman School in Rochester, New York, especially Mary Wallace Davidson, Jim Farrington, David Coppen, and the interlibrary loans office staff. Mark Horowitz and the librarians of the music department and especially the Leonard Bernstein Archive at the Library of Congress in Washington, D.C., made every effort to help me in my research, and to them I am greatly indebted. I also thank the librarians of the New York Public Library theater and dance divisions, especially Charles Perrier of the Jerome Robbins Archive. I would also like to thank Marie Carter and Charlie Harmon of the Bernstein Foundation for their assistance in locating and making available material relating to *West Side Story*. Christopher Pennington and the trustees of the Robbins Rights Trust graciously allowed me to look at Jerome Robbins's materials relating to the musical and to quote from them. I am indebted to the State Historical Society of Wisconsin in Madison, who gave me access to material in the Stephen Sondheim Collection. I would also

like to acknowledge Peter Higham and Hannah McNally of the Mount Allison
University Music Library and the interlibrary loans staff at Mount Allison for
providing assistance in the collection of this research, especially in the final
stages of writing. The Raymond Mander and Joe Mitchenson Theatre Collection in Kent, England, very kindly provided me with material relating to the
London production of *West Side Story*. I would also like to thank Peggy Schein
and Don McCormick of the Rodgers and Hammerstein Archive for assistance
with recorded material pertaining to my research. My thanks also go to Renée
Camus and Kellie Hagan, my editors at Scarecrow, for their careful and kindly
diligence in bringing the manuscript to completion.

This research has been generously funded by the Presser Foundation, the
Eastman School of Music, Eastman Opera Theatre, SYM, Mount Allison University, and the Susan B. Anthony Institute for Gender and Women's Studies.
John Sheridan and Walter Zimmermann kindly put me up in New York and
made the research process both possible and pleasant, and I would like to
thank Alicia and Charles Kopfstein in Washington for doing the same there.

Every effort was made to identify and reach the rights owners of certain
unpublished documents—letters, rehearsal notes, and tapes. I will happily
acknowledge additional permissions in any future editions of this book. My
thanks to the Robbins Rights Trust, Naxos Records, Schott Music, Sony Music, The Aaron Copland Fund for Music, the estate of Fred Fehl, Chris Paul
Harman, Paul Nolan, Harold Prince, Arthur Laurents, Alfred Music Publishing, Boosey & Hawkes, Stephen Sondheim, the New York Public Library,
the Library of Congress, the Leonard Bernstein Foundation, the New York
Public Library for the Performing Arts, and the Harvard Theatre Collection
for allowing permission to quote or reproduce unpublished and published
materials.

Thanks go to Rob Haskins, Marjorie Roth, Carol Moen, Michaela Harkins,
Jeremy Grimshaw, Randall Hall, Ellen Koskoff, Robert Fink, Joel Galand,
Daniel Albright, and Tim Scheie, and especially Ralph Locke, who unfailingly
saw every light at the end of every tunnel. I would also like to acknowledge
Martin Scherzinger, Patrick Macey, Gretchen Wheelock, Kerala Snyder,
Dean Bruce Jacobs, and Robert Wason, and my colleagues at Mount Allison
University, especially Edmund Dawe, Bonnie Johnson, Jim and Bindy Code,
Penny and Jamie Mark, Stephen Runge, and Margaret and Alex Fancy. Those

who supported me in mind, body, and spirit were Jean Pedersen, Russell, Lynne Sharp, Charles Emmrys, Meghan Barrett, and Sonam Targee.

Special thanks go to those who provided continuous support and from whom I learned the most about the world of musical theater performance: Steve Daigle, Steve Crowley, Anthony Maida, and Nic Minetor of Eastman Opera Theatre. For advice and support on my work on this project and Bernstein scholarship in general, I would like to thank Steve Swayne, Paul Laird, Jim Lovensheimer, Rose Rosengard Subotnik, Carol Oja, and the editors of *Echo*. Particularly I would like to thank all those who painstakingly read drafts of this work in progress: Adam Ricci, Kim Denis, Dale Chapman, Charles Hiroshi Garrett, John Sheridan, Cecilia Sun, Jennie Wood, and especially Stephen McClatchie, Nancy Vogan, and Kevin Stockall, who provided spiritual and editorial guidance above and beyond the call of duty. Greatest thanks should go to my able research assistant, Andrea Warren, who provided technical, editorial, and emotional support and was my right hand during the final stages of this project.

My family, especially my mother, Mary Wells, Carol Wells, Linda Wells, John McGuigan, Jerome Madden, and Debbie and Wayne Johnson, were of special help in the completion of this project, which would not have been possible without them. Lastly, I would like to thank Harold Prince, Arthur Laurents, and Stephen Sondheim for sharing their memories and thoughts about this work and for graciously allowing me to quote from their work.

Permissions

1

"There's a Place for Us"

Reflections on an American Musical

I don't like to theorize about how or if the show changed future musicals. For me what was important about *West Side Story* was in our *aspiration*. I wanted to find out at that time how far we, as "long-haired artists," could go in bringing our crafts and talents to a musical. Why did we have to do it separately and elsewhere? Why did Lenny have to write an opera, Arthur a play, me a ballet? Why couldn't we, in aspiration, try to bring our deepest talents together to the commercial theater in this work? That was the true *gesture* of the show.

—*Jerome Robbins, quoted in* "*Dramatists Guild Round Table Series, Landmark Symposium: West Side Story,*" Dramatists Guild Quarterly *(1985): 11–25*

Among the many legends of the New York stage, a special place is reserved for the Broadway flop. Entire books have been devoted to the subject; reading about scathing reviews, walk-out audiences, and failing box office receipts offers prurient delight to some and sleepless nights to others.[1] Despite the lip service paid to the importance of artistic integrity, originality, integration, or the power of the star, many musicals boasting quality in any and all of these areas have still fallen onto the ash heap of history, an ash heap much deeper than the analogous repository for the less successful works of Western classical music.[2] Whereas art music has remained carefully preserved through the efforts of librarians and archivists, and pop and jazz live on through their primary medium, recording, there are few who keep a candle lit for the failures of the

Broadway stage. No doubt Stephen Sondheim, arguably the towering figure in American musical theater in the last decades of the century, will be remembered, and not for the number of performances his works garnered, but for their artistic seriousness.[3] Indeed, even for the mature Sondheim, some shows have not had long runs, and it is a great surprise that *West Side Story*, his early break as a young lyricist, was not among them. Not only could it have been a significant commercial disaster, *West Side Story* could very well have been one of the worst musicals ever written. Our familiarity with the work makes it difficult to imagine the dubious qualities of the original concept: based on a regional and topical subject which would become quickly dated, exploiting a Hispanic musical style which was already overused and stereotyped, and written by four privileged middle-class men who, as Sondheim drily put it, "had never even met a Puerto Rican," this dark and tragic Broadway show about working-class juvenile delinquents would *neither* be funny *nor* attempt to deal analytically with social ills.[4] Even the original title (*Gangway!*) and the original setting (warring Catholics and Jews in a modern-day *Romeo and Juliet* story) held little promise for commercial or artistic success. In addition, the show would feature no stars, and the cast—consisting primarily of dancers—might be inexperienced kids pulled from the streets of New York (if the New York press was to be believed), not from dance rehearsal halls. The score, written by a classical music conductor, would be dissonant and fiendishly difficult to play and sing and would include—of all things—a fugue. The teenagers, whose dialogue was written by a middle-aged Jewish playwright, would speak in an invented street slang, uttering lines like "womb to tomb" and "cracko Jacko." The backers' meetings continually and repeatedly failed to attract investors for producer Cheryl Crawford, who finally dumped the project shortly before rehearsals were to begin. It is no surprise that no one thought this show would succeed. The question then remains, why did it? How did a show destined for commercial and artistic failure become one of the most successful, beloved, and iconic musicals of the century, paying off its original investors (once Harold Prince and Robert Griffith were able to secure them) 640 percent within the first fifteen years alone?[5] And, more importantly, how has this work carved itself a place in American culture, as has almost no other musical?

Indeed, within the canon of even the most wildly successful Broadway musicals *West Side Story* seems to hold a special place. William Weber, writing on the history of musical canon formation, identifies three primary kinds of canon: scholarly, performing, and pedagogical.[6] That *West Side Story* is included in two primary music history textbooks, the Peter J. Burkholder *A History of Western Music* and Mark Evan Bonds's *A History of Music in Western Culture*, suggests that the musical's prominence within popular culture is echoed in the selection of works considered by musicologists to be important to music histories focusing primarily on a classical tradition.[7] That Indiana University staged a production in the 2009–2010 season suggests that the work is considered serious enough to attract support in institutions where high standards of both musical research and musical performance are valued, including it in scholarly, performance, and pedagogical canons. Within the scholarly realm, the work has started to garner increased attention within a burgeoning field of musical theater scholarship. And, at this writing, a successful revival on Broadway (directed by original playwright Arthur Laurents) suggests that *West Side Story* has suffered no overexposure in its fifty-plus-year history and continues to lure Broadway audiences away from other shows that boast substantially greater production values, bigger stars, and more widely popular musical styles.

Despite this notoriety, however, *West Side Story* has as yet to earn a serious, full-length musicological study. Surprisingly, it is not alone. Musical theater in this mold (involving a strong directorial or choreographic element) falls more naturally within the purview of theater or dance studies, and it is these fields that have contributed most to the scholarly literature on this work.[8] The highly collaborative nature of the genre, its lack of one governing authorial voice, and the number of fundamental changes that may befall it over the course of a production history (as was the case with Bernstein's *Candide*) make it difficult for scholars to apprehend one definitive "text," let alone an urtext. More recent scholarship has approached musical theater through individual-work studies, like Tim Carter's monograph on *Oklahoma!* and bruce mcclung's study of *Lady in the Dark*, or has taken more broad perspectives on musical theater history and how a methodology might be constructed to deal with its complexities.[9] The considerable challenges posed by collaborative theater have meant that the relatively few musicologists who initially ventured into this territory were compelled to forge new methodological paths. The collaborative process demands the waiving of imagined inalienable rights of the composer and the immutable "work."[10] As well, the American musical theater poses special challenges for the music analyst. Standing anywhere from an array of songs and dance numbers scattered throughout a dramatic vehicle (*Anything Goes, A Funny Thing Happened on the Way to the Forum, A Chorus Line*) to an integrated symphonic-scale score (*Porgy and Bess, West Side Story, Sweeney Todd*), musical theater works suggest no one approach that can adequately address the multitude of styles, genres, and functions of music within one or between several musicals. In these yet-early days of musical theater scholarship, a plethora of approaches and methodologies have sought to address these large questions that musicals raise. Geoffrey Block has discussed canon formation within the repertoire, and Clum, Wolf, and Miller have brought gay and lesbian perspectives on characterization and audiences, which have contextualized musicals within cultural space.[11] Promising interpretive approaches on a larger body of musical theater works have emerged from Raymond Knapp (in his recent *The American Musical and the Formation of National Identity*, 2005).[12] Knapp combines a study of music and lyrics in selected important musicals in the Broadway tradition with a close reading of ethnicity, class, and difference within America and shows how these musicals function to reflect and contextualize national identity. Stephen Banfield's monograph on Sondheim's musicals presents a detailed and analytically eclectic study of each of the composer's major theater works, marshaling an impressive if occasionally daunting array of approaches, from critical and literary theory to Schenkerian-inspired analyses.[13] In the last few years, musical theater research has expanded further, providing the field with a plethora of genre and individual-work studies that have challenged or expanded methodologies on offer from the first generation of serious musical theater scholarship. Walsh and Platt's 2003 *Musical Theatre and American Culture* submits a large number of musicals (mostly from the Golden Age) to sociological and cultural critique, an approach not unlike Knapp's and one that promises to open up the field to even wider methodological and more rigorous critical apparatuses than have been obtained in some earlier scholarship.[14]

Perhaps not surprisingly, a series of books written by authors with some musical theater credentials (Mark Grant's *The Rise and Fall of the Broadway Musical*, 2004, and Bruce Kirle's *Unfinished Showbusiness*, 2005) have offered some of the most cogent and penetrating looks at the large-scale issues and trajectories of musical theater over most of the past century, bringing a deeper knowledge base to the study of this interdisciplinary artwork than musicologists or historians alone have done.[15] Scott McMillin, in his recent *The Musi-cal as Drama*, seemed to bring musicology full circle from the days of Joseph Kerman's *Opera as Drama*, arguing for a reassessment of musical theater that recognizes its theatrical and dramatic power while raising larger questions as to how that power is achieved and received by audiences and critics alike.[16]

Research on *West Side Story* in particular is as eclectic as the work itself. Although Joan Peyser and Keith Garebian have conducted preliminary re-search on the genesis of the piece,[17] documents only recently available in the Bernstein archive of the Library of Congress (along with material in the New York Public Library and the State Historical Society of Wisconsin) yield a more detailed picture of its conception and tortuous journey to the stage. Por-tions of Geoffrey Block's *Enchanted Evenings*, Joseph Swain's *The Broadway Musical*, and D. A. Miller's *Place for Us* treat the work in significant detail.[18] Miller, a professor of English and Comparative Literature, subtitled his cul-tural history of gay men and the musical "Essay on the Broadway Musical," and it falls more generally under the rubric of queer studies than musicology per se, taking its place next to a similar work by Wayne Koestenbaum, *The Queen's Throat* (in the latter case, a cultural commentary on gay men and op-era).[19] In a somewhat different vein, a collection edited by Mary E. Williams, *Readings on "West Side Story,"* is meant specifically as a primer for high school performers and audiences.[20] This wide variety of approaches and intended au-diences to whom the commentaries are directed speaks not only to the range of approaches taken to musicals but to the place of *West Side Story* in popular culture and the diversity of its audiences. My approach to *West Side Story* is informed by these precedents, exploring the work primarily as musical and cultural expression.

This study seeks in part to answer the question of how something that could have been so bad became so good, and a great part of that answer lies in the collaborative process, which allowed none of the creators to do what they re-ally wanted. Jerome Robbins, who originally conceived, choreographed, and directed the musical, envisioned a modern ballet with words. For Leonard Bernstein, the show was a shot at the major American "opera" that could be understood and appreciated by anyone,[21] and for playwright Arthur Laurents, it was an opportunity to bring social relevance to and graft archetypes of con-temporary urban life onto a Shakespearean classic. Although the younger Ste-phen Sondheim and Harold Prince seemingly had less at stake than their more illustrious counterparts, *West Side Story* would prove their first joint project and left an indelible mark on their future collaborations, now counted among the most important of our time.[22] So, although Robbins credits the act of collaboration with the work's success, the real "gesture" of the show might well have been competition and compromise. Sondheim's reserve pulled Bernstein away from overdone sentimentality while Bernstein's emotional openness prevented Sondheim from turning every song into a fascinating but crystal-cool psychological profile.[23] The young actors stopped it from becoming an opera by forcing Bernstein to write music that they could actually sing while dancing. Jerome Robbins prevented Bernstein from writing too symphonically by dictating the lengths and moods of the dance segments, and he also stopped playwright Arthur Laurents from getting too preachy and political by keeping the spoken dialogue exceptionally brief. Harold Prince toned down the violence. And no one could really stop Jerome Robbins from doing anything, but having an intricate and interesting score and clever lyrics allowed the show to expand beyond simply an ambitious modern ballet.

Most of us have gained our familiarity with this *West Side Story* through a number of different sources and so our reception of the musical becomes another stage in this unfolding process, a further collaboration between us and the various, sometimes competing, versions, which result in a collective, composite work. These include, most prominently, stage performances, although debatably fewer people have seen it live than in recorded formats; Bernstein's dance suite (*Symphonic Dances from West Side Story*), which exists as an orchestral standard in the classical repertory; the film version, which was central to its dissemination; various recordings of the show's song and dance numbers; or the composer's heavily operatic recording and the choreographer's all-danced *West Side Story Suite*, both valedictory statements that attempted to wrest each creator's work decisively and definitively from the collaborative process. Most pervasively, though, our knowledge of *West Side Story* springs from and in some cases is reduced to simply the songs themselves, which are so well known in both American and international culture—whether from these recordings or from the uncountable renderings by other performing artists—that they need no original context for ready identification. That the songs stand alone on their own aesthetic merits remains deeply ironic, considering that the score was dubbed "unsingable" by Columbia Records, Bernstein's record company, in the late 1950s.[24]

Not forty years later, a CD compilation entitled *The Songs from "West Side Story"* (see figure 1.1) attests to the work's enduring, extratheatrical life and seems to repudiate original charges of "unsingability." In the collection, musical numbers from the score are subjected to a wide variety of late-century popular styles by various urban recording artists. Divorced completely from their original context, the songs have become a kind of commentary on the contemporary American metropolis. It is difficult for us, then, to imagine this as a new work never heard or seen before. So many of the things that made *West Side Story* unique have become so commonplace today, both in classical and Broadway worlds, that we cannot fully experience its novelty and innovations for its own time, the late 1950s.

Several aspects of the original *West Side Story* either pioneered new methodologies or varied the usual pattern for Broadway productions. It was among the first shows for which Harold Prince claims he used voice miking. Even spoken stage plays are miked in the twenty-first century, but during this period actors were generally expected to sing and talk loudly enough to project into a theater.[25] It was reportedly the first Broadway show to employ a professional lighting designer, whereas before this the lighting would have been set by the scenic designer. As it was, there were usually only two different light

FIGURE 1.1
Cover art, *The Songs of "West Side Story."* Courtesy of Sony Music Entertainment.

levels: lower for dialogue and higher for songs and dances. *West Side Story* had an unprecedentedly long rehearsal period: eight weeks, which would have been costly given that performers had to be paid and rehearsal space secured. It also includes one of the shortest books of any Broadway musical.[26] This was striking, especially in the context of the Rodgers and Hammerstein model, then the standard for both composers and audiences. According to that model, substantial dialogue scenes set up dramatic and emotional situations that were then expanded in and separated by musical numbers. In contrast, *West Side Story* allowed dance to mediate where song or book would previously have carried the dramatic action.[27] The show was also novel in that the creators intentionally hired young, little-known singers and dancers, no stars to promote public interest or ticket sales. When it went on the road, instead of picking up a pit band in each city on the tour, several core members of the orchestra would be flown ahead to rehearse the difficult score with the new musicians before the rest of the company arrived. (This was in the days when companies normally traveled by train with sets and costumes in tow.)[28]

Moreover, the 1961 film version of *West Side Story* also included some significant variations from the usual mode of production. It was the first film musical that, when distributed in international markets, required inclusion of subtitles for the lyrics of the songs. Traditionally, only the dialogue portions would have been subtitled, and that in itself is odd when one considers that there is less need for this in a well-known and archetypal story than in more complicated and unconventional works such as *Carousel.*[29] *West Side Story* also broke new ground in the area of union concessions: the producers negotiated, in their contract with British Equity, that London's 1958 production would be cast entirely with American talent. After hearing testimony from theater experts, the union agreed to this on the condition that some British dancers be allowed to understudy the roles for a year, then gradually replace the Americans as the latter wore out or moved on to other shows. On an additional note, it was the first Broadway musical to be mounted in Israel, where it broke all box office records and grossed $250,000.[30]

All of these distinguishing features suggest a tremendous singularity for a show that was ready to close in 1960, when box office receipts were not sufficient to keep it running profitably. (During the first year, for instance, there were 142 cast changes, the equivalent of replacing every cast member approximately three times. Larry Kert alone, who played the part of Tony, wore out twenty pairs of shoes and went through three blue jackets in the first run of the show.)[31] Although it was certainly innovative in these various ways, many musicals before it had trodden much of the same ground. Why then is *this* musical so important, both then and now?

What seems to have happened is that from the protracted attempts at an initial staging to its eventual canonization, *West Side Story* merged artistic issues of its time, issues that continue to permeate and preoccupy our musical and artistic culture: difference and how it plays out in projections of the "other," the split between emerging rock music and traditional musical theater style, tensions between modernist and traditional paths within classical music, the gendering of ethnicity and musical styles, the place of the musical and the musical theater composer within popular music and classical music culture, issues of "borrowing" and pastiche within "original" music, and the importance of reception history and avenues of musical dissemination. These artistic issues expand to wider implications in American culture: the scourge of ethnic intolerance; the role of feminism in shaping our view of history in recent decades; the place of music (and particularly the musical) in reflecting or shaping ideas of Americanness; the perceived split between popular and art music and their attendant intellectual and socioeconomic followings; the binary oppositions of old/young, insider/outsider, and urban/rural; and modern scholarship's preoccupation with originality and authenticity. This study cannot hope to explain what has made *West Side Story* a great musical, nor retrace completely its tortured history, nor analyze its music to prove that it is organic and unified (others have done this already and better), but to tell a series of *West Side*'s stories, viewing this musical through different lenses so that we can see it as a product both of its own time and of ours. These perspectives afford glimpses of how musicals reflect and refract American culture and the creators of that culture and how that creation is a collaboration in which we all continue to partake.

This study begins by tracing the work's beginnings to its opening on Broadway, a circuitous path that left the creators at some points entirely hopeless that the work would see the light of day. From Jerome Robbins's initial ideas for an urban Romeo and Juliet story to the crisis of Cheryl Crawford's withdrawal from the project, we see *West Side Story* as perhaps more complex and nuanced than we might originally have imagined. The crucial issues of art and entertainment, popular and serious, converge in the music

of *West Side Story*, and chapter 3 examines some of Bernstein's motivations
and influences in writing the musical. Bernstein remains one of the most
renowned and enigmatic musicians in American history. Eschewing the imprimatur of a European training, he was hailed as the first great homegrown
talent, combining gifts as pianist, composer, conductor, educator, and cultural ambassador to forge one of the most glamorous and influential classical
music careers of the century. Following Toscanini's role as an arbiter of public
taste in classical music, Bernstein helped to define the nation's ideas on what
music was and how they should listen to it. Therefore, Bernstein's posthumous reputation has understandably rested primarily on his contributions to
education (through publications *The Joy of Music* and *The Infinite Variety of
Music*, the televised *Omnibus* and *Young People's Concerts* presentations, and,
later, his Harvard lectures) and his enormous recorded legacy.[32] However,
more lasting influence may well stem from his much-overshadowed efforts
as a composer, whether for the concert hall, to which he devoted most of his
professional life, or the Broadway stage. With a working knowledge of the demands of Broadway and fully cognizant of the European tradition, Bernstein
was poised to combine the best of both worlds in what he hoped would be a
new direction in American opera. Motivated by his desire for popularity, on
one hand, and haunted by the admonitions of his mentor, Serge Koussevitsky,
on the other, Bernstein had a very personal stake in creating a work that grew
as organically as possible from American roots and was grounded in tonality,
but measured up to European standards in its symphonic scope and perceived
progressiveness within its genre. Understandably, *West Side Story* is indebted
to precedents by Gershwin, Weill, and Blitzstein but also to classical operatic
models, especially in the treatment of ensembles and leitmotif (see figure 1.2).

Bernstein's high profile as a conductor and public figure (and his resultant
coverage in the popular literature) has rendered him until recently unattract-
ive to musicologists who seek the unities of oeuvre characteristic of the so-
called "serious" composer. Bernstein's own agenda as a composer was more
than adequately revealed through his writings on the Great American Opera,
and, indeed, Sondheim has commented on the (to him) irksome manner in
which Bernstein prided himself on having created the "Great Musical" in
West Side Story.[33] Although traditional scholarly, critical, and public attention
has attributed this "greatness" in part to its perceived originality and unity,
a closer study of the work suggests that much of its fascination lies in its

FIGURE 1.2
Leitmotif sketch by Bernstein of *West Side Story*. Courtesy of the Leonard Bernstein
Foundation.

disunities. Particularly, a more detailed look at the score reveals a substantial number of borrowings from other composers in style, content, or both. This stems in part from Bernstein's formidable knowledge of repertoire through conducting, but also from his ability to play anything from memory at the piano. As David Diamond recalls,

> Having known Lenny from the first days that he really began to compose and to build larger pieces, he always had models, of course, but people tell me who were with him at the Curtis Institute that he was the brightest of all when they were in Randall Thompson's class because he knew so much music and could just sit at the piano and play it off or sightread very easily. He *did* have this phenomenal gift and I think that goes through his *entire career*, right from the beginning at Curtis.[34]

Bernstein's incredible facility not only with recall but also with synthesis allowed many of the most famous or effective moments from music history to be melded together to create a score that seems on the outside to be completely integrated and organic, but upon further examination emerges as rather a "mosaic" in its final product than a proverbial "melting pot" of diverse sources.[35]

Using MacDonald Smith Moore's and Andrea Most's work as a starting point, I argue that Bernstein's efforts reflect in his own time the fictional composer's dilemma in the original play by Israel Zangwill, *The Melting Pot* (1909). In it, a Jewish immigrant composer attempts to write the Great American Symphony.[36] In many ways, Bernstein was able to create the Great American Musical, not through *West Side Story*'s originality, but through the integration of diverse elements into one seemingly homogenous whole. He shared Robbins's eclecticism (as expressed in dance styles) as a starting point for the creation of an accessible "American" art music, but at the same time labored more heavily under prevailing expectations of musical genre. Having earlier failed in his own mind to create what he considered a successful "opera" with *Candide*, Bernstein appropriated and experimented with operatic and musical theater models, notably some by Mozart and Gershwin. At the same time, pressure to create something "serious" within the compositional environment of the 1950s seems to have led him to employ dissonance both as a structural tool and as a unifying surface detail (as in the "Prologue").[37]

Chapter 4 expands the discussion of *West Side*'s music to explore the work's relationship to Hispanicism, in New York and beyond. Tellingly, Bernstein opens his Norton Lecture on "The Crisis of the Twentieth Century" not with Schoenberg or even Mahler or Debussy, but with Ravel's *Rapsodie espagnole*, music he describes as "blazing with self confidence into the twentieth century."[38] The castanets, rhythmic irregularity, and other Hispanic gestures of Ravel's work (including specific melodic phrases) are echoed in the particularly "Spanish" sound of *West Side Story*'s score. Here, "white" American jazz coexists with Hispanic dance music, which by then was integrated into American mainstream musical culture. Within this integration, however, there was tension. As Moore writes, traditional views of jazz were that "black was sensual; white was spiritual. Jazz was an assemblage of superficial mannerisms; classical music communicated an organic sense of substantive logic. Black jazz exuded violence; white classical music inspired love."[39] That Bernstein chose both idioms to express a universal and tragic story of intolerance, and that elements from both traditions inform the organicism of the work, shows a connection with the contemporary tensions over American civil rights that were not openly expressed until the more radical era of the 1960s and later, not least in Bernstein's own activism.[40] In *West Side Story*, the Puerto Rican "problem" (as will be seen in chapters 4 and 5) acts as a stand-in for the more pressing racial issues facing American society.[41]

Premiered during a period of racial and musical division, *West Side Story*'s combination of Hispanic, black, and white musical elements (from both classical and popular music realms) falls into a larger context of "crossover" musicals and shows such as *Carmen Jones* (specific scenes such as the mambo-inflected "Dance at the Gym" find precursors in the dance hall scene of this work), each attempting a successful blending of divergent ethnic strands.[42] Placed in the context of a massive Puerto Rican migration to New York City (and its attendant social pressures) and the vogue of Latin American dance bands both on Broadway and in film, *West Side Story* shows surprising adherences to and divergences from contemporary American interpretations of Puerto Rico and its music, more so than previously imagined. Resonances of Caribbean and South American music come not just from the "mambo craze" of the 1950s but also from Copland's and eventually Bernstein's connections with Mexican and South American culture.[43] Bernstein's own thoughts on the Hispanic, explored in his Harvard bachelor's thesis, link it explicitly with

African-American music and culture, in his opinion one of the cornerstones of an indigenous American music.[44] The interweaving of racial, social, and political agendas with the demands of the commercial Broadway stage provide new answers as to how *East Side Story*—a tale of warring Catholics and Jews—came to its eventual form as a Hispanic- and jazz-inspired musical.

Chapter 5 considers the ethnic "othering" of Hispanicism and how that eventually leads to consideration of gender. This discussion includes a reading of documentary sources from 1958 in which real juvenile delinquents who were taken to see the musical as a social program discuss the role of gender in the musical and in their lives. These tensions, which emerge in the work's portrayals of women, again draw interesting parallels with the world of the Hispanic, where females are relegated for the most part to "local color." It is in the most "operatic" portion of the musical, the duet "A Boy Like That/I Have a Love," that Anita and Maria break out not only from their differing opinions, but from the constraints of their Hispanic musical backdrop, and indeed from the norms of musical theater expression altogether. The "otherness" of composer, lyricist, bookwriter, and director through their leftist political leanings, homosexuality, and Jewishness seems also to find an outlet in *West Side Story*, also emerging through the treatment of gender. While both the musical and contemporary America concerned themselves with juvenile delinquency, the rise of "girl gangs" represented a new phenomenon that profoundly threatened the fabric of society. This tension found its way into the musical in the way gender roles are depicted and expressed, particularly the character of Anybodys. Among its many departures from Broadway musical traditions, *West Side Story* shows a strong emphasis on the male, ritualized through dance, and treats the female characters in a rather unorthodox way. The character of Anybodys encapsulates the gender struggle that permeates the musical. A tomboy who fits into neither male nor female worlds, this gender interloper is also the only character who has no precursor in Shakespeare's *Romeo and Juliet*, which the creators followed closely in their modern rendition. Does Anybodys represent the collaborators themselves, or, as the song "Somewhere" seems to suggest, the difficulties of reconciliation?

The considerable issues of equality lead to chapter 6, which addresses the musical's relationship to juvenile delinquency, one of the most pressing problems in American society in the 1950s. Although the creators did not particularly play up the more political ramifications of the musical, a reading of early lyric sketches reveals a work much more in tune with current sociological research than previously suggested. In addition, *West Side Story* premiered during a period in which juvenile delinquency, both in the popular press and in film, drew the public's attention to the youth movement, which would eventually dominate mainstream culture in the 1960s. Although seen in some ways as a culmination (as opposed to a progenitor) of trends, this aspect of *West Side Story* finds it slightly ahead of its time. Iconoclastic musicals such as *Hair* found a certain precursor in *West Side Story*'s placement of youths at the forefront of American social issues. Up until the present day, and perhaps even more so than before, *West Side Story* is being used in communities to help youth and concerned adults deal with the problems of juvenile delinquency. The Seattle *West Side Story* Project, started in 2007, has brought together hundreds of youths for summits on gang violence and crime prevention. Says Detective Kim Bogucki, "We used the musical as a springboard to discuss gang violence as it still resonates with today's youth, and captured the opportunity to raise awareness in a non-enforcement atmosphere."[45] Given the work's ostensible purpose as modern, avant-garde musical theater, it is fascinating to see it used in completely nontheatrical contexts for nontheatrical reasons.

Chapter 7 deals specifically with the ways in which the show's changing reception history have shaped our perceptions of the work. Part of the assertion of this study is that *West Side Story* has become symbolic of a kind of middle-class appropriation of the Hispanic, urban, and violent world it purports to represent. Arguably more popular today than it was when it opened, the work has entered a canon of "great" American musicals in that it has become iconic and beloved as, ironically, it becomes increasingly divorced from its original, fraught context. For example, a recent recording by the Paganini Ensemble on the Denon label is entitled simply *West Side Story* and includes on its cover a section of the 1960s film poster. However, the "Quintet" is the only track of twelve that comes from this musical, and none of the other music on the CD is by Bernstein. The work's archetypal story and characters, and the perceived seriousness of the music and choreography, have kept it continuously in the repertoire. Yet, many musicals of high quality and more manageable means of production have failed to reach *West Side Story*'s zenith of popularity, especially within the wider context of American culture as represented by regional theaters. The work has found a place not only in Broadway-scale revivals, but in amateur and stock productions, and especially in high schools. Considering the work's strenuous performance demands—from instrumental, vocal, staging, and dance perspectives—it is an exceptionally odd choice for any venue other than the professional musical theater, and yet it is here in such modest surroundings that it has had its longest and most enduring life. Although Stephen Sondheim has gone on record as saying that the piece is more about theater than anything else, the fact that so many ensembles approach it that are too inexperienced to rise to its theatrical, vocal, and instrumental demands— although some high schools, as I shall point out, are better than others in this regard—suggests that the McLuhanesque "medium is the message" has been reversed.[46] The social message attracts us today perhaps even more than it did in the late 1950s, so much so that we are willing to try to perform it, however unadvisedly, in high schools again and again.[47] I argue that its popularity has as much to do with its artistic merit as with what I would call its "posthumous reception," that is, the culture's immediate dismantling and remaking of it as soon as it opened on Broadway. To be sure, many works of American musical theater suffer from being seen as just "the songs themselves," divorced from their theatrical corollaries and contexts. However, *West Side Story* is different in that most of the score, not just select "hit" numbers, is treated and remembered as one piece, not many.[48]

This reification dovetails with a now ubiquitous concern for authenticity. Recently, Kenneth Schermerhorn and the Nashville Symphony Orchestra released a recorded version of *West Side Story*, advertising the authenticity of this performance as adhering to Bernstein's "original" score (see figure 1.3). This, in spite of the fact that Leonard Bernstein had *already* released his definitive, final version of the work with a handpicked orchestra and the opera singers of which he had always dreamed (see figure 1.4). To be sure, Bernstein's operatic version was often critically panned. But, if Schermerhorn's recording can be seen as a response to Bernstein's "definitive" version, for whom then does it speak? Bernstein's recording, I argue, failed not because the performances of José Carreras and Kiri Te Kanawa were inept (for all of Carerras's discomfort with the American idiom, his vocal quality was not in question), but because the composer's vision of the work rubs up so harshly against *our West Side Story*, the one we have created in our own communal image. We, like Bernstein, want to wrest it from a context that does not feel right to us, even if that means out of the composer's own hands.

AMERICAN CLASSICS

LEONARD BERNSTEIN
West Side Story
The Original Score

Morrison · Eldred · Cooke · Dean · San Giovanni
Nashville Symphony Orchestra · Kenneth Schermerhorn

FIGURE 1.3
Cover art, Nashville Symphony's *Bernstein's Original Score: "West Side Story."* Courtesy of Naxos.

Authenticity, then, to what or to whom? To one of two different Bernsteins, to Robbins, or to the "work" itself? This leads to the ultimate question: what does authenticity mean in a Broadway musical? As the most collaborative of art forms, as the product of so many creators, both advertised and unsung, the genre defies any sense of authenticity by its very nature. I open this discussion asking one of the first and most important of questions: "Whose *West Side Story*?" The final chapter will answer, finally, "Our *West Side Story*." What falls between are many intervening stories, differing visions of this radical musical theater work, by its creators, its performers, its audience, its critics.

FIGURE 1.4
Cover art, *Leonard Bernstein conducts "West Side Story."* Courtesy of Deutsche Grammophon.

NOTES

1. See, for instance, Ken Mandelbaum, *Not Since* Carrie: *Forty Years of Broadway Musical Flops* (New York: St. Martin's Press, 1991); or Rick Simas, *The Musicals No One Came to See: A Guidebook to Four Decades of Musical Comedy Casualties on Broadway, Off-Broadway, and in Out-of-Town Tryout, 1943–1983* (New York: Garland, 1987). Similar books exist on "turkeys" of the film industry (Harry Medved and Michael Medved, *The Golden Turkey Awards: Nominees and Winners, the Worst Achievements in Hollywood History* [New York: Perigee, 1980]; and *The Hollywood*

Hall of Shame: The Most Expensive Flops in Movie History [New York: Perigee, 1984]), although the emotional response to artistic and commercial disaster must surely be moderated by the fact that the performers and creators do not usually witness the audience response to their works in person, an unavoidable element of live theater.

2. A myriad of genre designations and descriptors have been applied to the body of work which constitutes America's commercial musical theater, especially those shows created specifically for the Broadway stage. For the sake of simplicity and inclusiveness, I will restrict myself throughout this study to the terms "musical" and "American musical theater," representing the genre and its milieu, respectively.

3. For a discussion of canon formation and its relationship to number of performances, see Geoffrey Block, "The Broadway Canon from *Show Boat* to *West Side Story* and the European Operatic Ideal," *Journal of Musicology* 11 (1993): 525–44.

4. Quoted in Craig Zadan, *Sondheim & Company*, 2nd ed., updated (New York: Da Capo, 1994), 14. Sondheim's comment (retold by his agent Flora Roberts) seems particularly disingenuous, as Puerto Rican maids were no doubt common currency in upscale Manhattan.

5. *Variety*, February 16, 1972.

6. William Weber, "The History of Musical Canon," in *Rethinking Music*, ed. Nicholas Cook and Mark Everist (New York: Oxford University Press, 2001), 336–55. Weber's work continues a theme explored by Joseph Kerman in "A Few Canonic Variations," *Critical Inquiry* 10 (1983): 107–26. Weber defines canon as "the complete construct of activities, values, and authority that surrounded the music" (338). Although musicologists have followed the lead of literary scholars in questioning the validity and nature of canons, the very need to deconstruct them presupposes their existence and, presumably, influence. See particularly Katherine Bergeron and Philip V. Bohlman, eds., *Disciplining Music: Musicology and Its Canons* (Chicago: University of Chicago Press, 1992); and Marcia J. Citron, *Gender and the Musical Canon* (Cambridge: Cambridge University Press, 1993).

7. Peter J. Burkholder, Donald J. Grout, and Claude Palisca, *A History of Western Music*, 8th ed. (New York: W. W. Norton, 2010); and Mark Evan Bonds, *A History of Music in Western Culture* (Upper Saddle River, NJ: Prentice Hall, 2003). Bonds compares "Tonight" to Verdi's "Bella figlia dell'amore" from *Rigoletto*, making connections between the works in the anticipation that the participants feel about the

encounter. Although Bonds treats the musical as part of the tonal tradition along with works by Shostakovich and Cole Porter, he links it most closely to traditional opera.

8. See James Winston Challender, "The Function of the Choreographer in the Development of the Conceptual Musical: An Examination of the Work of Jerome Robbins, Bob Fosse, and Michael Bennett on Broadway between 1944 and 1984" (PhD diss., Florida State University, 1986); Gregory Dennhardt, "The Director-Choreographer in the American Musical Theatre" (PhD diss., University of Illinois at Urbana-Champaign, 1978); Eugenia Volz Schoettler, "From a Chorus Line to *A Chorus Line*: The Emergence of Dance in the American Musical Theatre" (PhD diss., Kent State University, 1979); Raphael Francis Miller, "The Contributions of Selected Broadway Musical Theatre Choreographers: Connolly, Rasch, Balanchine, Holm, and Alton" (PhD diss., University of Oregon, 1984).

9. Tim Carter, "*Oklahoma!*" *The Making of an American Musical* (New Haven, CT: Yale University Press, 2007), and bruce d. mcclung, *Lady in the Dark: Biography of a Musical* (New York: Oxford University Press, 2007).

10. Richard Crawford makes the distinction between composer's music (with detailed musical instructions, and in which the composer maintains artistic control) and performer's music (giving access to the consumer marketplace, but where the composer cedes some control). Crawford identifies these two strands as forming the roots for musical categories for American music (see Richard Crawford, *America's Musical Life: A History* [New York: Norton, 2001], 226–30). It seems that musical theater falls more into the latter than the former category, although *West Side Story* is somewhat of an anomaly in that the published piano/vocal score is significantly more detailed than are musical theater scores generally available for commercial sale.

11. Block, "The Broadway Canon"; John M. Clum, *Something for the Boys* (New York: St. Martin's Press, 1999); Stacy Wolf, *A Problem Like Maria: Gender and Sexuality in the American Musical* (Ann Arbor: University of Michigan Press, 2002); D. A. Miller, *Place for Us: Essay on the Broadway Musical* (Cambridge, MA: Harvard University Press, 1998).

12. Raymond Knapp, *The American Musical and the Formation of National Identity* (Princeton, NJ: Princeton University Press, 2005).

13. Stephen Banfield, *Sondheim's Broadway Musicals* (Ann Arbor: University of Michigan Press, 1993).

14. David Walsh and Len Platt, *Musical Theater and American Culture* (Westport, CT: Praeger, 2003).

15. Mark Grant, *The Rise and Fall of the Broadway Musical* (Boston: Northeastern University Press, 2004); and Bruce Kirle, *Unfinished Show Business: Broadway Musicals as Works-in-Process* (Carbondale, IL: Southern Illinois University Press, 2005).

16. Scott McMillin, *The Musical as Drama: A Study of the Principles and Conventions behind Musical Shows from Kern to Sondheim* (Princeton, NJ: Princeton University Press, 2006); and Joseph Kerman, *Opera as Drama* (New York: Knopf, 1956).

17. Joan Peyser, *Bernstein: A Biography* (New York: Beech Tree Books, 1987); and Keith Garebian, *The Making of "West Side Story"* (Toronto: ECW Press, 1995).

18. Geoffrey Block, *Enchanted Evenings: The Broadway Musical from "Show Boat" to Sondheim* (Oxford: Oxford University Press, 1997); Joseph Peter Swain, *The Broadway Musical: A Critical and Musical Survey* (New York: Oxford University Press, 1990); D. A. Miller, *Place for Us*; also, Jennifer Harrison Powell, "Unity and Tragedy in the Libretto and Score of Leonard Bernstein's *West Side Story*" (master's thesis, Southern Methodist University, 1994).

19. Wayne Koestenbaum, *The Queen's Throat: Opera, Homosexuality, and the Mystery of Desire* (New York: Poseidon Press, 1993). See also Wolf, *Problem.*

20. Mary E. Williams, ed., *Readings on "West Side Story,"* Greenhaven Literary Companion to American Literature Series (San Diego: Greenhaven, 2001). All the pieces in the Greenhaven anthology—many of them magazine articles—were previously published.

21. "If I could write one real, moving American opera that any American can understand (and one that is, notwithstanding, a serious musical work), I shall be a happy man," Bernstein wrote almost a decade earlier, quoted in *Findings* (New York: Simon & Schuster, 1982), 129. The musical *On the Town*, growing out of Bernstein's and Robbins's *Fancy Free* ballet, premiered on Broadway in 1944; in 1953 *Wonderful Town* opened; Bernstein's one-act opera on the trials of marriage, *Trouble in Tahiti*, enjoyed a limited run on Broadway in 1953 (it was later incorporated into the opera *A Quiet Place*); *Candide*, first opening in 1956 to commercial failure, was reworked throughout the composer's life and beyond. *1600 Pennsylvania Avenue* opened in 1976, with book and lyrics by Alan Jay Lerner, and failed immediately (substantial fragments were incorporated posthumously into *A White House Cantata*).

22. Stephen Sondheim might well challenge my assertion that he had less at stake. As Meryle Secrest reports in her 1998 biography, he remembers an audience member hurriedly walking out on a performance, no doubt a tired businessman

expecting from *West Side Story* a panacean evening-long diversion instead of an experimental work. "I can't blame him," recalls Sondheim, "but that's when I knew my career was in trouble." For a complete account from Sondheim's recollection, see Meryle Secrest, *Stephen Sondheim: A Life* (New York: Alfred A. Knopf, 1998), 127.

23. Although sentimentality and a certain "purpleness" (as Sondheim puts it) in a musical might seem a desirable thing, the creators clearly wanted to avoid many of the stereotypical aspects of the mainstream genre.

24. Bernstein remembers, "Steve and I, poor bastards that we were, trying by ourselves at a piano to audition this score for Columbia Records, my record company. They said no, there's nothing in it anybody could sing, too depressing, too many tritones, too many words in the lyrics, too rangy—'Ma-ri-a'—'nobody could sing notes like that, impossible. They turned it down. Later they changed their minds, but that was an afternoon Steve and I will never forget" ("Landmark," 17).

25. For a more complete discussion of this phenomenon, see J. Kenneth Moore, "The Mixing and Miking of Broadway: Changing Values of a Sound/Music Aesthetic," in *To the Four Corners: A Festschrift in Honor of Rose Brandel*, ed. Ellen C. Leichtman (Warren, MI: Harmonie Park Press, 1994), 169–88. Although certainly amplification was used before this time, *West Side Story* seems to have standardized the use of miking for more than just the principal characters. Prince claims to have used it here for the first time in his own productions (Harold Prince, *Contradictions: Notes on Twenty-Six Years in the Theatre* [New York: Dodd, 1974], 165).

26. The "book" is the spoken portions of the musical, akin to a stage play. In general, and especially in this time period (with the notable partial exception of Hammerstein's involvement in some of his show's books), the bookwriter would often be a separate individual from lyricist and composer, respectively.

27. Although there are certainly examples within the operatic repertoire where there is very little "book" as opposed to music, this is not generally the case for the musical.

28. "Los Angeles Next: 'West Side Story' Nears End of Run," *Denver Post*, July 8, 1959. Conductor Joseph D. Lewis and six key musicians flew ahead to pick up an extra twenty musicians in each town. Meanwhile, four railroad baggage cars moved scenery, electrical equipment, props, and costumes from one town to the next. For a sense of stage management in this time period, see Bert Gruver, *The Stage Manager's*

Handbook, 1st ed. 1952, revised by Frank Hamilton (New York: Drama Book Publishers, 1972).

29. This makes sense to the extent that the lyrics, often involving allusions to concrete aspects of contemporary life or heavily vernacular, go by at such rapid-fire speed at some points that subtitles might well be helpful for an English-speaking audience as well. Sondheim later criticized his own lyric writing for this reason. As he states, "'America' has twenty-seven words to the square inch. I had this wonderful quatrain that went, 'I like to be in America/OK by me in America/Everything free in America/For a small fee in America.' The 'For a small fee' was my little zinger—except that the 'for' is accented and 'small fee' is impossible to say that fast, so it went '*For* a smafee in America.' Nobody knew what it meant!" Quoted in Zadan, 23.

30. "Tel Aviv—March 21," *New York Times*, March 21, 1961.

31. Stuart W. Little, "Theater News," *New York Herald Tribune*, December 15, 1960; and "*West Side Story* Is Back after 10 Months on the Road," *New York Herald Tribune*, April 27, 1960, 19. Kert left the show after his 1218th performance, the only principal cast member left from the original production. He reported that he was leaving to promote his new recording, "Larry Kert Sings Leonard Bernstein" ("*West Side Story* Is Losing Star after 1,218 Shows," *New York Herald Tribune*, September 3, 1960). Kert, interviewed in the early 1970s, confirms that he found himself doing the role of Tony repeatedly in a variety of venues and was unable to get ongoing successful employment as an actor until his breakthrough in Sondheim's *Company*. See Norma McLain Stoop, "Tony & Larry & Bobby & Larry," *After Dark*, June 1971, 40–43.

32. Leonard Bernstein, *The Infinite Variety of Music* (New York: Simon & Schuster, 1966); *The Joy of Music* (New York: Simon & Schuster, 1959); *Young People's Concerts* (New York: Simon & Schuster, 1970); *The Unanswered Question: Six Talks at Harvard* (Cambridge, MA: Harvard University Press, 1976). The "Young People's Concerts" were presented between 1958 and 1972, and Bernstein appeared on the first *Omnibus* program in 1954, with subsequent appearances.

33. Sondheim recalls, "All Lenny was saying was, 'I wrote a great musical and nobody else can do it.' He was making that statement all the time. But he wasn't leading the pack at all. He was just blowing his own trumpet and it always pissed me off." Quoted in Secrest, 131.

34. David Diamond, interview with the author, July 14, 2002, Rochester, New York.

35. These two terms have been used since at least Israel Zangwill's play of 1909, *The Melting Pot*, to describe two approaches to cultural integration in American society. See also Richard C. Harper, *The Course of the Melting Pot Idea to 1910* (New York: Arno Press, 1980).

36. MacDonald Smith Moore, *Yankee Blues: Musical Culture and American Identity* (Bloomington: Indiana University Press, 1985); and Andrea Most, "'We Know We Belong to the Land': Jews and the American Musical Theater" (PhD diss., Brandeis University, 2001).

37. See also Leonard Bernstein and Gene Krupa, "Has Jazz Influenced the Symphony?" *Esquire*, February 1947, 47, 152–3.

38. Leonard Bernstein, *The Unanswered Question*, 263.

39. Moore, *Yankee Blues*, 88.

40. Bernstein's attempt to assist the Black Panthers by arranging a meeting between the Panthers and some of Bernstein's friends at the composer's elegant apartment is now legendary. The most famous commentary on this incident was the famous "Radical Chic" essay by Tom Wolfe, found in *Radical Chic and Mau-Mauing the Flak Catchers* (New York: Farrar, Straus and Giroux, 1970).

41. Joseph Swain's chapter on the "ethnic musical" (Swain, *Broadway Musical*) as well as *The Exotic in Western Music*, edited by Jonathan Bellman (Boston: Northeastern University Press, 1998), will provide a starting point.

42. In a similar spirit, almost fifty years later, pop artist Beyoncé Knowles recreated an African-American *Carmen* for television.

43. The mambo craze seems to actually continue, not begin, a fascination with this particular brand of exoticism, dating back to Gottschalk.

44. Bernstein's undergraduate thesis, reprinted in *Findings*, 36–99. A reexamination of the musical's roots reveals why *West Side Story* has continued to speak eloquently to American culture, especially in the context of the late 1990s vogue of Latin American music, when references (both musical and textual) to *West Side Story* abounded in the most pervasive media: popular music, advertising, film, and prime-time television drama.

45. Seattle Police Department, "*West Side Story* Project," www.seattle.gov/police/programs/youth/WestSide.htm, accessed July 23, 2009.

46. Sondheim claims, "*West Side* is about theater. It's not about people. It's a way to tell a story. What was best was its theatricality and its approach to telling a story in musical terms." Quoted in Zadan, 28.

47. The aforementioned Williams, *Readings on "West Side Story,"* for example, is intended specifically as a primer for high school performers and audiences.

48. See chapter 3 for Bernstein's own very clear statement that the unifying aspects of the score make it one piece, not many. This may be an unusual case in which a composer's intent is instantly and enduringly seized upon by his public.

2

From *Gangway!* to Broadway

Genesis of the Musical

I don't remember the exact date—it was somewhere around 1949—this friend of mine was offered the role of Romeo. He said to me, "This part seems very passive, would you tell me what you think I should do with it." So I asked myself, "If I were to play this, how would I make it come to life?" I tried to imagine it in terms of today.

—*Jerome Robbins ("Landmark," 11)*

As I recall, the origins of *West Side Story* were indeed in 1949. Jerry called up and gave us this idea and said, "Come over and let me explain it to you." Arthur and I were quite excited by it. I remember that evening in Jerry's apartment as though it were yesterday *because* of the excitement.

—*Leonard Bernstein ("Landmark," 13)*

West Side was originally dreamed up in 1945 by Robbins and Laurents as a story about a Jewish girl and a Gentile boy on the streets of New York. Soon after, Leonard Bernstein joined them, and for a time Betty Comden and Adolph Green were to write the lyrics and Leland Hayward to produce.

—*Harold Prince* (Contradictions, 30)

I asked Arthur what he was doing, and he told me he was beginning to work on this musical. I asked him who was doing the lyrics, and he said, "We don't have anybody because Comden and Green were supposed to do them, but they're in California and may be tied up with a movie contract.

Would you like to come and play your songs for Leonard Bernstein?" I
said, "Sure" and the next day I met Lenny.

—*Stephen Sondheim ("Landmark," 13–14)*

One of the overarching issues addressed in this study is the many perspectives
from which *West Side Story* can be viewed and the continual remaking of this
musical by different audiences with different agendas. Although the work
underwent very few changes in the tryout period (unlike many shows, which
are torn apart and retried with new numbers often very late in the rehearsal
process), there were many changes to the musical in its early stages, which
reflected the conflicting visions and priorities of its creators. Indeed, the genesis of *West Side Story* is as complicated as the many issues it raises. In 1985,
Leonard Bernstein, Arthur Laurents, Jerome Robbins, and Stephen Sondheim
convened for a Dramatists Guild Landmark Symposium in which they shared
reminiscences of the creation of *West Side Story* some thirty years later.[1]
The accounts were framed, by agreement of the participants, in Rashomon
fashion—a kind of storytelling in which each person retells the same narrative from his own perspective.[2] The accounts elucidate not only the vagaries of
human memory decades after the fact, but also the competing priorities under
which *West Side Story* took shape. Investigation of this crucial phase of the
musical's history reveals not only the conflicting expectations and demands of
initial producer Cheryl Crawford and the four collaborators, but the cultural
and commercial milieu from which the piece was born and the competitive
forces at work within Broadway musical theater at the time. Although Keith
Garebian, Joan Peyser, and Humphrey Burton's research has outlined the
most important aspects of the work's genesis, and the reminiscences of each
of the creators has added detail about this creative phase, it is not well known
that *West Side Story* began as a much more operatic and integrated show than
the final version we know. Specifically, longer versions of the balcony scene
(with more parlando, recitative-like sections for Tony and Maria) and the
"I Have a Love/A Boy Like That" duet (made into a trio by the inclusion of
Tony behind a scrim) suggest that the work included even more music than
remains in the published score.[3] Indeed, the earliest plot outline was not simply about conflict between Catholics and Jews, but took place mostly in Jewish
settings (a Passover seder, for instance), addressing strictly anti-Semitic rather
than anti–Puerto Rican sentiments.

In considering the ultimate success of a work whose creation seems to have taken so many turns, we cannot underestimate the role that the collaborative process played in shaping the final product. Although each collaborator remembered somewhat differently the very beginnings of the work, which was for a time humorously titled *Gangway!*, there is no doubt that the roots of *West Side Story* may well date back to the early- and mid-1940s, and certainly to an idea by Jerome Robbins. At that time Robbins was a young dancer performing in Antony Tudor's setting of *Romeo and Juliet*, with music by Prokofiev. He played the parts of both Mercutio and Benvolio, prefiguring the characters of Riff and Bernardo, respectively, in *West Side Story*. As a budding choreographer as well as a dancer, Robbins would no doubt have been influenced by Tudor in his own approach to the subject matter only a decade later. Although this early exposure to *Romeo and Juliet* certainly must have played an important part in Robbins's mind, *West Side Story* lore recounts that the idea came to Robbins after friend and actor Montgomery Clift approached him at a party on Fire Island. Cast as Romeo, Clift was looking for some direction in rehearsing and preparing his role, and this gave Robbins the idea of setting the story in the present.[4] However, as fellow dancer Janet Reed recollects, the idea may also have come from classes given by director Mary Hunter. Hunter was producing plays in Greenwich Village in the 1940s and would later collaborate with Robbins on *Peter Pan*. At the time, Reed and Robbins were regularly taking Hunter's classes. On one occasion they were assigned an improvisation on the Romeo and Juliet theme, with Robbins as a Jewish boy and Reed as a Catholic girl. "I remember talking to him about it on the subway. I think that's where he might have first come up with the idea for *West Side Story*. It was already on his mind," she recalls.[5]

It would not take ten years, however, for Robbins to explore the subject of star-crossed lovers in his own choreographic work. The theme first appeared in his ballet *The Guests*, which he was rehearsing for City Ballet in the 1940s (music by Marc Blitzstein). The scenario for the ballet followed two groups, one with stars on their foreheads, the other without. After the dancers perform with masks over their faces, a pas de deux couple who has formed a romantic relationship is unmasked only to reveal that each are from a different contingent. Both groups ostracize the couple as a result of the disclosure.

Although not connected explicitly with *Romeo and Juliet*, the themes explored in the ballet seem to foreshadow the central problem in *West Side Story*.[6]

With the Romeo and Juliet concept clearly on his mind, Robbins approached Bernstein and Laurents as early as January 1949 with the idea (while *The Guests* was in rehearsal).[7] As he recalls, "I wrote a very brief outline and started looking for a producer and collaborators who'd be interested. This was not easy. Producers were not at all interested in doing it. Arthur and Lenny were interested, but not in getting together to work on it at that time, so we put it away."[8] The initial plotline set the story between Catholic and Jewish groups on the Lower East Side of Manhattan. Bernstein claims that he was indeed quite interested in the project, knowing little about Laurents except as the author of *Home of the Brave*, at which Bernstein "cried like a baby."[9] Laurents had heard Bernstein's music for *On the Town* ("electrifying" was what he called it) and was eager for a collaboration as well as to write his first musical. The trio met with Robbins with the idea of setting the work in the tenements of the East Side of Manhattan, with the Montagues as Catholic and the Capulets as Jewish. The action would take place over Easter/Passover. "At the first meeting at Jerry's, all three of us overlapped one another, blathering excitedly, bubbling with ideas, stumbling only momentarily over the obstacle Lenny always put in the way: he wanted to write 'an American opera.' Neither Jerry nor I wanted to do an opera any more than we wanted to do a musical comedy. What we did want, what all three of us agreed we wanted, was impossible to categorize because we couldn't define it."[10] It seemed that all parties wanted to create something never seen on Broadway before, and furthermore something they could write quickly. The *New York Herald Tribune* announced that the show would be out the following year, even though the collaborative team had only just started with a concept. Bernstein recalls that the early days of the project were stimulating:

> What was basically different from the way *West Side Story* turned out was that it was conceived as taking place on the *East* Side of New York. It was an East Side version of *Romeo and Juliet*, involving as the feuding parties Catholics and Jews at the Passover-Easter season with feelings in the streets running very high, with a certain amount of slugging and blood-letting. It seemed to match the Romeo story very well, except that this was not a family feud, but religion-oriented. As a matter of fact, Arthur and I were so excited about it that Arthur

wrote some sketched-out scenes, one of which was pretty complete. I can tell
you exactly where I was, I was in St. Louis, Missouri conducting that orchestra
when I received the opening scene and an outline of the second scene. I was
really excited.[11]

However, things did not take off as quickly and easily as the authors might
have wished. Laurents particularly came to the conclusion that the Catholic
and Jewish dichotomy was not as timely as it could be given the demographics
of the Lower East Side, which had changed considerably over the decade. As
planned, the musical would come dangerously close to *Abie's Irish Rose*, a play
from the 1920s that covered much the same ethnic conflict. Imagining that the
work might become a warmed-over *Rose* with music, Laurents decided not to
continue with the project and turned his attention to other things. Bernstein,
too, had other commitments, and the collaboration quickly fizzled out before
any substantial work had been done on Laurents's original outline. Robbins
decided to keep the show on the back burner until he could get Bernstein and
Laurents enthused about it again. During that hiatus, he claims that he didn't
seek out different collaborators. "I thought these were the best people for the
material," he recalls. "I stuck to trying to get these guys, and when they came
back to me I had the bait to grab them."[12] When they did come back, however,
it was in June of 1955, and they approached Robbins with a completely different project: an operatic version of James M. Cain's *Serenade*. The topic, relevant for both Bernstein and Laurents at the time, was about an opera singer
who discovers his own homosexuality. Composer and playwright were both
interested in pursuing *Serenade*, but Robbins argued for his original Romeo
concept instead. As he put it, "I don't know why you're wasting your time on
that trash when here I'm presenting you with an idea which is a much more
noble thing to do."[13] Laurents was still not excited about the Jewish-Catholic
setting and worked on other projects in the interim. Fortuitously, it was during this period that he was introduced to a young composer-lyricist, Stephen
Sondheim. Sondheim was in New York trying to break into the business as a
composer, and Laurents met him during an audition for him and producer
Martin Gabel.[14] Sondheim played through his score of *Saturday Night*, and
Laurents was impressed with Sondheim's lyrics.

The turning point came in Los Angeles, where Laurents and Bernstein
happened to meet up at a poolside at the Beverly Hills Hotel. Laurents was in

Los Angeles writing the screenplay for *Summertime*, a film based on his play *The Time of the Cuckoo*, and Bernstein was conducting the Hollywood Bowl orchestra.[15] In a conversation about something entirely different, Bernstein spied a copy of the *Los Angeles Times* with headlines concerning rioting gangs in the streets of Los Angeles.[16] Both men considered setting the story not on the East Side of Manhattan (whose tenements had by then been torn down) but on the multiracial West Side, the site of Puerto Rican gang warfare. "It would have Latin passion, immigrant anger, shared resentment," recalls Laurents.[17] Immediately they got in touch with Robbins, who was thrilled at the prospect. As it turned out, Robbins was also in Hollywood late that summer choreographing "The Small House of Uncle Thomas" for *The King and I*.[18] Work started in greater earnest, with Bernstein writing both music and lyrics. The collaborators approached Betty Comden and Adolph Green, who had worked with Bernstein on *On the Town* some years previously. They were busy with *Bells Are Ringing* but did complete a several-page outline for the musical and met with Laurents and Bernstein a few times. However, it didn't seem to be the project for them, and this, along with their prior commitments, prevented them from taking the musical further. Bernstein's own intention to write the lyrics turned out early on to be something of a mistake, since the composition demands on Bernstein were already heavy. At the opening-night party for Ugo Betti's *Isle of Goats*, Laurents met up again with Sondheim, the young composer who had previously auditioned for him to write the songs for *Serenade*. "In the corner I spotted Arthur Laurents," Sondheim recalls. "I went over to make small talk and I asked him what he was doing and he said that he was just about to begin a musical of *Romeo and Juliet* with Leonard Bernstein and Jerry Robbins. I asked, just idly, 'Who's doing the lyrics?' and Arthur literally smote his forehead, which I think is the only time I've ever seen anybody literally smite his forehead, and he said, 'I never thought of you and I liked your lyrics very much. I didn't like your music, but I did like your lyrics a lot.' Arthur is nothing if not frank. So he invited me to meet and play for Bernstein, which I agreed to because I thought it might be very glamorous to meet Lenny."[19] Bernstein had already decided to attempt the lyrics, but had second thoughts. "When we began I had—madly—undertaken to do the lyrics as well as the music. In 1955, I was also working on another show, *Candide*, and then the *West Side Story* music turned out to be extraordinarily balletic—which I was very happy about—and turned out to be a tremendously greater amount of music than I had expected, ballet music, symphonic music, developmental music. For these two reasons, I realized that I couldn't do all that music, plus the lyrics, and do them well. Arthur mentioned that he'd heard a young fellow named Stephen Sondheim sing some of his songs at a party."[20] At first Sondheim was not sure whether he wanted to take on the project, as he was trying to establish himself as a composer, not a lyricist. "I've never been that poor and I've never even *known* a Puerto Rican," he argued. However, his mentor Oscar Hammerstein II urged him to take on the show, claiming that it would be good experience to work with such fine collaborators. Sondheim agreed and started meeting with Bernstein on a regular basis to work on song composition.

By the time Sondheim joined the team, Laurents already had a three-page outline.[21] At their first meeting he told Bernstein that he himself was a composer, with the recent *Saturday Night* under his belt and the aspiration to be a Broadway success. Bernstein was delighted with this; as he says, "I could explain musical problems to him and he'd understand immediately, which made the collaboration a joy."[22] It turned out rather quickly that Bernstein and Sondheim discovered they worked very differently. Sondheim liked to take the Laurents material away and think about it for some time before producing a lyric, whereas Bernstein preferred to work in intense bursts. Early in 1955 Bernstein was having regular meetings with Laurents and Robbins, and Sondheim seems to have come on board in October. Indeed, Bernstein's date book shows multiple dates starting in October. He would meet with Sondheim for afternoon sessions day after day through the fall. To entertain themselves during meetings, and to dispel tension, Sondheim and Bernstein would play word games and anagrams with each other. "I introduced him to the *Listener* crossword puzzle and at the anagram table I drove him crazy because, to his dying day, he never beat me," claims Sondheim.[23] This was an activity in which they would indulge long after *West Side Story* was completed.

Bernstein already had musical material underway by the time Sondheim joined him. He was able to write snatches of music and lyrics after getting material from Laurents. At first, Bernstein started writing from the outline without having seen the first scene, but Sondheim needed to see the scene so that he could understand the characters. "The totality of the collaboration," writes Laurents, "left both Lenny and Steve free to do what Steve called 'raiding the dialogue.' . . . For the second act there was the 'Officer Krupke' dispute. I'd had to talk them and Jerry into the Krupke scene. There was a need, I thought, for comedy relief which, by lessening tension, would increase the impact of the tragedy that followed. After getting nowhere with dramaturgical arguments, I invoked Shakespeare's use of clown, his porter scenes, etc. Pretentiousness, however shameful, can be used: it worked."[24] "Maria" was the first composed piece, with a dummy lyric by Bernstein. The huapango from his clarinet sonata became the basis for "America," one of the many borrowings from Bernstein's own previous works in the piece.[25] Sondheim suggested that the song be about the name "Maria" instead of the actual personage, since Tony had just met Maria for a short time. Laurents encouraged the tendency of composer and lyricist to steal from the dialogue scenes. He even wrote lead-ins to songs, such as "A Boy Like That," as he felt that the musical aspect was as important as any other.[26] Bernstein also found inspiration in the city itself:

> It's this town that still gets me. No wonder I keep composing about it. I've lived here for so long, sometimes I don't even notice it anymore—and then I open my eyes and, my god! It's so dramatic and so alive! Like the time I was coming out of the Henry Hudson Parkway. I'd been mulling over *West Side Story* and I didn't take the right exit, I think. Somehow I was under a huge causeway somewhere right by the river up around 125th street. All around me Puerto Rican kids were playing, with those typical New York City shouts and the New York raucousness. And yet this causeway backdrop was in a classic key, pillars and Roman arches. The contrast was a fascination. It really contained the theme of *West Side Story*. You know, contemporary content echoing a classic myth. Suddenly I had the inspiration for the rhumba scene. We even used that wonderful causeway in the set.[27]

Although Bernstein's working relationship with Sondheim was fairly equal, he was more deferential to Robbins, clearly the leader in this project. "We worked closely together. I remember all my collaborations with Jerry in terms of one tactile bodily feeling: his hands on my shoulders—composing with his hands on my shoulders. This may be metaphorical, but it's the way I remember it. I can feel him standing behind me saying, 'Four more beats there,' or 'No, that's too many,' or 'Yeah—that's it!'"[28] Not every moment was so inspiring. "There was only one moment when I was really scared to play something." Bernstein recalls. "It was the 'Cool' fugue. He liked it so much he freaked out. I was so happy."[29] The collaborative process did not always result in consensus between the authors. Laurents pushed for more passion and edginess in the songs, feeling that "One Hand, One Heart" (originally planned for the balcony scene) was not impassioned enough for that moment, and preferring a harder version of the "Jet Song." Another number that was originally conceived more collaboratively was the "Prologue," which was originally sung throughout. Robbins had asked Laurents before dance rehearsals were to begin to write essentially a one-act play that would serve as the basis for the drama unfolding in the prologue.[30] Many of the lines taken from the ensuing dialogue and from the "Jet Song" first found their way into this danced, sung, and acted tour de force. For logistical as well as artistic reasons, the text was dropped and the number was transmuted into pure ballet.

In the meantime, Robbins was trying to find a producer for the show. George Abbott, Leland Hayward, and Rodgers and Hammerstein all turned the project down, feeling that it was too depressing a scenario to make into a hit musical.[31] "No one should be shocked by that," recalls Robbins. "A *fait accompli* is one thing, but it's not surprising that people said, 'I don't understand what that's about' in the case of a work in the embryo stage that was quite radical in its time. They hadn't heard Lenny's score, they hadn't read the script, they certainly hadn't seen what was going to be danced."[32] Finally Cheryl Crawford, who had directed at the Group Theatre along with Harold Clurman and Lee Strasberg, agreed to take on the project and started to find backers. She found this extremely difficult. The same reasons why the other producers turned the team down had an equally chilling effect on those who could provide the financial backing. The serious story, the lack of the usual Broadway production values, and the absence of a star meant that the show would have to succeed on its own artistic merits. There were also casting problems as the collaborators tried to find relatively unknown dancers who could also manage the singing and acting challenges of the work. The drama continued to unfold in a backers' audition held in April of 1957 in the West Side apartment of a woman named Bea Lawrence. There was no air conditioning, so the audition (for about thirty or forty people) took place in front of the open windows of the apartment, which looked out onto the river. The sound of tugboats wafted through the window and eventually became incorporated into the score itself. Crawford and her partner Roger S. Stevens hosted the evening, and the team did the best they could in singing and acting their way through the drama. The audience responded poorly, seemed bored,

and offered no money. Before they left for the evening, Stevens gave Arthur
Laurents his number in London and asked him to call if there was any trouble
with the show. No doubt Stevens sensed Crawford's shaky faith in the project
and wanted to help the collaborators as much as he could.

The following Monday morning, April 22, 1957, the team was summoned
to Crawford's office, where she let them know that she would not be able to
produce the show. Over the weeks that preceded the meeting, she had been
sending memos to the collaborators, blaming one to another for the weaknesses of the piece. Her reasoning on that morning was that the book was not
good enough and that the collaborators would have to rewrite the show before
she could consider producing it. Laurents recalls, "Cheryl Crawford didn't like
the book, she was on my back from the very beginning about the vocabulary
of invented slang. She told me, 'No place do they say, "That's how the cookie
crumbles."' She wanted it in very badly. I think maybe if I'd put it in she might
have produced the show."[33] Crawford's major concern was that the musical
should trace the juvenile delinquent problem by showing how WASP neigh-
borhoods became Jewish, then African-American, and then finally became the
racial mix that was portrayed in the show. As Arthur Laurents drily put it, "Set
that to music." Gerald Freedman reports that Elia Kazan cautioned Crawford
against doing the show because it wasn't realistic enough.[34] In fact, the most
important reason was that she could not raise the money. Laurents asked her if
Roger Stevens felt the same way about the show, and she assured them that he
did. In a corner, Stevens's assistant Sylvia Mazzola shot Laurents a glance that
suggested that Crawford was lying about Stevens's disavowal. Laurents then
said, "Cheryl, you are an immoral woman," and the four men left the office.[35]

Finding themselves on the corner of 44th Street and 6th Avenue, the team
came apart and tried to find somewhere to sit down, have a drink, and re-
group. They tried the Algonquin, but they could not be served because Arthur
Laurents was not wearing a tie. Instead they went to the nearby Iroquois,
where Stephen Sondheim convinced Laurents to use the Roger Stevens number. After the collect call to London, Laurents reported, "Roger says, whatever
happens, keep working. He will guarantee everything somehow. Just don't
worry about it." The collaborators even thought of having the show produced
at City Center, which would have meant a two-week run, even though they
didn't know yet whether they would be able to stage it there. They were hopeful, but they were also desperate.

That night Stephen Sondheim was on the phone with his friend and colleague Harold Prince. Prince was in Boston rehearsing a Gwen Verdon show called *New Girl in Town*, and things were not going well. A show that had been meant to be a musical version of *Anna Christie* was turning more and more into a dance vehicle for Verdon, who was also ill very close to the show's opening. Prince was afraid that he and his partner Robert Griffith had a flop on their hands. Sondheim regaled Prince with his own sad tale, and then each hung up the phone. A couple of sleepless hours later, Prince called Sondheim back and asked him to send the script of *West Side Story* to himself and Griffith. Prince already knew the score, as Sondheim had played it for him throughout the previous year, but Prince had to pretend that he had never heard it before, since Bernstein did not want anyone to hear the music before the show went in to production. The following Sunday at 10:00 a.m. Prince and Griffith were back in New York and listened to the show at Bernstein's apartment at the Osborne, with Prince occasionally singing along. "That's what I need! A producer who understands music,"[36] remarked Bernstein, unaware of Prince's prior intimacy with the score. The producing team agreed to take on the musical on the condition that they would do no work until *New Girl in Town* opened. They also had to contend with Bernstein's availability, since he was scheduled to conduct in Israel and South America in the fall, very close on the heels of an expected opening. It took only a week for Griffith and Prince to raise the three hundred thousand dollars needed to get *West Side Story* on stage. Most investors contributed on the strength of the producers' reputation, imagining that they might lose their money on *West Side Story*, but would be able to recoup this on future, successful musicals. Of that budget, sixty-five thousand dollars was allocated to costumes, which Irene Sharaff was building. Prince later recalls,

I remember I didn't have much patience for the blue jeans Irene Sharaff "designed" for *West Side Story* at the cost of $75 a pair (today they would cost $200). I thought, How foolish to be wasting money when we can make a promotional arrangement with Levi Strauss to supply blue jeans free for program credit. So I instructed the wardrobe mistress in New York to replace them as they wore out with Levi's, not with costumes. A year later I looked at *West Side* and wondered, Why doesn't it look as beautiful as it used to? What's happened? What 'happened' was that Sharaff's blue jeans were made of a special fabric,

which was then dipped and dyed and beaten and dyed again and aged again and
so on, so our blue jeans were in forty subtly different shades of blue, vibrating,
energetic, creating the *effect* of realism.[37]

Once the show was back up and running, Jerome Robbins dropped a bomb:
he felt that it was too much work for him to both choreograph and direct, so
he wanted to direct only and have Herbert Ross hired to do the choreography.
Prince remained calm but reminded him that the reason he had agreed to
produce the show was because Robbins was going to choreograph, and if he
wasn't, Prince wasn't sure he wanted to continue as producer. Robbins acqui-
esced but asked for eight weeks of rehearsal, when the norm was four (he also
had to clear with Equity to start rehearsals four weeks early). Prince agreed to
this. Robbins also wanted four rehearsal pianists, and Prince agreed to give
him three. The show was on again, and now the team needed to finish auditions and get ready for rehearsals to start in very short order. Roger Stevens
was instrumental in securing the Winter Garden Theatre for the show, and
rehearsals were to take place in the Chester Hale Studio, on 55th Street near
Carnegie Hall, a loft above a garage. Gerald Freedman, who had worked with
Robbins on other shows, was assistant director, although Laurents claims he
did a fair amount of direction himself, staging some scenes in the restroom
lounge.[38] Peter Gennaro, who had worked on *Seventh Heaven*, was brought in
as co-choreographer, and he staged most of "America" and the Latin dance
styles for the Sharks in the "Dance at the Gym."[39]

Originally the creators wanted a show which went against some of the
conventions of Broadway: a show that had much of the story danced instead
of sung and spoken and had no stars that would take attention away from the
very serious subject matter. They apparently auditioned a number of street
kids, hoping to come up with authentic representations of the characters in
the show. "It was the hardest show to cast I've ever heard of," recalls Bernstein. "Everybody has either to be or seem to be a teenager, to sing a very difficult score, to act a very difficult role and dance very difficult dances. Everybody had to seem to be doing all of these things, so that Larry Kert and Carol
Lawrence had to seem to be dancing as much as anybody else. Part of Jerry's
magic was to make it seem that way. We were also very lucky to find people
like Mickey Calin, who played Riff. He sang 'Cool'—not like an operatic star,
but the way it should be sung, I felt—and he was a fabulous dancer."[40] The

casting process was also collaborative. As Robbins recalls, "As part of our collaboration, we had to sort out whether a specific actor was going to sing, or dance, or just act, and how to put him together with the rest of the show. We were very fortunate in getting the cast that we did, from a great dancer like Chita Rivera to someone like Larry Kert who had a wonderful voice and could do acrobatic things when we needed it."[41] Kert, who eventually won the role of Tony, auditioned some sixteen or so times for various different roles. His voice was not high enough to sing the tenor parts written by Bernstein, and his dancing was not strong enough to win a role as one of the other characters. Kert recalls that he auditioned for the musical several times while a chorus member in a show called *Mr. Wonderful.* After that show he auditioned for Bernardo, but wasn't good enough as a dancer; subsequently he auditioned for Riff, but again his dancing abilities got in the way. Similarly, Carol Lawrence, who most recently was performing in a Ziegfeld show, came to the audition heavily made-up and bedecked in jewelry. The auditioners told her to go home and have a shower and come back looking like a young girl. To improve their chances, she asked if she and Kert could go away for a couple of days and work on "Tonight." After three or four days they returned to audition. "When I was doing the audition," Kert recalls, "I looked around for Carol on stage and couldn't find her. Without any plan to do it, she had gone up a back fire escape she had seen there, just to project the feeling of a balcony. When I had to sing 'I'm coming up,' I shimmied up the pole, also on instinct. It lent a sense of urgency to the moment and showed some physical prowess on my part." Later that night Kert got a call from Arthur Laurents telling him he had been cast as Tony. By the time the auditions were complete, there was only one person who came with some star status: Chita Rivera, who had worked with Robbins previously on *Seventh Heaven.* Casting took place over a period of approximately six months, and during the last couple of weeks auditions took place in Griffith and Prince's office after Crawford had dropped the show.

The rehearsal period was intense, with Robbins's high standards and his tendency to pick on dancers readily in evidence (he also allegedly had sexual relationships with both Lee Becker, who played Anybodys, and Tommy Abbott, who played Gee-Tar, during rehearsals for the show).[42] Jay Norman (one of the Sharks) recalls that Mickey Calin (playing the part of Riff) was chosen as Robbins's whipping boy.

I was so proud that he didn't come in one day with a gun and kill the man. I just wouldn't have been able to take what he took. It would have killed me. I wouldn't have had a career. What I saw happen was . . . when we started rehearsals, Mickey Callan [sic] was not Riff. He was a nice-looking guy, not a bad tap dancer, but couldn't dance as well as the rest of us as far as the other stuff. Jerry tore him apart . . . just totally dissected him. But Jerry put him back together. Perhaps I'm wrong, perhaps Mickey pulled himself back together, but when he came back together, he was Riff, and he was a damn good Riff. By that time, Mickey understood what Jerry wanted. In that sense, it was wonderful, but to watch it happen as a fellow human being was horrible. I would go home really despising Jerry for that. . . . It was amazing. Mickey couldn't even click in tempo. Jerry had him so rattled . . . in 'Cool,' his mouth was in time to the music and his hand was out of time. Now figure that. . . . But when the two of them were finished, when rehearsals finally came to performances, we had a Riff.[43]

During the rehearsal for the bedroom scene, Carol Lawrence had hit Larry Kert's chest so many times that she was loosening his lungs from his ribcage. Robbins suggested she start hitting him in the head instead; "you won't hurt anything there," he quipped.[44]

Robbins decided to use Method techniques, asking the cast to identify as closely as possible with their roles. Cast members cut out gang articles from the newspapers and papered the backstage area with them. They were also not allowed to call each other by their real names, only their character names. As Carol Lawrence recalls,

> To keep us from slipping out of character, Jerry would suddenly ask us questions about our parents—not our real parents, but the parents of the characters we were playing, even if those parents were not mentioned in the show. He trained us to imagine what it would be like to *be* the characters we played and discover why we were the way we were. . . . We humane, civilized actors were becoming the hate-filled, violent street gangs we were portraying. If you think onstage was exciting, it didn't compare to backstage! The Sharks and the Jets lived! Violence and sexual intimidation, fights and injuries, you name it—it was going on and getting worse.[45]

Carol Lawrence recalls how tough was the competition. During one rehearsal she fell to the floor in a botched choreographic move, and she could see the faces of her three understudies peering hopefully from the wings. That was all the encouragement she needed to get up and keep rehearsing. Tony Mordente, one of Robbins's favorites and eventually cast in the film version, was ostracized by his fellow Jets when he started dating Chita Rivera (they had a child together shortly before the British tour).

Sondheim credits Robbins's method with the success of the direction. "It helped that Jerry kept the Jets and the Sharks apart as groups separate during rehearsals, even having their meals as separate gangs. I thought it was pretentious, but of course it was perfect, because, without any animosity or hostility, there was a sense of each gang having its own individuality, so that you had two giant personalities onstage. And I believe this is the first show whose chorus had individual characterizations. Maybe one or two people would be characterized, like Agnes de Mille's The Girl Who Falls Down in *Oklahoma!*, but in *West Side Story* each of the members of the chorus had a name and a personality and was cast accordingly. Everybody takes that for granted now, but in those days it was a startling notion."[46]

Grover Dale recalls in Greg Lawrence's *Dance with Demons* how intimately the dancers associated with their roles.

> He encouraged us to keep the war going offstage as well as on. During a rehearsal lunch break, a couple of the Jets found a large piece of cardboard in the alley by the stagedoor entrance. We got an idea. Within ten minutes, we climbed the ladder to the fly floor above the stage with a giant shark cutout stuffed with newspaper. We knew Jerry was onstage promptly. No one ever dared to be late for a Robbins rehearsal! Sure enough, at two p.m. the stage was occupied by a full contingency of Sharks standing there, like, Aren't we good boys! Jets were nowhere in sight. Jerry paced furiously, demanding an explanation from the stage manager, Ruth Mitchell, why the Jets weren't onstage. Perfect. Without a word, we tossed the cardboard shark onto the stage. It landed inches from Jerry's feet. Plop. He loved it.[47]

Robbins's demands were on not just the dancers but the other collaborators. Bernstein harbored a certain awe for Robbins that stopped him from arguing with the choreographer. As Sondheim recalls, "at one point in Washington during the *West Side Story* tryout . . . Robbins took over the orchestra from Lenny and inserted some music to fit a choreographic idea that he had just created. Lenny was in the back of the theater and when he saw what was happening he started to storm down the aisle. I thought he was going to go after Jerry. But then he stopped, turned around and practically ran out of the theater. I ran after him and found him in the bar next door to the theater with five shots of whisky in front of him."[48] That said, none could deny Robbins's mastery as a director. "'Gee, Officer Krupke,' which stopped the show every night, was staged in record time." Sondheim recalls, "There are some good jokes there. Parenthetically, Jerry staged it in three hours by the clock, three days before we went to Washington. Jerry had been staging everything else, and we kept reminding him that this was a comedy number, and he kept saying, 'I'll get to it. I'll get to it.' One afternoon he did it in almost no time at all. Maybe the ideas had been cooking, but the staging of 'Krupke' is one of the most brilliant inventive in one numbers I've ever seen."[49] Robbins is more self-effacing about the direction of the song: "By the end of the rehearsal period you're really into the work, you know the actors, you know the scenes. It isn't like the first days of rehearsals when you're fishing around and going tentatively toward what you want. You're on course. It's like those numbers you write in rehearsal or out of town. By that time, the wheels are rolling, you are into the character, the mood, the energy. Also, I find I do a lot of my best work when I'm tired and have less tension inside of me."[50]

The set, by Oliver Smith, also produced some tense moments. Smith had designed a dark blue background with red fire escapes, which Robbins wanted to replace in the second-act ballet with a clear stage, bringing in a sense of light and space. The ballet followed a bedroom scene between Tony and Maria, and there was no way to get the bed off because Smith had designed what was essentially a box. Robbins asked for a saw and sawed through the set while Smith stood by helplessly.[51] The bed was able to be cleared through the hole in the side of the set as a result.

Most of the changes to the show were made in early summer, omitting a very aggressive gang number called "Mix!" (it would later find its way into Bernstein's *Chichester Psalms*) and dropping the lyrics for the prologue, which became an all-danced introductory number. Although Arthur Laurents liked "Mix!" Harold Prince felt it was too violent for the opening of the show. The song "Somewhere" was originally meant for the balcony scene, but it was altered to the dream ballet and "Tonight" was substituted. There was also a liberal amount of sharing of material between the concurrent *Candide* and *West Side Story*, most significantly the use of "One Hand, One Heart," originally intended for Cunegonde and Candide, and "Gee, Officer Krupke," also coming from *Candide*. Similarly, the song "O Happy We" was originally intended for Tony and Maria. "One Hand, One Heart" particularly irked Sondheim, who had to deal with Bernstein's original lyrics.

> I had two street kids singing, "Today the world was just an address, a place for me to live in," Now, you know, excuse me, that's okay for Romeo and Juliet, that's a perfectly good line, but. . . . That was Lenny's idea of poetry, very purple. . . . He wrote a lyric for a tune, "I Have a Love." His lyric was—it's hard for me to do this with a straight face— "Once in your life, only once in your life/Comes a flash of fire and light." Wait for it! "And there stands your love/The harvest of your years." That was his idea of poetry. As for my words to "One Hand, One Heart," we used to break up laughing when they did it during the out-of-town tryouts. We had to leave the room. But one person stayed and wept over it every single time. That was Lenny.[52]

By the time the show went into tryouts in Washington, there were very few changes made, fewer than in any of Sondheim's shows that he could remember, with the exception of *Sweeney Todd*.[53] The collaborators had been working on the show for so long (thirteen months, according to Laurents) that there were very few changes needed. Sondheim recalls, "On the way to the airport in Washington after a very nice run, I said rather ingenuously to Jerry 'Gee, this is my first show, and I wanted to have the experience of sitting up until three o'clock in the morning in a smoke-filled room rewriting the second act.' He looked at me in such anger and said, in effect, 'Take that back, don't ever say that out loud. Until you've been through it, you don't know what it's like.' I thought it would have been glamorous. I learned that Jerry was right, at two or three o'clock in hotel rooms in subsequent years. But the show was changed very little. It was what it was when it opened."[54] Richard Rodgers saw the show in rehearsal, and his contribution was to suggest they drop a death scene for Maria, who was going to commit suicide as in the Shakespeare original. "She's dead already, after this all happens to her," he averred.[55] One song, "Like Everybody Else," was written after the Washington opening but dropped for the New York production because Laurents argued that it seemed to shift the work into musical comedy, which none of the creators wanted.[56] In particular, Stephen Sondheim, the youngest and most inexperienced of the team, saw flaws in his lyrics that he eventually wanted to correct. Sondheim realized that the lyrics he was writing, particularly for Maria, were too wordy and articulate for a young girl who just got off the boat from Puerto Rico. He wrote a simpler version of "I Feel Pretty," but the rest of the team rejected it. It became one of Sondheim's least favorite of his lyrics. "I was outvoted. I changed the lyric of 'I Feel Pretty' after seeing the run-through in New York because I was ashamed of it. Later the others said they liked it better the way it was before, so I went home. I'm not fond of a lot of the *West Side Story* lyrics. To me, they seem very 'written.' I like 'Something's Coming' and 'Jet Song' because they have a kind of energy to them. The more contemplative lyrics I find very self-conscious and a mite pretentious every now and then. I hear a writer at work instead of a character."[57] The collaborators remark in their joint reminiscences about how story became song sometimes rather organically. "There was a generosity on everybody's part that I've rarely seen in the theater," Bernstein recalls. "For example, the song 'Something's Coming' was a very late comer. We realized we needed a character-introduction kind of song for Tony. There was a marvelous introductory page in the script that Arthur had written a kind of monologue, the essence of which became the lyric for this song. We raped Arthur's playwriting. I've never seen anyone so encouraging, let alone generous, urging us, 'Yes, take it, take it, make it a song.' Almost all the 'Something's Coming' lyrics had been written as a poetic prose by Arthur."[58]

In late June orchestration started in earnest. Brought on board were Bernstein's childhood friend Sid Ramin and fellow orchestrator Irwin Kostal. Long orchestration meetings would go on after rehearsal, with the orchestrators finishing numbers as they were completed by Bernstein. Typically Broadway composers do not orchestrate their own works but use orchestrators who specialize in creating the Broadway sound behind the composer's intention. In Bernstein's case, his notes were so detailed that he knew exactly what he wanted for each number and would no doubt have orchestrated the score himself had he had time. Bernstein wanted the best orchestra he could get for his show and intentionally did not write viola parts because he had no faith in the violists in the Winter Garden Theatre orchestra. He also used a soloist in the cello section rather than entrust the entire section to handle much of the music.

The first run-through was on August 10 for a "gypsy" audience (other actors and theater people) without sets or costumes. The tryouts in Washington opened on August 19 and proved more successful than anyone had dreamed.

A late rehearsal (at 3:00 p.m.) on the opening day helped to keep the show tight and in good shape for the first Washington audience. Tickets were sold out for the run of the show. There were seventeen curtain calls, and as a result the creators became temporary local heroes. The keys to the city of Washington were presented to Robbins, Laurents, and Bernstein for all they had done for juvenile delinquency. The show then went to Philadelphia for more tryouts, and there they had also a warm reception, with mounted policemen on duty to keep the ticket lines in order. The critics and audiences were very supportive, even if not as explosive as those in Washington. In an act of generosity, Bernstein agreed to remove his name from the lyrics attribution and let Sondheim have the sole program credit. "And we'll make the financial adjustments, too," Bernstein added, to which Sondheim said he really only cared about the credit. It was a decision that would cost him a great deal in royalties over the years.

Sondheim's note to Bernstein on the day of the New York premiere sums up his feelings about the experience: "*West Side Story* means much more to me than a first show, more even than the privilege of collaborating with you and Arthur and Jerry. It marks the beginning of what I hope will be a long and enduring friendship. Friendship is a thing I give or receive rarely, but for what it's worth, I want you to know you have it from me always."[59]

SYNOPSIS OF THE MUSICAL

West Side Story opens on the streets of Manhattan in the last days of summer. To the sound of the characteristic whistle that has become emblematic of the show, the "Prologue" music starts as members of two gangs, the Sharks and the Jets, populate the stage. Entirely in dance we see a series of scenarios typifying the interaction of these two rival gangs. The predominantly Puerto Rican Sharks and the mostly "white" Jets stage a series of ambushes, hazing, and intimidation; just when one gang seems to have the upper hand, another scene shows the other gang on top. The prologue establishes for the audience the time, place, and mood of this piece—a New York City portrayed almost like a scene of ruins. Walls full of graffiti, industrial and urban landscapes form the backdrop to this struggle over who owns the streets. In the final conflict, the Sharks accost the more vulnerable A-Rab, throw him to the ground, and pierce his ear. The sound of the policeman's whistle brings the youths to their senses, and the Sharks run off. Enter Lieutenant Schrank and

Officer Krupke, two policemen who represent to both gangs the adult world, a world that neither understands nor accepts them. Schrank tries to intimidate A-Rab into revealing who attacked him, but Riff, the charismatic leader of the Jets, deflects the question and levels a sarcastic response to Schrank. The police warn the young gang members that they don't own the streets, and we see starkly the divide between adult and youth, authority and gang, that will characterize the interactions of these groups throughout the musical.

Left to their own devices, Riff builds up the Jet members with talk of retaliation and Jet pride. His first number, the "Jet Song," glorifies the life of the Jet gang member, who finds a home with his buddies in a way he cannot with any other group. The gang vows to officially challenge Bernardo, the Shark leader, to a rumble. They agree to meet that night at the dance at the gym, looking their best, to issue a challenge that will change their lives forever. In the next scene, Riff goes to former gang member Tony to secure his support for the rumble and to make sure he comes to the dance that night. Tony is painting a sign for Doc's candy store, where he now works. He has started to grow up and no longer wants the gang life he once enjoyed with Riff and the others. Riff prods and cajoles him to join the gang this one last time, and Tony begrudgingly agrees. He tells Riff that every night he wakes up reaching out for something, although he knows not what. Maybe that something will be "twitching at the dance tonight," Riff reminds him. Alone on stage, Tony sings "Something's Coming," a restless song that encapsulates Tony's sense of anticipation and prefigures the life-altering events that will unfold at the gym that night.

The story moves to the bridal shop, where the wily Anita and the younger Maria work as seamstresses. Maria is getting ready for her first night out in America, and she cajoles Anita to lower the neckline on her party dress. Anita is firm—Maria is still young and promised to her countryman, Chino. There is no need for a sexier dress. Maria finally gets the dress on and admires herself in the mirror. Bernardo and Chino arrive to escort the girls to the dance, and the charismatic and knowing Bernardo is a good foil to the timid and inexperienced Chino.

As Maria readies herself for her first night as a young lady of America, the scene dissolves to the gym, where both Sharks and Jets dance with their girlfriends. Gladhand, a nervous and ineffective emcee for the evening, tries to convince the gang members to partake in a mixer dance that would potentially see girls and boys from rival gangs dancing together. To the tune of a pedantic *pasodoble*, the teenagers at first acquiesce, but quickly break into their own mambo. What follows is one of the great set choreographic pieces of the show, as each gang tries to outdance the other, the Jets in a more modern, jazz idiom, the Sharks with a flamboyant Latin dance style. Before either group can be declared a winner, Tony and Maria see each other across the crowded room and are immediately transfixed. As most of the dancers leave the stage, the young couple approach each other slowly and enter into their own gentle cha-cha. The dancers left on stage mirror their movements, as though in slow motion, and a dialogue ensues between Tony and Maria. They seem instantly in love, and their words echo the sense of wonder and amazement that each has found the other in this unlikely place. As Tony slowly goes to kiss Maria, the scene changes rapidly; now the "jump" music intervenes, and Bernardo is quickly at Maria's side, defending her against what he perceives as the advances of one of the enemy. Maria is sent away with Chino, and Bernardo and Riff determine the time for a war council meeting at Doc's store.

Tony, in an altered state from this dramatic meeting, wanders into the street singing about "Maria," an expansive, lyrical song in which he repeats the name over and over. Eventually he finds his way to Maria's balcony and climbs up to speak to her. In "Tonight," the young lovers remark on the sudden change that this meeting has brought to their lives. Maria is worried that her parents will discover her with Tony; she sends him away with promises that they will meet at the bridal shop the next night after work. They declare their love and their fate is sealed.

The Shark men and women enter the scene, relaxing after the dance. Bernardo and Anita reveal themselves as playful, teasing partners. Bernardo complains of the inequities of the Puerto Rican life in America; Anita celebrates its rights and freedoms. Anita informs Bernardo that she is an American girl now and does not want to wait until he is finished with his war council. They reach a momentary truce, but after the men leave, Anita regales the remaining Shark women with her view of this new home, "America." The song is funny and clever and allows the Shark women an opportunity to show their dance skills. This is the first fully entertainment number in the musical, showcasing the acting and dancing talents of Anita.

Meanwhile, the Jets are at Doc's drugstore, nervously awaiting the arrival of the Sharks and the ensuing war council. Anybodys, a tomboy, is desperate to become a Jet member, but she is ridiculed and belittled by both the men and the Jet girlfriends. We start to see different personalities emerging in the Jets: Baby John, young and inexperienced; Action, a fighter; A-Rab, ready to burst with violent energy. Riff admonishes the group to play it "Cool," not to reveal their emotions to the enemy. In a dance sequence much different in style from Anita's, the Jet men and women perform an angry, barely controlled expression of their frustration, longing, and disillusionment. Bernardo and the Sharks arrive on the scene, and the gangs start sparring verbally. True to his promise to Maria, Tony arrives and challenges them all to a fair fight, no weapons. The best man from each gang will fight the best man from the other. Bernardo shakes on it, so eager is he to get his hands on this Tony. He is taken aback when Riff announces that Bernardo will fight Diesel, instead. Their exchange is interrupted by the arrival of Schrank, who tries to extract from the kids the location of the fight. He dismisses the Sharks and tells the Jets that he's on their side and will help them if they only reveal the location of the rumble. But the gang will not give in, and Schrank leaves in disgust. Tony reveals to Doc the reason he wanted to make it a fair fight; he now has a girl, and she is Puerto Rican. Doc, seeing the danger, urges Tony to be careful.

The next day Maria and Anita are getting ready to close up the bridal shop; Maria promises to lock up and encourages Anita to be on her way. When Tony arrives, Anita guesses at the nature of their relationship and immediately disapproves. However, she sees their sincere emotions. Anita agrees to leave them alone for fifteen minutes and not to tell Maria's family about Tony. Like playful children, Tony and Maria describe their wedding ceremony, with dressmakers' mannequins taking the place of their parents and friends. However, when Maria dons a veil, they both look at each other and understand the gravity of their situation and their love. In "One Hand, One Heart," they kneel and sing their vows to each other. In one of the great ensemble pieces of the show, the Jet and Shark gangs, Tony, Maria, and Anita all sing of their anticipation of "Tonight," the night of the rumble. Tony and Maria long for the day to end so that they can see each other, Anita looks forward to a passionate night with Bernardo, and each gang is determined to beat the other once and for all. Tony is sure that with his intervention he will fulfill his promise to Maria and there will be no fight.

Under the highway the gangs meet. Riff tries to have Diesel shake Bernardo's hand, but the Shark leader will have none of this. He wants to get down to the fight, and he's not interested in the Jets' traditions. When Tony appears on the scene, no one believes that he is there to make peace. Bernardo taunts him, and soon a fight erupts. Knives appear and before they know it Riff is killed by Bernardo. In anguish, Tony kills Bernardo and then cries out for Maria. As the police sirens close in, Anybodys pulls Tony away from the gruesome scene. A distant clock chimes as the curtain descends.

The beginning of Act II takes us to a bedroom where Maria is chatting with her girlfriends. No one can figure out why she is so happy, until she reveals to them that tonight is her wedding night. To a light Spanish number Maria explains "I Feel Pretty," as she is loved by a "pretty wonderful boy." Their frivolity is interrupted by the arrival of Chino, shaken and dirtied. Maria does not believe him when he tells her that there was a fight and is stricken when he reveals that Bernardo has been killed. When she asks desperately if Tony is safe, Chino guesses at their relationship and storms out. Maria kneels in prayer, hoping against hope that Chino's story is not true. When Tony sneaks in through her window, her first reaction is rage, and she beats against his chest crying, "Murderer, murderer." He calms her and explains that he spontaneously avenged Riff's life. He offers to go to the police, but Maria wants him to stay with her. As they dream of a world far away from this conflict, the stage clears and the music of "Somewhere" becomes the backdrop for the second-act ballet, the main set choreographic piece of the musical. After the central drama of the work is enacted through the ballet, we return to the bedroom, where Tony and Maria take solace in each other.

In another alley, A-Rab and Baby John reconnoiter, badly shaken and worried about what will happen next. A short encounter with Officer Krupke sends the boys running in different directions until they meet up with more of the Jet gang. In one of the comic highlights of the show, the boys sing "Gee, Officer Krupke," in which they enact various social approaches to juvenile delinquency. As the song ends, tomboy Anybodys appears on the scene to let them know that Chino is looking for Tony and that Chino has a gun. The Jets disperse to spread the news and find Tony, and Anybodys finally gets some recognition from Action—she has earned favor from the all-male Jets.

Anita comes to Maria's room, awakening Tony and Maria and knocking insistently at the door. Tony leaves through the window, promising to get money and to meet Maria at the candy store, from which they will make their escape to the country. When Maria finally lets Anita in, Maria's state of undress and the open window tells Anita that the lovers have met. In disbelief and grief, Anita launches into the fiery, "A Boy Like That," warning Maria of the kind of man that Tony is and how he will hurt her. In a stylistically operatic number, Maria intervenes with "I Have a Love," appealing to Anita's love for Bernardo to understand her situation. By the end of the number, Anita is won over and agrees to help the couple. Schrank arrives and starts to interrogate Maria about the scene in the gym. She asks Anita in coded language to tell Tony to wait for her and continues her interrogation by Schrank.

Anita goes to Doc's store, where Tony is hiding. She tries to convince the Jets that she is there to make peace and to give Maria's message to Tony, but the Jets harass her mercilessly and attack her. Doc interrupts the assault, but Anita is so angry that she tells the Jets that Maria is dead; Chino found out about the couple and shot her. Doc goes to the basement to tell Tony, who can only talk about his happy future with Maria. Once he hears the terrible news, he runs out into the street, calling for Chino to come and kill him, too. Suddenly, he sees Maria emerging from the shadows, but as they run toward each other, a shot rings out. Tony falls and, in a short reprise of "Somewhere," dies in Maria's arms. Maria, now bereft and with nothing left to lose, takes the gun from Chino and threatens both Sharks and Jets, all of whom killed Tony. She blames them for the life they have created out of conflict and hatred. As the police arrive, both Sharks and Jets slowly come together to carry Tony's body away, and Maria walks slowly behind the cortege, nothing left to live for. As the last chords ring out in the orchestra, the music reminds us that the truce is only temporary, and that the "Somewhere" for which they all hope is still very much out of reach in their troubled world.

NOTES

1. Landmark symposia, organized by the Dramatists Guild, have focused on a number of musicals, including *Fiddler on the Roof* and *The Fantasticks*, and the proceedings have been published by *The Dramatist* (formerly *Dramatists Guild Quarterly*).

2. *Rashomon* was a 1951 film by Japanese director Akiro Kurosawa (who also directed the acclaimed 1954 film *Seven Samurai*) in which the plot was told separately through the perspectives of individual characters. It questioned the validity of one "truth" by presenting four different viewpoints on one incident.

3. Geoffrey Block lays out these changes throughout chapter 12 of *Enchanted Evenings*.

4. Opinions differ on whether or not Montgomery Clift ever played the part of Romeo, let alone went to Robbins for help. Russ Tamblyn, who played the part of Riff in the film version, recalls that Robbins substantiated the Clift story during the filming of *West Side Story*.

5. Quoted in Greg Lawrence, *Dance with Demons: The Life of Jerome Robbins* (New York: G. P. Putnam, 2001), 52–53.

6. Lawrence, *Demons*, 139.

7. Lawrence, *Demons*, 231. Meryle Secrest reports the January date in *Leonard Bernstein: A Life*, 212.

8. "Landmark," 11.

9. See Bernstein, "*West Side Story* Log," in *Findings*, 144–47.

10. Laurents, *Original Story By: A Memoir of Broadway and Hollywood* (New York: Applause, 2000), 329.

11. "Landmark," 13.

12. "Landmark," 12.

13. Quoted in Humphrey Burton, *Leonard Bernstein* (New York: Doubleday, 1994), 248.

14. Laurents, *Original Story By*, 334.

15. As it turns out, Robbins was also in Los Angeles that summer, choreographing "The Small House of Uncle Thomas" for the film version of *The King and I*.

16. "Landmark," 13. Bernstein claims that the headline read, "Gang Riots on Oliviera Street" and Laurents, in his autobiography, claims it was "More Mayhem from Chicano Gangs" (Laurents, *Original Story By*, 338).

17. Laurents, *Original Story By*, 338.

18. Lawrence, *Demons*, 233.

19. Craig Zadan, *Sondheim & Company*, 12.

20. "Landmark," 13.

21. "Landmark," 12.

22. Quoted in Burton, *Bernstein*, 255.

23. Quoted in Secrest, *Leonard Bernstein*, 215.

24. Laurents, *Original Story By*, 350.

25. Burton, *Bernstein*, 96.

26. Laurents, *Original Story By*, 350.

27. Quoted in Secrest, *Bernstein*, 212.

28. "Landmark," 20.

29. "Landmark," 20.

30. Laurents, *Original Story By*, 356.

31. Lawrence, *Demons*, 248.

32. "Landmark," 12.

33. "Landmark," 17.

34. Lawrence, *Demons*, 248.

35. Laurents, *Original Story By*, 328.

36. Secrest, *Bernstein*, 216.

37. Harold Prince, *Contradictions*, 36.

38. Lawrence, *Demons*, 241; and Laurents, *Original Story By*, 359.

39. "Landmark," 20.

40. "Landmark," 17.

41. "Landmark," 16.

42. Lawrence, *Demons*, 247.

43. Lawrence, *Demons*, 252. Stephen Sondheim wrote to Lawrence about Robbins's difficult working relationships: "I think the reason for Jerry's success at intimidation with everyone was that he had a knack for spotting essential weaknesses in people almost instantly on meeting them, and he would file the knowledge away in his memory for future use. One of his most effective ploys, which worked with Lenny as

well as me, was public humiliation—that is to say, brazen criticism in front of one's own colleagues. . . . Jerry's artistic ruthlessness was combined with real sadism. Also, he always felt intimidated by anybody educated, so people like Lenny were prime targets. To my knowledge, the only two men who were never afraid of him were Arthur and Jule Styne. . . . In fact, Arthur and Jule were the only ones I ever saw tell Jerry off" (*Demons*, 247–48).

44. Lawrence, *Demons*, 254.

45. Carol Lawrence, *Carol Lawrence: The Backstage Story* (New York: McGraw-Hill Ryerson, 1990), 43.

46. "Landmark," 23–24.

47. Lawrence, *Demons*, 251.

48. Quoted in Secrest, *Bernstein*, 218.

49. "Landmark," 20.

50. "Landmark," 21.

51. Laurents, *Original Story By*, 362.

52. Meryle Secrest, *Stephen Sondheim: A Life*, 115.

53. "Landmark," 16.

54. "Landmark," 16.

55. "Landmark,' 14.

56. Laurents remembers that a song called "Kid's Stuff" was part of the Washington tryout period.

57. "Landmark," 20.

58. "Landmark," 14.

59. Quoted in Burton, *Bernstein*, 277.

3

"Music about Music"

Bernstein and West Side Story

Take *Le sacre du printemps*, which is supposed to be the work that
revolutionized music and changed the world, and just analyze it page by
page, bar by bar. You'll find that every bar of it comes from somewhere
else. But it has just been touched by this magic guy.

—*Leonard Bernstein, interview by Paul R. Laird in "The Best of All Possible Legacies: A
Critical Look at Bernstein, His Eclecticism, and* Candide," Ars Musica Denver 4, no. 1
(Fall 1991): 34

I can't imagine that he is going to convert anybody to Stravinsky and
Bartók by *West Side Story.*

—*Robert Evett, "Music: Bernstein's 'Romeo and Juliet,'"* New Republic, September 9,
1957, 21

West Side Story is a work whose music deserves more detailed study than it
has received thus far. Listeners and scholars alike tend to take Bernstein's
contribution for granted, perhaps because many of its numbers have become
so familiar and because they make their effect so powerfully and directly—or
at least so we think. The present chapter explores the remarkably diverse
materials that Bernstein drew upon in building up his score. As he said about
Stravinsky's *Rite of Spring (Le sacre du printemps)* in the first epigraph above,
many elements in it "come from somewhere else." By becoming aware of
these borrowings and (possible) allusions, we can understand better the

artistry with which another "magic guy"—Bernstein himself—melded them together into a coherent and durable whole. Although gestures from Robbins's choreography continue to resonate in popular culture, and imagery and language from Arthur Laurents's adaptation of Shakespeare have become in some ways synonymous with the work, it is undoubtedly Bernstein's music that has accounted for the longevity of *West Side Story*, not only in the theatrical world but in both classical and popular music realms.[1] Although clearly Bernstein's score was to a certain extent ballet music made to order, catering to many of the demands of Robbins's choreography, much of its notoriety has rested on the quality and originality of the songs, the "modernity" of the score in terms of complexity and dissonance treatment, its colorful orchestration, and the perceived organic unity Bernstein achieved through the careful deployment of leitmotifs (see figure 3.1). The tritone motive, one of the most enduring symbols of the musical's unity, is outlined with the assertion by the composer that this is what makes it one piece, not many. Transcription of figure 3.1: "Impossible to send analysis by mail—But one little clue: in West Side—look for the relation among songs and dance pieces in terms of these three notes (sort of a leitmotif)—Then, in Maria: (same three notes in different order). Then, in Cool: (same notes, different pattern). There are many of these, if you can find them! Good luck. (all this holds the work together and makes it *one* piece instead of many different pieces—)."

This perceived progressiveness of genre and style prevails because *West Side Story* has been able to live a crossover existence in two separate but complementary musical camps. Anyone familiar with the Broadway musical repertoire will know that as early as *Show Boat* and *Porgy and Bess* (as well as in the operetta tradition) reminiscence motives, reprise, underscored dialogue (as in the "Jet Song" and the "Balcony Scene"), and leitmotifs were common in musicals that aspired to a sense of continuous musical and dramatic argument. Yet, Bernstein's score emerges as somewhat remarkable within the Broadway genre, many of whose better-known works tend to rely on variety rather than unity for effect. That a non–musical theater audience has become familiar with *West Side Story* has led many less conversant with the genre to believe that its apparent novelties (continuous musical scenes, spoken dialogue over music, integration of ballet, etc.) are somewhat innovative, even though the works of Rodgers and Hammerstein (especially *Oklahoma!* and *Carousel*) had long before set these standards.[2] Within the Western art-music

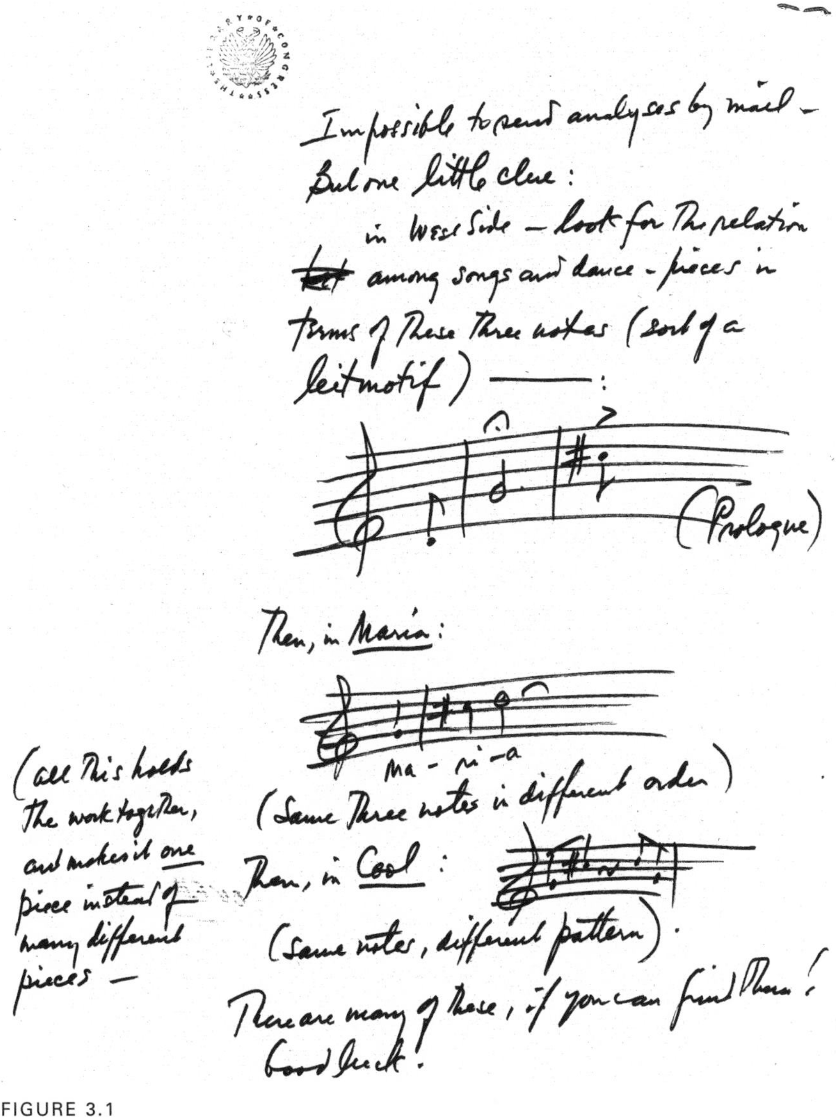

FIGURE 3.1
Aerogram from Bernstein to Dutch student's request for clues to analyzing *West Side Story* for a school project, 3 February 1969. Bernstein Collection: Writings series, Box 83, Folder 33. Courtesy of the Leonard Bernstein Foundation.

repertoire, the motivic and leitmotivic approach, as well as deployment of the tritone both structurally and as a surface detail, date back to the nineteenth century, hardly "progressive" or even modern by 1957 standards (the most famous example, perhaps, being the Wolf's Glen scene from Weber's 1821 *Der Freischütz*, in which two interlocking tritones create the diminished seventh chord that represents the satanic Samiel). Yet, to a Broadway audience, the music emerges as more avant-garde and dissonant than much of the music written up to that point for the genre. It is this very crossover existence that *West Side Story* enjoys that has left the impression in both camps that it filled a unique gap within the other, bridging ballet and musical, opera and musical, classical and popular.[3] Certainly, there is some truth to this, but *West Side Story* was more the culmination of prevailing traditions rather than a work pioneering new trends.[4]

Some of what made *West Side Story* seem so avant-garde was its presentation of Americanism as urban, dangerous, "cool." The same year, *The Music Man* (which beat out *West Side Story* for the coveted Tony Award) reflected a different America, a small-town America whose innocence is polluted by the city slicker's cynical and deceitful ways. The machinelike ensemble that opens that work replicates the sounds of train travel, the mechanized harbinger of the evil, industrialized world from which the protagonist unleashes his moral turpitude on an unsuspecting little town. The resonances of innocence vs. experience, urban vs. rural, and natural vs. manufactured become increasingly echoed in more general musical culture during the late 1950s, where integral serialism and the ascendancy of electronic music abandoned (or set themselves in opposition to) the tonal tradition epitomized by Bernstein, Shostakovich, and Britten (resulting in an oft-cited separation between composer and audience).[5]

Bernstein's attempt to be modern in terms of dissonance and complexity perhaps seems unusual for a work intended for a general audience, especially considering the composer's own belief in tonal music, but it accords with his views on twentieth-century music in general and presumably *West Side Story*'s role in it in particular. "All the truly great works of our century have been born of despair or of protest or of a refuge from both. But anguish informs them all," he avers in his Harvard lectures.[6] Although the music for *West Side Story* reflected the subject material, both in form and content (even negative reviews at least admitted that the score suited the drama), Bernstein approached the work with deeper issues than simply finding a suitable tone for an urban tragedy. Bernstein sought to stretch the boundaries of mainstream musical theater expression while creating a work that could stand on its own outside of its theatrical context. One way to create both aural recognition in his listeners and organicism was to employ the tritone both on a structural level and as a surface detail.

This, along with a tight integration of dance, drama, music, and design, did signal a certain kind of turning point in the popular musical theater, but I argue that it is not the organicism of *West Side Story* that places it among the important musicals of this era, but those aspects of it that diverge from a homogeneous, organic, and singular artwork.[7] Indeed, even Stephen Sondheim remarks that for all the acclamation of the piece, "What the critics didn't realize—and they rarely realize anything—is that the show isn't very good. By which I mean, in terms of individual ingredients it has a lot of very serious flaws: overwriting, purpleness in the writing and in the songs, and because the characters are necessarily one-dimensional."[8] Despite this, the musical continues to dominate musical consciousness, viewed by most as an integrated and cohesive work. Looking at the musical from the perspective of Bernstein's many models, however, reveals much of the richness of the work and, simultaneously, another way of reading *West Side Story* as a collaborative piece of musical theater.

He was a facile virtuoso, a clever vaudevillian, a talented ballet-composer parading as a symphonist, a thieving magpie and—the most unforgivable sin—he didn't restrict his thieving; he was an eclectic. He wrote music about other music, "music about music."

—*Leonard Bernstein on Stravinsky, Harvard lectures*[9]

Paul Laird, as early as 1991, posited the idea that eclecticism was at the heart of Bernstein's most important compositional contributions. It was also, clearly, what defined Bernstein as a composer in his own mind.

> BERNSTEIN: If you go into anybody, including Bach, Beethoven, you can make a case for eclecticism. The greater the composer, the better case you can make for eclecticism.
>
> LAIRD: So, to you every composer is to some extent eclectic.
>
> BERNSTEIN: Every painter, every poet, everybody.
>
> LAIRD: You've got to be basing your work on what's coming before it.
>
> BERNSTEIN: Otherwise, you don't exist.[10]

Bernstein goes on to cite Stravinsky, and *Le sacre du printemps* in particular, as an example of great, groundbreaking music based entirely on music by Stravinsky's predecessors. Is Bernstein simply trying to absolve himself of any unintended plagiarism by allying himself with the most canonical composers? Is he, in a moment of self-aggrandizement, trying to prove his own artistic pedigree by placing himself in this legacy? Or, does he see himself as the American Stravinsky, and so his own music, too, can therefore be justified despite its coming "page by page, bar by bar," as he put it, from somewhere else? For the typical composer who is the subject of a musicological study, one often needs to read between the lines of the composer's letters or biographies or to apply what is already known about a compositional process or aesthetic stance to tease out a compositional intent. With Bernstein, material such as Laird's interview augments an already rich documentation of the composer's life, among the most extensively covered of any classical musician of this century. In addition, Bernstein has certainly left writings on his aspirations and issues as a composer. But even without such direct statements about eclecticism, we could well infer some of these aesthetic values simply from looking at Bernstein's music, in general, and *West Side Story*, in particular. Falling as it did at Bernstein's very ascendancy as a musical figure, it held a special place in his development as a musician and directly addressed his own inner conflict between composition and conducting, between classical music and the popular realm. Just a few weeks before *West Side Story* was to open for previews in Washington, Bernstein wrote to his wife, Felicia,

> The show—ah, yes. I am depressed with it. All the aspects of the score I like best—the "big," the poetic parts—get criticized as "operatic"—& there's a concerted move to chuck them. What's the use? The 24-hour schedule goes on—I am tired & nervous & apey. You wouldn't like me at all these days. *This is the last show I do.* The Philharmonic's board approved the contract yesterday, & all is set. I'm going to be a conductor, after all![11]

As much as the collaborative process obviously took its toll on the composer, the work's subsequent popularity made it the music most closely associated with Bernstein, further problematizing his conflict between conducting and composition.[12] As David Diamond recalls,

> When he came to Florence we were in the Piazza, and from all the loudspeakers came this song, "Maria." It just took over every place in the world including the

Soviet Union. And, typical Lenny, he said "Oh, that's me," you know. And of course, he was right. It was a catchy song, and it was a beautiful song.[13]

Many commentators have noted the similarities between moments from *West Side Story* and music by the very composers Bernstein invoked in the name of eclecticism. Indeed, there are so many suggestions of borrowings, coming from the scholarly literature as readily as from online discussions, that an entire book could be written entirely on the music's influences. The "Quintet" ("Tonight") may be modeled on the Mozart ensemble finale, and certainly this is an easy comparison to make. With Bernstein having a wide background by that time as an operatic conductor, including his debut as the first American conductor at La Scala in 1953, there is no doubt that he used the operatic ensemble finale, especially as perfected by Mozart, as the model for "Quintet." Bernstein's modulations, mostly vacillating between major and minor, are more restricted than the tonal framework of Mozart's ensembles (e.g., the notoriously long and complex act 2 finale in *Figaro*), but this is to be expected considering the vocal ranges Bernstein has to work with and the brevity of the number when compared to an equivalent excerpt from a purely operatic work. Perhaps closer operatic models might include the *Rigoletto* quartet, the *Meistersinger* quintet, or a number of similar moments from a host of nineteenth-century sources. Or, the "Quintet" could be an extension of a standard Broadway technique of combining numbers (this is especially prevalent in the contemporary *The Music Man*). William Marvin's work suggests that in fact the "Quintet" might well fit in to the category of quodlibet, in which a composer can combine at least one "hit" song with other material. A typical example from the repertoire would be the simultaneous reprise of Jerome Kern's "The Way You Look Tonight" and "A Fine Romance" from *Swing Time*.[14]

Other composers have also been identified as sources for material in *West Side Story*. Joan Peyser specifically draws attention to resemblances between "Maria" and Blitzstein's *Regina* and connections between the "Goodnight" motive from Britten's *Rape of Lucretia* and Bernstein's setting of the same text in his balcony scene.[15] Stephen Banfield has suggested Beethoven's *Grosse Fuge* and the "Emperor" Concerto among *West Side Story*'s many influences.[16] However, it is not simply these momentary echoes of famous composers that make up the most interesting aspects of Bernstein's borrowings, but the more subtle correspondences between his art and the composers with whom he feels most closely allied, especially as expressed through his own writings. Originality and organicism have, up until this point, been the linchpins on which the musical's reception and analysis have been held. Indeed, the originality upon which many early commentators remarked was seen as one of the most important achievements of Bernstein's score and has continued to attract audiences and analysts for this reason. Accolades for and analyses of the music have tended to focus on these aspects of unity, originality, and use of motivicism, especially Jack Gottlieb's in-depth analysis of Bernstein's music in general and Joseph Swain's discussion of this work in particular.[17] It is precisely these features that, for the analyst, provide a sufficient and, moreover, comforting proof that *West Side Story* clearly deserves its place in the Broadway canon, if not the wider standard repertoire of Western classical music in general.[18]

To be sure, these approaches no doubt reflect traditional musicological and analytical values that reify works that are seen as organic and unified, a stance that has broken down over the last several decades through the advent of postmodern criticism and the opening up of the field to wider methodologies and repertoires. Although the aim of this study is not to challenge the work's organicism (and Bernstein clearly planned this organicism in his compositional process), this study looks at the work in a more postmodern light, teasing out what lies under the musical text and surface structure to reveal layers of subtle influence and borrowings. Not relying solely on the dispassionate observation of a harmonic or structural analysis, nor seeing the work as an autonomous, individual creation, a close reading of some of the eclecticism and "borrowing" of the score renders it even more fascinating and compelling than do the supposed unities that have always accounted for its renown and which have been written about extensively by other authors. Further, Bernstein's own very public commentaries, ostensibly not on his music but on that of others, reveal a rich analytical reading of his own composition. Specifically, his Harvard lectures of the early 1970s, written twenty years after *West Side Story* and ostensibly the mature musings of a master musician, purport to reflect on the meaning and structure of music; not Bernstein's music, but all music. Here we find some of the most striking correspondences between the composer's interpretation of music history and *West Side Story*. Bernstein must have realized that much of his notoriety as a composer from 1957 on would come from the musical, but also that its familiarities would allow it to become a conduit through which other works from the repertoire could be discussed in the wider project of music appreciation to which Bernstein devoted much of the rest of his life. In turn, important moments and models from the classical repertoire not only informed the work's composition, they became justification after the fact for the many qualities for which *West Side Story* was lauded. I would like to isolate a few instances of (in Goethe's term) "elective affinities" that have thus far eluded comment or sometimes even notice in the vast sea of writings on *West Side Story*, especially in relation to the Harvard lectures.

Part of Bernstein's agenda in the lectures was to apply Chomsky's ideas on grammar to music, specifically teasing out musical language and syntax by looking in part at how composers borrow works from each other to use as "deep structures"—underlying grammars—for their own works. Ultimately, *West Side Story* becomes one of those works. Bernstein's understanding of Chomsky (or at least his use of Chomskyan ideas) has been criticized as too reductive or general, and his role as master musician–cum–academic has also inspired some commentary.[19] Indeed, he himself felt the weight placed on him in creating the Harvard lectures, very different in tone and expectations than his other forays into musical explication, the *Young People's Concerts*, or his *Omnibus* programs. He needed to lay out a large intellectual project about music, and he chose Chomsky as a springboard to his own ideas about a universal musical language or syntax. How effectively one can apply linguistic theory to music is not at issue in this discussion, nor is how well or convincingly Bernstein linked these elements in his talks, but instead how Bernstein's response to some of his own influences reads along some of the lines he describes in the Harvard lectures. Over the first two of six lectures, Bernstein describes and then applies ideas from the field of linguistics to musical structures. Starting with a brief explanation of Chomsky's theories, he postulates whether there can be within music similar ideas of deep structure (i.e., musical meaning that underlies surface structures) as well as whether or not the harmonic series is a starting point for some kind of universal musical language, among other topics. He starts with an analysis of the opening movement of Mozart's G Minor Symphony as a model of balance, concision, and structure, then extrapolates from it ideas about symmetry, elision, repetition, and deletion. Creating a rather pedantic but literal version of the opening bars of the movement that renders them perfectly symmetrical and balanced, Bernstein shows how Mozart (and, indeed, all good composers) worked with structure and musical syntax to create interesting and unique musical expression. Using linguistic grammar as a starting point, he discusses the difference

between surface structure and deep structure, meaning that accrues underneath the surface of language and which allows it to be altered while retaining
certain core meanings (i.e., "Jack loves Jill" and "Jill is loved by Jack," etc.).
His discussion then goes on to comparisons of works by Berlioz and Wagner
(discussed below) and finally to Stravinsky, whose "transformational grammar" (to use the linguistic term) allows meaning and syntax to exist even
when surface structures themselves may not be as literal or as pedantic as
Bernstein's Mozart example. Although these ideas could readily be applied to
any number of Bernstein's influences, it is interesting to see which of these
show up in the Harvard lectures and which do not, and how they relate to
West Side Story's score.

SURFACE STRUCTURE: CHOPIN AND DIAMOND

One of the more striking moments of convergence between Bernstein's Harvard lectures and his compositional life surrounds a Chopin mazurka that he
performs in his lecture "The Delights and Dangers of Ambiguity" (concerning
Debussy and the early twentieth-century music-historical period). The composer discusses the Chopin Mazurka op. 17, no. 4 as a perfect example of not
only tonal but rhythmic ambiguity, two features that characterize West Side
Story. The opening of "Maria" evinces the same sense of ambiguity, with the
parlando-style opening to the song that includes the same triplet subdivision
of the beat found in the Chopin (example 3.1). The parallels are astonishing,
as the end of Chopin's mazurka (which is the part Bernstein singles out to perform in the Harvard lectures) sounds nearly identical to early bars of "Maria"
(example 3.2). Even more compelling, the first setting of the song was set a minor third higher, rendering this section originally at the identical pitch class to
the Chopin (example 3.3). Although the reasons for lowering it seem obvious
(Larry Kert's limited vocal range, as well as charges by the other collaborators
that Bernstein's music was "too operatic"),[20] the song was intended not only to
be identical with Chopin's tonal framework, but to provide the high C at the
climax that is the hallmark of the operatic (not necessarily the Broadway) tenor
(example 3.4). The original, more "operatic" version bowed to the demands
of the Broadway stage, but Bernstein originally wanted this moment to be, for
all intents and purposes, a more operatic utterance with more classical roots.

   Bernstein's "borrowing" on one level suggests simply inspiration by another composer. But it is more than this: the ambiguity of the Chopin that

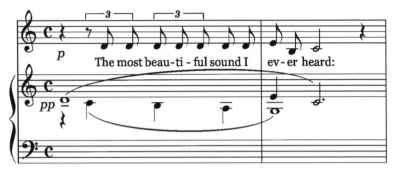

EXAMPLE 3.1
Leonard Bernstein and Stephen Sondheim, *West Side Story*, "Maria," mm.
1–2. Copyright © 1956, 1957, 1958, 1959 by Amberson Holdings LLC and
Stephen Sondheim. Copyright Renewed. Leonard Bernstein Music Publishing
Company LLC, publisher. Boosey & Hawkes, Inc., sole agent. International
Copyright Secured. Reprinted by permission of Boosey & Hawkes, Inc.

Bernstein remarks on in his lecture is improved, concluded, "resolved" by
Bernstein's own composition. The end of the mazurka, which he isolates
as leaving the listener "hovering as we began, in the bliss of ambiguities,"[21]
continues and is completed in "Maria" with the cadence in measure 11:
here the E♭ chord becomes V to a B major chord (F to C major in the
original key), with an accented lower neighbor on the word "Maria" (example 3.2). So in the listener's mind, something vaguely familiar, something
"hovering," finds a resolution and continuation in Bernstein's own work, a
resolution that is not just satisfying because it continues or resolves a harmonic ambiguity but because it also continues the lyric, "Maria, I've just met
a girl named Maria"—the lyric is repeated and intensified by the repeat of
the girl's name just as the harmonic and melodic underpinning is also driving that moment forward. It is a beautiful example in which an allusion to
another work takes flight into a new composition. It is an almost alchemical
moment, and it is entirely Bernstein's, as "Maria" was written before the rest
of the musical, with both lyrics and music by the composer.

The relationship to Chopin, although only a few bars in duration, is hardly
coincidental. Only a year after *West Side Story*'s premiere, Bernstein used the
genre of the Chopin mazurka as a touchstone on the relationship between
word meaning and music meaning: "If it were possible for words to 'tell' a

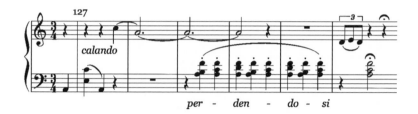

EXAMPLE 3.2
Chopin, Mazurka Op. 17, no. 4, mm, 127–32, and Bernstein, *West Side Story*, "Maria," mm. 10–11. Leonard Bernstein through Boosey.

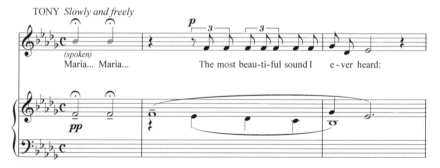

EXAMPLE 3.3
Bernstein, *West Side Story*, "Maria," mm. 1–2. Original key. Leonard Bernstein through Boosey.

EXAMPLE 3.4
Bernstein, *West Side Story*, "Maria," mm. 34–39. Original key. Leonard Bernstein through Boosey.

Chopin mazurka—its sad-gay quality, the abundance of its brevity, the polish of its detail," as he writes in an article in *The Atlantic*.[22] The relationship between word and music, word and meaning, which was such an important part of *West Side Story*'s perceived integration, emerges in Bernstein's discussion of Chopin outside of the context of the musical, as part of a larger question of musical harmony and ambiguity. It represents the beginning, for him, of the kind of ambiguity that springboards the twentieth century and that will find its ultimate resting place in Stravinsky, as we shall see.

Perhaps the most poignant reference of Bernstein's *West Side Story* "alchemy" comes not from classical models, but closer to home in the work of fellow composer David Diamond. As Diamond remembers, "Around 1944, I think it was, I had read some poetry by Logan Piersall Smith and one of the poems that I set was called 'Somewhere.' And Lenny was *crazy* about my song, just crazy about it. Most people don't know that he was very influenced by that song."[23] Bernstein and Diamond were longtime friends, but Bernstein also sincerely regarded Diamond as among the most important contemporary American composers.[24] In notes to himself for lectures on American music in 1947, Bernstein describes Diamond as a prolific composer who "always wins prizes in contests" and also "writes all the time and very fast"[25] (perhaps a thread of jealousy lies behind these words). Diamond's song, dedicated to Bernstein's friend and assistant Helen Coates, is remarkably similar in tone to Bernstein's "Somewhere," particularly the motive Diamond uses for "I am

EXAMPLE 3.5
Diamond, "Somewhere," mm. 28–29.

near my destination" (example 3.5) and Bernstein's "Somewhere" motive
(also at identical pitch). Although again operating more as a surface detail
than a deep structure, the influence of Diamond can be seen as a way of
grafting *West Side Story* onto a canon of American music of which Bernstein
hoped his musical would become a part, putting together the contemporary
American and the art-music tradition.

DEEP STRUCTURE: BERLIOZ AND WAGNER

Although the surface similarities of Chopin and Diamond (and many other
composers, as others have pointed out) provide one type of borrowing or influence, Berlioz and then in turn Wagner provide a kind of scaffolding, a deep
structure for *West Side Story* that tends to run through the entire work rather
than appear as surface structures in the musical. The Berlioz *Romeo and Juliet*
must have been in the forefront of Bernstein's mind when he turned to *West
Side Story*.[26] An unusual and sometimes awkward programmatic symphony
(classified as a "semi-opera" by Daniel Albright),[27] it was a favorite in Bernstein's repertoire, one he felt compelled to promote.[28] A performance as far
back as 1950 prompted a self-professed fan letter from fellow musical theater
composer Marc Blitzstein, describing Bernstein's interpretation as bringing
out "a beautiful sober romanticism, an innate tragic sense."[29] Bernstein also
toured the work with the Israel Philharmonic in Italy in 1955, pairing it with
his own composition, *Serenade*, another study of aspects of love.[30] Within
a few months of the tour, he had signed to do a musical play with Arthur
Laurents entitled *East Side Story*. Not just the subject matter was strikingly

similar; Berlioz dealt with the Shakespearean tale in many of the same ways that Bernstein (and Robbins) would.

Both composers chose to start the work with a prologue that depicted musically the war between the rival factions. Here, the fight sequences from Tchaikovsky's *Romeo and Juliet* fantasy overture must surely have provided a precedent as well. The fugal texture of Berlioz's opening is mirrored in the imitative sections of Bernstein's prologue, as well as the climactic moment—the intervention of the prince—that brings the action to a stop. In Berlioz the fugal section returns, whereas in *West Side Story*, the intervention of Schrank signals the beginning of the first spoken dialogue portion of the musical. Even more striking is that Berlioz's warring prologue has text—precisely as did the original "Prologue" for *West Side Story*, quickly abandoned by the creators as the performers had trouble singing it and dancing at the same time.[31] The reasons for including a prologue with text in a heavily choreographed Broadway musical have always been assumed to be related to the creator's desires for maximum integration of dance, music, and text elements. However, it could be that Bernstein attempted to rewrite Berlioz's opening for his own, up-to-date "semi-opera." Another point of comparison is the use of leitmotifs. Although certainly the deployment of reminiscence motives and leitmotif were nothing new in Bernstein's time, the combination of scenes is similar: Berlioz recalls motives from "Romeo Alone" in the dance segment, just as Bernstein brings back the driving motive from "Something's Coming" (which we might call "Tony Alone") in the "Dance at the Gym." This might not seem so striking if it were not for the fact that Bernstein spends a great deal of time in his Harvard lectures outlining the theme from "Romeo Alone" and showing how it is combined with a new motive at the dance. He then proceeds to conduct with orchestra the entire scene.

Although the reasons clearly seem quite different (Berlioz attempting a kind of symphonic work, Bernstein's music supporting a choreographic work), the result is that much of the most important action of both dramas is expressed entirely through instrumental music instead of music with text. Specifically, in *West Side Story*, the "Prologue," the "Dance at the Gym," the "Rumble," the taunting of Anita, and the second-act ballet are musically dramatized without the use of the standard Broadway "song." As Bernstein points out about Berlioz, the important scenes are purely orchestral, "told by the orchestra alone in highly pictorial terms."[32] Similarly, Berlioz chooses never to give vocal parts to the characters of the two protagonists, but instead bestows most of the music with text to the chorus (analogous perhaps to the

predominance of chorus dance in *West Side Story*'s narrative). Perhaps one of
the most striking similarities is the "Strophes" for female solo, which presents
a kind of disembodied love song that does not move the Shakespearean drama
forward, but instead focuses on the nature of love. Similarly, Bernstein's use
of the song "Somewhere," sung from offstage while the second-act ballet
unfolds the central story and themes of the musical, fulfills a similar function
through similar means. Berlioz's decision to write a wordless vocalization into
the last movement of *Romeo and Juliet* likewise finds an apparent counterpart
in the truncated reprise of "Somewhere" that brings *West Side Story*'s drama
to a close (see figure 3.2 for a comparison of the structure of the two works).

On a more detailed musical level, it seems that Bernstein used at least one
technique of Berlioz's in his own work. In his Norton lecture, Bernstein accounts for "Romeo Alone"'s musical style as representing Romeo's particular
agitation: "He's alone, lovesick, vague, restless, waiting for his imminent
destiny," is how Bernstein describes it. Consider not only the lyrics but the
dramatic setup for "Something's Coming":

TONY: OK . . . Every single damn night for the last month, I wake up—and I'm
reachin' out.

RIFF: For what?

TONY: I don't know. It's right outside the door, around the corner. But it's
comin'!

And, Bernstein's description of the song: "We wrote a new song for Tony
that's a killer, & it just wasn't the same not playing it first for you. It's really
going to save his character—a driving 2/4 in the great tradition—but it gives
Tony balls—so that he doesn't emerge as just a euphoric dreamer."[33] Bernstein describes Romeo's theme as a melodic line with harmonies only implied,
chromatic tones "on the fringe" that occur in chromatic descents that imitate
lovesick sighs. If one looks at the melodic intervals in "Something's Coming,"
it is certainly the semitone appoggiaturas that give the melody its interest and
tension. Otherwise, the opening melody would simply be a reiteration of $\hat{1}\,\hat{5}$
and then an alternation of $\hat{5}\,\hat{6}\,\hat{5}$—hardly a catchy tune by any contemporary
standards (example 3.6) and certainly not agitated nor lovesick. Consider the
"Somewhere" motive (example 3.7), as well as the semitone motive that Bernstein outlines in figure 3.1 (making up a tonic, tritone, and fifth, respectively),
as unifying the entire work.

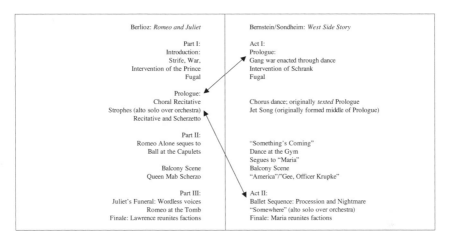

FIGURE 3.2
Comparison of *Romeo and Juliet* and *West Side Story*.

In Tony's solo, certainly the agitation of anticipation is clearly evoked in the motive itself, a kind of distillation and encapsulation of the same musical figure that Berlioz extended to a greater melodic degree (in keeping with his own more expansive nineteenth-century melodic style). However, the entirety of *West Side Story* can be encapsulated in the semitonal motion that infuses most of its leitmotifs (see chapter 1, figure 1.2).

Bernstein's hero, then, is not just the euphoric dreamer of the nineteenth century, but is imbued with the "cool" modernist aesthetic that characterizes *West Side Story*, an extension of, but also once again an improvement on, the "great tradition." As Daniel Albright has remarked, *Romeo and Juliet* "became one of the most generically challenging works of the Nineteenth Century,"[34] and this perhaps helps to explain why the work required the championing of Bernstein in the mid-1950s. *West Side Story* was also considered a new genre of musical theater, unclassifiable by previous standards; as such it fulfilled a similar role to that of the Berlioz work approximately one hundred years later. Was it perhaps, again, a desire on Bernstein's part to improve upon, by somehow rewriting, his favorite works from the repertoire for a new century?

Perhaps the most important relationship between Bernstein and Berlioz in fact also relates to a third figure, Wagner. As Bernstein points out, in *Romeo and Juliet*, the two initial themes of Romeo's longing become, when conflated, the opening to Wagner's *Tristan* prelude and prefigure the *Tristan* chord (example 3.8).

EXAMPLE 3.6

Bernstein, *West Side Story*, "Something's Coming," mm. 1–18. Leonard Bernstein through Boosey.

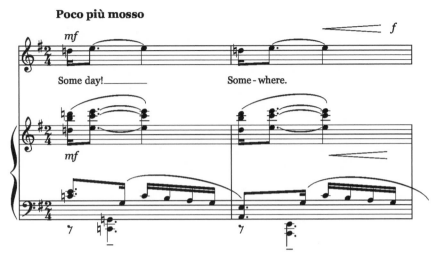

EXAMPLE 3.7
Bernstein, *West Side Story*, "Somewhere" motive. Leonard Bernstein through Boosey.

Linking Wagner's work to Berlioz's, Bernstein asserts that *Tristan* is a giant metaphor of *Romeo and Juliet*.[35] The borrowing by Wagner of Berlioz's
themes is "the phenomenon of transformational grammar in the most
Chomskyan sense: where one surface structure, namely Berlioz's, has become
the deep structure of another surface structure, namely Wagner's." Perhaps
Tristan, so completely removed in structure from what a Broadway musical (however choreographic) could be, could not provide an appropriate
model for Bernstein's work. Berlioz, though, as an important predecessor of
Wagner, certainly could. So, if Wagner is, as Bernstein argues, "a transformational magician" (rather like Stravinsky, a "magic guy"), is not Bernstein the
transformational magician of Wagner? Certainly, *Tristan*'s tonal plan was in
Bernstein's mind. The "double tonic complex" identified by Robert Bailey in
the *Tristan* prelude involves the polarity between A-major and C-major re-
gions.[36] These are in fact the two key areas juxtaposed and treated quite similarly by Bernstein in the "Prologue," and they are pitted against each other
in the equally combative and dramatically polarized "Rumble" (for a fuller
discussion of this polytonality, see Joseph Swain's discussion in *The Broadway
Musical*).[37] Perhaps the comparison between Wagner and Bernstein is not one
that the latter composer would presume to make, but it is interesting that
Bernstein's perceived personal failure to make *West Side Story* operatic was

EXAMPLE 3.8
Bernstein's combination of the two themes from "Romeo Alone" in Berlioz's *Romeo and Juliet* to form the opening of the Prelude to Wagner's *Tristan und Isolde* and implying the *Tristan* chord. Leonard Bernstein, *The Unanswered Question: Six Talks at Harvard* (Cambridge, MA: Harvard University Press, 1976), 226. Courtesy of the Leonard Bernstein Foundation.

not simply the result of the other collaborators cutting back on his operatic music ("my poor little mashed-up score. All the things I love most in it are slowly being dropped—too operatic, too this & that," he wrote in July 1957)[38] but of his failure to musicalize Maria's final speech. As Bernstein explains it:

At the denouement, the final dramatic unraveling, the music stops and we talk it. Tony is shot and Maria picks up the gun and makes that incredible speech,

"How many bullets are left?" My first thought was that this was to be her biggest aria. I can't tell you how many tries I made on that aria. I tried once to make it cynical and swift. Another time like a recitative. Another time like a Puccini aria. In every case, after five or six bars, I gave up. It was phony.[39]

Although the creators may have been disappointed with this ending, the critics certainly weren't. Richard Watts Jr., in his review in the *New York Post*, called the last few minutes of the show "poignant to a degree almost unheard of in the popular musical theatre."[40] To a certain extent, his beloved Gershwin did not provide a model that Bernstein could follow here. As Joseph Swain has pointed out, Gershwin fails to create a true tragedy in *Porgy* precisely because he provides the uplifting and brief "O Lawd, I'm on My Way" for the final musical number, and at the moment of greatest sadness.[41] But perhaps the weight of the "great tradition" was too heavy for Bernstein (as for Gershwin) at this point, as he must have had looming over his shoulder the work of the composer whom he had "magicalized," Wagner's *Tristan*. Maria's final speech, given over the dead body of the lover who had sacrificed himself, would have had to measure up to the "Liebestod" in terms of both musical and dramatic scope. Among the original books for the musical, in which Maria kills herself, there might have been room for a final number of this type. But, with Maria still alive and the specter of continued violence looming on the horizon, it would not have been possible for Bernstein to "resolve" this particular unfulfilled love in the way that Wagner did. Indeed, the "double tonic complex" that characterizes the entirety of *Tristan*'s tonal structure, and which is resolved at the end of the "Liebestod," could not find a place within Bernstein's tritone-juxtaposed tonal framework, since the last moments of the musical reverberate with the opening prologue: the impossibility of a "Somewhere" amidst the racial chaos within which *West Side Story* operates. Perhaps Bernstein has not actually failed in terms of his Wagnerian precedent: considering the ways in which Wagner's *Tristan* chord were deconstructed in the decades that followed him, Bernstein's own tritone "chord" perfectly represented in his own time the "crisis of the twentieth century," the works "born of despair or of protest or of a refuge from both," of which *West Side Story* is a part. If he had been able to write a kind of "Liebestod" for Maria, he would have negated the musical and artistic premise on which *West Side Story* is based—that there are no resolutions, no answers—and not allowed it to stand for the values of a mid-twentieth-century America.

TRANSFORMATIONAL GRAMMAR: STRAVINSKY AND GERSHWIN

Although certainly the classical repertoire with which Bernstein was most familiar, and which was by definition most canonical, informed the composer's choices of style and structure, it was also the music of his own contemporaries and immediate predecessors that demanded the most compelling responses from him as a composer. Wanting as he did to write the Great American Opera, Bernstein naturally turned to one of the important American operatic achievements of the 1930s for his closest model, Gershwin's *Porgy and Bess*. Not only did this work also attempt to bridge a gap between opera and Broadway,[42] it forged new ground in combining operatic styles and precedents with contemporary vernacular, in this case that of African-Americans (Gershwin's "final amalgamation," as Bernstein put it).[43] But there were more personal reasons for this relationship, primarily Bernstein's own affinity with Gershwin's background and aspirations as a composer. To get a sense of how deeply Bernstein empathized with Gershwin's musical and social lives, consider this interview on Gershwin that Bernstein did for WGBH-TV in Boston.

> He was from the other side of the tracks. He came from the pop song side of the tracks. And at a certain point in his life he wanted to write real pieces, real honest to god pieces. With form. And he wrote the "Rhapsody in Blue," and he wrote "American in Paris" which was better, and he orchestrated it himself, which he did not do for the "Rhapsody in Blue". . . . And he played the piano, like crazy. At Hollywood parties. And he was the belle of the ball. He was just terrific. He was the toast of Paris and he was the toast of London and he was the toast of Hollywood and New York and everything.[44]

In his essay "Why Don't You Run Upstairs and Write a Nice Gershwin Tune," Bernstein credits Gershwin with being one of the musical geniuses of the century, but bemoans the fact that his art was not that easy to achieve.[45] "Time and history may even show him to be the truest and most authentic of his time and place," he writes in a preface to Charles Schwartz's book on Gershwin. "Gershwin was, and remains, one of the greatest voices that have ever rung out in the history of American urban culture."[46] Bernstein was so overwhelmed by his feelings about Gershwin that he ended the WGBH interview as follows.

> LB: So that's the story. What else is there to say? George Gershwin lived. And changed our history.

> Q: What about Concerto in F?

LB: Same thing. Better. Another step. Another triumph. Big triumph. *Porgy* was the big triumph and the great success. The great achievement. But god think what could have happened after *Porgy*.

Q: Were you . . .

LB: One can't think. One can't. It's just too . . .

Q: You're going to work on an opera . . .

LB: I have to go.

Q: OK. Thank you so much.

LB: I have to go. It's much more than eight minutes. And I'm too emotional about it. I can't talk.

Q: OK. Thank you. Cut.

LB: I have never in my life done an interview in tears. I don't know what the hell has happened to me. I thought I was more professional than that. . . . He just touched something.

Q: Are you all right?

LB: Yes. . . . George was unprofessional. Same kind of genius.

Q: Are you OK?

LB: No. I loved him so much.[47]

Bernstein especially credits Gershwin with succeeding in what Bernstein was also seeking, to develop "from shows to real theater pieces (works)." Bernstein admits that when he was young he took Gershwin for granted, knew his shows, but *Porgy and Bess* changed his life.

> When I was a freshman at Harvard "Porgy and Bess" came to Boston. Brand new. In 1936. Tryout in Boston. This is pre-Broadway. And I had the luck to attend it. And I went ape. Freaked out. And I tried to buy the piece, I couldn't afford it, I couldn't buy the music, but I chanced on a score a year later, and learned it all by heart. I knew it all anyway, I had it all in my ears.[48]

Not surprisingly, *Porgy and Bess* forms an important "deep structure" to Bernstein's musical, and not just in the music but the conception of the work as a whole. The two worlds of African-American and white, which polarize characters in *Porgy*, find their equivalent in the worlds of adult and teenager in *West Side Story*. Consider the following police interrogations of Heyward and Laurents in *Porgy and Bess* and *West Side Story*.

Porgy and Bess

Act 3, scene 2

DETECTIVE: (*white man*) Come on down, Serena Robbins and make it damn quick! (*there is silence for a moment, then the shutters open and Annie looks out*)

ANNIE: Huh! Serena been very sick lately in her bed three day an' I been here with her all de time. (*closes shutters*)

DETECTIVE: The hell she has. Tell her if she don't come down I'll get the wagon an' run her in. (*there is a moment's silence then the window opens and loud groans are heard as Serena is helped to the window. Serena sprawls on sill as though too ill to hold herself up. She groans. Her head is wrapped in a towel.*) Where were you last night, Serena Robbins?

SERENA: I been sick in dis bed three day an three night.

ANNIE: An' we been nursin' her all dat time.

WOMAN: Dat's Gawd's truth.

CORONER: Would you swear to that?

WOMEN: Yes boss, we swear to that.

CORONER: There you are, an airtight alibi. (*regards Coroner with scorn*)

DETECTIVE: Just two months ago right here Crown killed your husband, didn't he? (*silence from women*) (*advances*) You'll either talk here or in jail. Did Crown kill your husband, yes or no?

WOMEN: We swear to dat boss.

DETECTIVE: And last night Crown got his right here, didn't he?

ANNIE: Ha ha ha ha ha! Go 'long boss, ain' dat gentleman say we is a alabi?

DETECTIVE: (*shouting with rage*) Was Crown killed here, yes or no?

WOMEN: We ain' seen nuttin' boss, we been in dis room three day an' night An' de window been closed.

DETECTIVE: Look at me, Serena Robbins. Do you mean to tell me that the man who killed your husband was bumped off under your window, an' you didn't know it?

WOMEN: We ain' seen nothin' Boss, we been in dis room three days an nights.

ANNIE: An' the window been closed.

DETECTIVE: (*furiously*) You needn't do that one again. (*turning away disgustedly*) Oh hell! You might as well argue with a parrot, but you'll never break their story.

West Side Story

Act 1, scene 6

SCHRANK: Beat it! (*A second. Then Riff nods once to Bernardo, who nods to his gang. Slowly, they file out. Bernardo starts to whistle "My Country 'Tis of Thee" as he exits proudly. His gang joins in, finishing a sardonic jazz lick offstage.*) From their angle, sure. Say, where's the rumble gonna be? Ah, look: I know regular Americans don't rub with the gold-teeth otherwise. The river? The Park? (*silence*) I'm for *you*. I want this beat cleaned up and you can do it for me. I'll even lend a hand if it gets rough. Where ya gonna rumble? The playground? Sweeney's lot? (*angered by the silence*) Ya think I'm a lousy stool pigeon? I wanna help ya get rid of them! Come on! Where's it gonna be? . . . Get smart, you stupid hoodlums! I oughta be taken down the station house and have your skulls mashed to a pulp! You and the tin-horn immigrant scum you come from! How's your old man's d.t.'s, Arab? How's the action on your mother's mattress, Action? (*Action lunges for him but is tripped up by Riff. Schrank crouches low, ready for him. Quiet now.*) Let him go, buddy boy, just let him go. (*Action starts to his feet but Diesel holds him.*) One of these days there won't be nobody to hold you. (*Riff deliberately starts for the door, followed by the others, except Tony.*) I'll find out where ya gonna rumble. But be sure to finish each other off. Because if you don't, I will!

Act 2, scene 3

SCHRANK: Anybody home? (*Goes to the bedroom door. Pleasantly.*) Sorry to disturb you. Guess you're disturbed enough.

MARIA: (*gathering her robe*) Yes. You will excuse me, please. I must go to my brother.

SCHRANK: There are just a coupla questions—

MARIA: Afterwards, please. Later.

SCHRANK: It'll only take a minute.

ANITA: Couldn't you wait until—

SCHRANK: (*sharply*) No! (*a smile to Maria*) You were at the dance at the gym last night.

MARIA: Yes.

SCHRANK: Your brother got in a heavy argument because you danced with the wrong boy.

MARIA: Oh?

SCHRANK: Who was the boy?

Furthermore, just as Gershwin further differentiates the two groups within the scene by having the African-American characters sing instead of speak, the creators of *West Side Story* limited singing and dancing to the juvenile protagonists throughout. The similar sense of encroachment and imposition by the police along with resistance and defiance by the teenagers is found in both scenes. In both cases, the detective is infuriated by the interviewees' lack of responsiveness.[49] Note also that the strategy of feigned illness (for both Maria and Serena) is used to attempt to excuse them from testifying (the initial interrogation at Robbins's funeral also provides a similar dramatic moment). In both cases, the police try to intervene in solving crimes that the main protagonists (African-American and teenage, respectively) have already resolved in their own world and attempt to hide from the outside. *West Side Story* also originally was planned as a three-act work (like *Porgy*), not the standard two acts of a Broadway show, although Robbins early on put a stop to that. In addition, Gershwin's use of the "Crown" motive during the storm scene of act 2 anticipates Bernstein's treatment of leitmotifs within the more purely orchestral moments of *West Side Story* (the "Maria" theme recurring at the top of the balcony scene). Individual song types also find some resemblances between the works, with Maria's "I Feel Pretty" echoing the sentiment, style, form, and placement (the first "charm" song of act II) of Porgy's "I Got Plenty o' Nuttin'" (even the rhythm of the opening words, Porgy's "nuttin'" and Maria's "pretty," are similar—see example 3.9). Both songs evince a kind of contented feeling—Porgy's in his everyday life and Maria's in her new love for a "pretty wonderful" (but otherwise ordinary) boy.

For all that Bernstein felt the shadow of Gershwin looming behind him, however he may have felt the weight of the "great tradition" from Mozart, through Beethoven, Berlioz, and Wagner, one specter became the touchstone for Bernstein's creativity as a composer: the music of Igor Stravinsky. We see time and again responses in Bernstein's own work to Stravinsky's oeuvre, certainly considered one of the most important in Bernstein's lifetime. The elder composer is, in Bernstein's mind, the "genius-alchemist" who "makes every note he writes unmistakably his own," keeper of "some private alchemy, some secret magic" and achieving, as Bernstein himself desired, "honors heaped upon him as upon no other composer of this age—from the Kremlin to the Vatican, from heads of government to Texas cowboys."[50] In Bernstein's own

EXAMPLE 3.9
Gershwin, *Porgy and Bess*, "I Got Plenty o' Nuttin'," mm. 1–4, and
Bernstein, *West Side Story*, "I Feel Pretty," mm. 3–6. Gershwin: Words
and Music by George Gershwin, Du Bose and Dorothy Heyward, and Ira
Gershwin. Copyright © 1935 (renewed) by George Gershwin Music, Ira
Gershwin Music, and Du Bose and Dorothy Heyward Memorial Fund.
All Rights Administered by WB Music Corp. All Rights Renewed, Alfred
Music Publishing. Bernstein: Leonard Bernstein through Boosey.

description of Stravinsky, we see an encapsulation of what Bernstein strove
for and, in part, achieved, through *West Side Story*'s legacy.

His textures go from the richest to the leanest; his spirit was both devout and
irreverent; his music is at once tender and spiky, emotional but antiromantic;
it can be popular and esoteric, nationalistic or intercontinental. In this sense he
was probably the most universal composer who ever lived.[51]

This description is not unlike Bernstein's of Gershwin, suggesting that perhaps it was those qualities that he felt he possessed (or wanted to possess) that he projected onto his favorite composers. Similarities abound in their creative outputs. *Prelude, Fugue, and Riffs* follows Stravinsky's highly similar work, the *Ebony Concerto* (also written for Benny Goodman—another moment of crossover for both of these composers). Stravinsky's opera of the early 1950s, *The Rake's Progress*, is a political and allegorical eighteenth-century morality play resurrecting baroque operatic styles and forms, followed closely by Bernstein's *Candide*, a Broadway opera on a political and allegorical eighteenth-century morality story resurrecting a wider variety of operatic styles and forms. Whether or not *Candide* was meant as a direct response to Stravinsky (which I suspect it was), it was certainly an attempt to master this particular kind of genre in a more American, eclectic fashion than Stravinsky achieved, and very soon afterward.[52] In *West Side Story*, Bernstein hoped to some extent to "revolutionize" musical theater at midcentury, and the strong ballet aspirations that Robbins brought to the work might well have brought Bernstein to consider the legacy left by Stravinsky's ballets.

Bernstein's descriptions of Stravinsky in his Harvard lectures sound almost like descriptions of his own self-styled primitivist music, the "Rumble" or the "Prologue" from *West Side Story*, another case in which a vernacular music is embedded in, as he calls it, "stylish sophistication."

> But the most striking semantic effects of Stravinsky's primitivism results from the utterly modern sophistication with which it is treated. There is an exciting friction here of conflicting forces: after all, here's a thoroughly twentieth century composer writing prehistoric music. It's a glorious earthy vernacular embedded in stylistic sophistication.[53]

Although Bernstein's idea for a tritone motive could have come from a multitude of precedents from Liszt on, the fact that Stravinsky immortalized and focused on the tritone relationship in *Petrouchka*, a kind of nose-thumbing to conservative musical factions, seems to resonate with Bernstein's own vision of the tritone relationship, "the absolute negation of tonality," as he called it. Indeed, in Bernstein's extensive discussion and analysis of *Prélude à l'après-midi d'un faune* in his Harvard lectures, he singles out the tritone relationships found in the opening of that piece as signaling the ultimate in "ambiguity."[54] And although the tritone plays a fairly large role in Bernstein's compositions as a whole, there well could be a parallel drawn between his use of and Stravinsky's identification with this interval. The tritone interval became for Bernstein the touchstone of *West Side Story* (see figure 3.3, a birthday greeting sent to Stephen Sondheim in 1980, an A–E♭ tritone enclosed in a heart). The tritone still encapsulates the *West Side Story* experience for Bernstein, "almost a quarter century" later.

Perhaps the most significant points of intersection between *West Side Story* and Stravinsky come in the latter's *Rite of Spring*, a work that Bernstein identified on a number of occasions as the one that revolutionized music. The ritualistic, tableau-oriented vision of this ballet accords well with Robbins's visceral and aggressive choreographic vision, and certainly the idea of rites of passage such as the "Dance at the Gym" and the "Rumble" (not to mention the "Taunting Scene," perhaps a nod to the sacrifice of the virgin represented in Stravinsky's work) fits well with the earlier work. Stravinsky's rhythmic displacement, most notable in the Augurs of Spring section, is not unlike Bernstein's constant shifting of rhythmic accents at the beginning of the rumble, the kind of rhythmic play that Bernstein refers to in the Harvard lectures with Harold Shapero's colorful phrase "Igor's asymmetry racket" (see example 3.10).[55] But it is this moment from the "Somewhere" ballet which provides an even more striking Stravinsky "fingerprint" (example 3.11, one measure before rehearsal 102, and example 3.12, rehearsal 45).

If *West Side Story* attempts to rewrite musical history (in the case of Chopin or Berlioz), or at least tries to revolutionize Broadway, then how does Bernstein "improve upon" Stravinsky? In one way, it is the integration of the elements, the kaleidoscopic or cinematic quality (as the collaborators put it), that was singled out as one of the most important qualities of the musical. Film could not have played such a part in the time of Stravinsky's ballet as it would in the late 1950s (indeed, the collaborators, as we will see in chapter 6, used certain films as a model, if not inspiration, for the juvenile delinquency aspect of *West Side Story*). The juxtapositions that serve to amaze and perhaps jolt the listener in Stravinsky's ballet score become the "seam" moments in *West Side Story*, where pure dance expression melts into word expression. Further, it is at the moments when Bernstein becomes *most* similar to Stravinsky that the older composer's music falls away and allows a segue to something new. In the last measures of the *Rite*'s "Adoration of the Earth" and at measure

LEONARD BERNSTEIN

Dearest Steve:

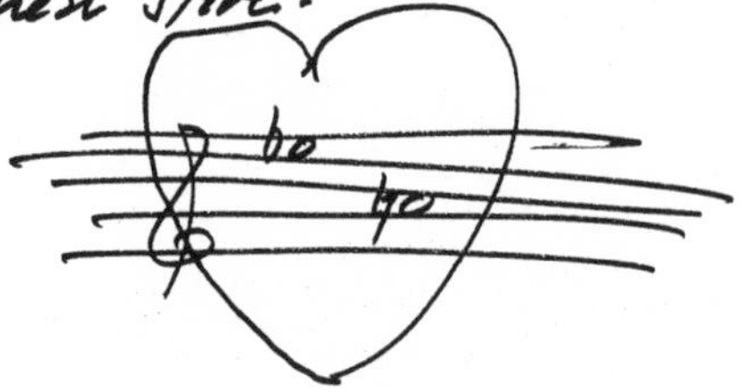

This Es/La tritone comes with warmest memories of work and play and friendship. S-L is almost a quarter-century old, and it seems all wrong that I should not be in attendance on your glorious 50th. But I'll be down in the Caribbean with my children on that date, and will be thinking strongly and affectionately of you. More power to you, and much Merriment . . .

L = 50 = Love = Lenny

16 March '80

FIGURE 3.3

Birthday greeting from Leonard Bernstein to Stephen Sondheim on the latter's 50th birthday. Transcription: "Dearest Steve: This Es/La tritone comes with warmest memories of work and play and friendship. S-L is about a quarter-century old, and it seems all wrong that I should not be in attendance at your glorious 50th. But I'll be down in the Caribbean with my children on that date, and will be thinking strongly and affectionately of you. More power to you, and much Merriment . . . L = 50 = Love = Lenny. 16 March 80." Courtesy of Stephen Sondheim, Bernstein Collection, Library of Congress, Correspondence Series.

EXAMPLE 3.10
Bernstein, *West Side Story*, "Rumble," mm. 7–10. Leonard Bernstein through Boosey.

153 of Bernstein's "Prologue," for example, the intrusion of the police whistle (and, probably not by accident, the intrusion of the adult "non-music" world into the teenager "music world") into the texture ends the Stravinsky moment abruptly and brings back the original motives from the prologue.

In a similar vein, the end of the last bars of the "Rumble" (example 3.13) are eerily similar to the last bars from the *Rite of Spring* (example 3.14). Since both the prologue and rumble are among the most "ritualistic," and certainly purely violent, tableaux of the respective works, the references here to *Rite of Spring* are particularly relevant. But whereas Stravinsky concludes these bars with a giant, definitive chord (example 3.14) to end his ballet, Bernstein's act 1 ends with the vaguest and most inconclusive of moments, a chime striking 9:00 p.m. above a tremolo E♭. Does Bernstein, in a kind of subconscious way, "wake up" from these Stravinsky moments like Debussy and Mallarmé's Faun, which he describes in such great detail in the Harvard talks? Or, does Bernstein "improve upon" Stravinsky by providing in these moments the disjunctures, the vacillation, and the sense of twentieth-century angst that *West Side Story*'s subject matter demanded, the sentiments most poignantly expressed in "Somewhere"?

Bernstein's relationship to Stravinsky in this work has more overarching meaning, however. In his lectures, Bernstein hails Stravinsky as an almost godlike, deus ex machina figure for tonality. "But it was precisely this Stravinsky, this very child of Satan, bag of tricks and all, who appeared like an angel of deliverance, just in time to lead the great rescue operation, the huge project

EXAMPLE 3.11
Stravinsky, *Le sacre du printemps*, "Sacrifice," Reh. 101.

EXAMPLE 3.12
Bernstein, *West Side Story*, "Transition to Scherzo," 2nd Act Ballet, Reh. 45. Leonard Bernstein through Boosey.

EXAMPLE 3.13
Bernstein, *West Side Story*, "Rumble," mm. 143–147. Leonard Bernstein
through Boosey.

of saving tonality in those critical years before World War I,"[56] he claims near
the end of the lecture series. Was not this, in essence, also part of Bernstein's
overall agenda as a composer? Although he used twelve-tone methods in a
number of his works, he remained a staunch champion of tonality—in a kind
of artistic credo at the end of the Harvard lectures he lays it out explicitly: "I
believe that from that Earth emerges a musical poetry, which is by the nature
of its sources tonal. I believe that these sources cause to exist a phonology of
music, which evolves from the universal known as the harmonic series."[57]
Was not Bernstein himself, through a work like *West Side Story*, not only trying to recreate the "final amalgamation" that Gershwin did in *Porgy and Bess*,
but also trying to prove that, just like Stravinsky, tonality could go on forever,
only needing to be "freshened up," as he put it, by great composers? And did
Bernstein hope that he, too, could be one of those great composers? Indeed,
his identity as a composer continued to be an area of great sensitivity to him
throughout his life.

    Diamond or Berlioz? Gershwin or Stravinsky? So many of these moments
from the repertoire (and many more) can be read as either direct quotations
and allusions to other works, or as part of a continuing dialogue, a "deep
structure" to which Bernstein adds his own compositional voice, his own
transformational grammar. Part of this interest in Chomsky no doubt stems
from Bernstein's intention to be scholarly, to be current with developments
within the academy. But it also reflects the composer's own attempts to cre-

EXAMPLE 3.14
Stravinsky, *Le sacre du printemps*, "Sacrifice," final measures.

ate a canon of works within the Western classical tradition that are linked through similar compositional processes and the reliance on models, a kind of Chomskyan deep structure for music cognition. These works, perhaps not surprising given Bernstein's own feelings on the importance of tonality, come from the tonal tradition. Although Ives's *Unanswered Question* forms the title of his lecture series and is indeed the most dissonant or avant-garde work he discusses, Bernstein includes few American composers in his talks. This seems strange, considering how important the championing of American music was even from his early days as a conductor. In the examples I have discussed, the surface structure of Diamond and the deeper structure of Gershwin play perhaps the largest roles in his borrowing, and yet these works were never mentioned in the Harvard lectures. Only the European, high-art examples appear in Bernstein's talks, and he never directly refers to *West Side Story* nor any other of his own compositions during his Harvard lectures (nor his talks on musical theater or American music in other venues). To be sure, the lecture series was not a place for shameless self-promotion. Ultimately, did Bernstein feel that some of his American composers did not measure up, he among them? Certainly the elements of tonality and syntax in their works could have been just as compelling or useful in his series, and they would or should have been just as "classical" as any of the European works Bernstein chose. Or were they too close to home? Of all the borrowings and influences in *West Side Story*, it is these resonances that Bernstein comments on in later life that remain fascinating, an almost subconscious reference to what informed probably his most influential (and some would argue, best) composition. At the same time, talking about and reflecting on these very pieces bolsters his own works, provides an exegesis explored in the intimate (and, ultimately, authoritative) setting of the Harvard lectures, and also reflects the dichotomy between self-doubt and self-confidence which made up Bernstein's unique psychology. By creating a kind of evolutionary narrative of musical style, Bernstein ultimately places himself within a tradition that extends back at least to Berlioz (if we take this as the earliest music linked explicitly to *West Side Story*) without appearing to be so presumptuous as to baldly state this. Indeed, it is more likely that these connections were made for Bernstein than for his audience, who could not have been expected to hear or find the similarities between the work Bernstein composed and the works that preceded it. Perhaps this was his unconscious need to find his place within a historical continuum. Either way, Bernstein's manipulations of previous models, some subtle, some obvious, have created in *West Side Story* a kind of compendium of notable moments from the canonic works of Western classical music. But, more than that, Bernstein's own commentary on music, widely read and heard by generations of "music appreciation" audiences, and its intersections with Bernstein's own work make him a kind of apologist for his compositional output after the fact, and in turn act as a lens through which the classics are perceived and filtered. *West Side Story* is subtly sold to the audience through Bernstein's presentation and reification of a repertoire that comes from sources outside the musical.

If we see the musical in this light, then, does it still emerge as a unified, organic, and modernist musical? Or is it the first postmodern musical, relying on intertextual allusion to such a subtle and extensive degree that it is in fact a masterpiece of eclecticism? Bernstein did not suffer from any lack of inspiration or creativity, nor was he a musical plagiarist. Instead, his incredible memory and facility with music of different periods and in different styles allowed him to pull musical gestures from a larger language that he and, for the most part, his audiences found understandable, a larger syntax that he only was really ready to explain in words long after the fact. Is Bernstein, then, one of the first postmodern composers? Whatever statement Bernstein hoped to achieve through his own recording of a "definitive" version of *West Side Story*, the process at work in the Harvard lectures perhaps does more to promote the "classical music" status of the work than anything Broadway could have provided. After all, Bernstein wanted this work to be more of an opera than the finished product would suggest. A much longer balcony scene, including a parlando/recitative-like section, continues to show up in the piano/vocal score for a fairly long time in the creative process. Particularly striking is a version of "A Boy Like That/I Have a Love" that includes Tony as one of the singing characters; a scrim was meant to reveal him in the drugstore, adding his (again, operatic) high Cs to Maria and Anita's duet. More integrated, yes, but also much more classically oriented and conceived than the number that remains in the finished score.

Why did Bernstein feel he needed to provide, either for himself or others, the imprimatur of the classical tradition? Particularly in the early 1970s, Bernstein was, more than ever, becoming aware that his dual lives as composer and conductor would mean that one of those endeavors would probably suffer. As it turned out, Bernstein was not able to spend as much time composing as he had wanted, and when he came to the composition of *A Quiet Place*, he was finding that composing was not coming as easily to him as it once had. The Harvard lectures, although prestigious and rewarding in their own way, no doubt reminded him of the time pressures he was under and that *West Side Story* might be remembered as his greatest work. Sondheim complained in later years, "All Lenny was saying was, 'I wrote a great musical and nobody else can do it.' He was making that statement all the time. But he wasn't leading the pack at all. He was just blowing his own trumpet and it always pissed me off."[58] However, Bernstein didn't want to just write a great musical; he wanted to write a great opera. As Arthur Laurents says, "The real problem, and it exists to this day—Lenny, like most Classical musicians—the culture is snobbish—thinks opera is art, Broadway is not. His greatest theatre piece is *West Side Story*—a Broadway musical. What interfered with his other theatre pieces was his desire to be accepted as a classical composer. He didn't accept that *West Side* was a masterpiece."[59]

The diversity, then, the models that come from both the popular and classical realms that he loved, showed the composer as torn, within that one work and beyond, between the desire to be accepted as an art-music composer and to be the next Gershwin and Diamond. Pedigree notwithstanding, *West Side Story* is Bernstein's greatest musical; it was his own inner struggles that perhaps did not allow him to recognize that it was also his great American opera.

NOTES

1. See chapters 7 and 8 of the present study for more on this issue. Certainly, the expressions "womb to tomb," "daddy-o," and "cracko Jacko" have become associated with the work, as well.

2. Indeed, Joan Peyser recounts that Bernstein saw *Oklahoma!* and it impressed him greatly (Joan Peyser, *Bernstein: A Biography*, 265). In an *Omnibus* program on musical theater, he takes apart a larger scene complex (twin soliloquies) from *South Pacific*, clearly intimate with its structure.

3. See Heidi Owen, "Broadway Opera and Opera on Broadway: 1934–1958" (PhD diss., University of Rochester, forthcoming).

4. This is asserted even by the original producer, Harold Prince. See Harold Prince, *Contradictions*.

5. Milton Babbitt's famous essay, "Who Cares If You Listen?" (*High Fidelity* 8, no. 2 [February 1958]: 38–40), has become not only the touchstone for this debate, but also coincides with *West Side Story*'s peak of popularity.

6. Leonard Bernstein, "The Twentieth Century Crisis," *Unanswered Question*, 315.

7. Indeed, a wide variety of intentionally antiorganicist works in the tradition of Weill and Brecht's *Threepenny Opera* may have provided an impetus for Bernstein's approach.

8. Stephen Sondheim quoted in Meryle Secrest in *Stephen Sondheim: A Life*, 117.

9. Bernstein, *Unanswered Question*, 389.

10. Laird, *Best of All Possible Legacies*, 34.

11. Leonard Bernstein to Felicia Monteleagre Bernstein in Chile, 26 July 1957, Bernstein Collection, correspondence, box 5, folder 33, Library of Congress, Music Division.

12. Joan Peyser interprets Brooks Atkinson's comment that Bernstein "capitulated to respectability by accepting the post of conductor of a famous symphony orchestra" as a criticism of Bernstein's choice of classical over Broadway. Peyser, *Bernstein*, 279.

13. David Diamond, interview with the author, July 14, 2002, Rochester, New York.

14. See William Marvin, "Simulating Counterpoint in Broadway Musicals: The Quodlibet as Compositional Procedure" (paper read at the Joint Meeting of the American Musicological Society and Society for Music Theory, Columbus, OH, 2002).

15. Peyser summarizes Gradenwitz's arguments in Peyser, *Bernstein*, 374. For more, see Peter Gradenwitz, *Leonard Bernstein: The Infinite Variety of a Musician* (New York: Oswald Wolff Books, 1987).

16. Banfield, *Sondheim's Broadway Musicals*, 37.

17. Joseph P. Swain, *The Broadway Musical: A Critical and Musical Survey* (New York: Oxford University Press, 1990), 208–46; and Jack Gottlieb, *The Music of Leonard Bernstein: A Study of Melodic Manipulations* (Doctor of Music diss., University of Illinois at Urbana-Champaign, 1964).

18. For more on this issue, see Geoffrey Block, "The Broadway Canon."

19. Allan Keiler, "Bernstein's '*The Unanswered Question*' and the Problem of Musical Competence," *The Musical Quarterly* 64, no. 2 (April 1978): 195–222; Joseph Horowitz, "Professor Lenny—Leonard Bernstein's Young People's Concerts," *New York Review of Books* 40, no. 11 (June 10, 1993): 39–44. More recently Naomi Thomas has written more extensively on Bernstein's understanding and use of Chomsky. See Naomi Thomas, "Bernstein's Unanswered Question: A Journey from Deep Linguistic Structure to the Metaphysics of Music" (MA thesis, Florida Atlantic University, 2004).

20. Larry Kert reported that after wobbling on a high C, "They said not to mind about the wobble—I had the guts to see it through, and that's part of what they wanted. Then they gave me a version that was transposed down a tone, and after a few days of work I got through it without a wobble on the High B Flat." Quoted in Patterson Greene, "Baritone Sings Tenor in *West Side Story*," *Los Angeles Examiner*, July 5, 1959, section 7, 1.

21. Bernstein, *Unanswered Question*, 211.

22. Leonard Bernstein, "Speaking of Music," *The Atlantic* 200 (December 1957), 104–6.

23. Diamond, 2002.

24. Indeed, Joan Peyser relies heavily on Diamond's reminiscences in her biography of Bernstein.

25. Notes for talks on "American Music," 1 August 1947 at Berkshire Music Center, Bernstein Collection, writings series, box 71, folder 27.

26. Bernstein even refers to the project simply as "Romeo" throughout all his early correspondence and date book entries.

27. Daniel Albright, *Berlioz's Semi-Operas: "Roméo et Juliette" and "La damnation de Faust"* (Rochester, NY: University of Rochester Press, 2001).

28. About performing his own *Serenade* and Berlioz's *Romeo* on tour he writes, "Imagine, with my funny modern music and unpopular Berlioz." Bernstein to Felicia Monteleagre Bernstein, quoted in Burton, *Leonard Bernstein*, 247.

29. Quoted in Burton, *Leonard Bernstein*, 196.

30. Quoted in Burton, *Leonard Bernstein*, 247.

31. Bernstein recalls, "Another example of how closely we worked together was the prologue. Believe it or not, it originally had words. That extraordinarily instrumental

music was sung. It didn't take us long to find out that wouldn't work. That was when Jerry took over and converted all that stuff into this remarkable thing now known as 'the prologue to *West Side Story*,' all dancing and movement. We all learned something from one another. We learned how to re-learn and to teach. It was an extraordinary exchange." "Landmark," 15.

32. Bernstein, *Unanswered Question*, 218–19.

33. Bernstein to Felicia Monteleagre Bernstein, 8 August 1957. Bernstein Collection, correspondence, box 5, folder 33.

34. Albright, *Berlioz's Semi-Operas*, 47.

35. Bernstein, *Unanswered Question*, 227.

36. Robert Bailey, ed., *Prelude and Transfiguration from "Tristan und Isolde,"* *Richard Wagner* (New York: Norton, 1985).

37. Swain, *Broadway Musical*, 216–17 and 228–29, identifies this tonal duality.

38. Bernstein to Felicia Monteleagre Bernstein in Chile, 28 July 1957. The excerpt reads in its entirety: "Where does the time all go to? [This is an allusion to a song from *On the Town*: "Some Other Time"] In a minute it will be August, and off to Washington—and people will be looking at West Side Story in public, & hearing my poor little mashed-up score. All the things I love most in it are slowly being dropped—too operatic, too this & that. They're all so scared & commercial success means so much to them. To me too, I suppose—but I still insist it can be achieved with pride. I shall keep fighting." Bernstein Collection, correspondence, box 5, folder 33.

39. Quoted in David Stearns, "*West Side Story*: Between Broadway and the Opera House," *Leonard Bernstein Conducts "West Side Story,"* 1985 by Deutsche Grammophon, 415 253-1. This is augmented by the collaborators: "Laurents: "We all hold certain set beliefs, and I've always believed that the climax of a musical should be musicalized. Well, the climax of *West Side Story* is *not* musicalized. It's a speech that I wrote as a dummy lyric for an aria for Maria, with flossy words about guns and bullets. It was supposed to be set to music, and it never was." Bernstein: "Yes, it was discarded, four or five times. It's not that I didn't try," "Landmark," 15.

40. Richard Watts Jr., "Two on the Aisle: Romeo and Juliet in a Gang War," *New York Post*, September 27, 1957.

41. Swain, *Broadway Musical*, 205.

42. See John Andrew Johnson, "Gershwin's 'American Folk Opera': The Genesis, Style and Reception of *Porgy and Bess*" (PhD diss., Harvard University, 1996).

43. Bernstein, *Findings*, 305.

44. Television interview on Gershwin for WGBH-TV, Boston for Unitel, fall 1972, Bernstein Collection, writings series, box 89, folder 15.

45. Leonard Bernstein, "Why Don't You Run Upstairs and Write a Nice Gershwin Tune," *The Joy of Music*, 52–64.

46. *Findings*, 305–6.

47. Television interview on Gershwin for WGBH-TV.

48. Television interview on Gershwin for WGBH-TV.

49. For more on these scenes, see Ralph P. Locke, "The Border Territory between Classical and Broadway: A Voyage around and about *Four Saints in Three Acts* and *West Side Story*," in *Liber Amicorum Isabelle Cazeaux: Symbols, Parallels and Discoveries in Her Honor*, ed. Paul André Bempéchat (Hillsdale, NY: Pendragon Press, 2005).

50. Bernstein, "Homage to Stravinsky," *Findings*, 299–302.

51. Bernstein, "Homage to Stravinsky," *Findings*, 299–302.

52. Interestingly, Stephen Sondheim, in a discussion of purely Broadway lyrics, refers to Auden's "lyrics" for *The Rake's Progress* as being too packed. His inclusion of the work in a discussion of Broadway seems to suggest that Sondheim's familiarity with *The Rake's Progress* stems from the *Candide* and *West Side Story* period (the article, based on an earlier talk, was first published in 1964). See Stephen Sondheim, "Theatre Lyrics," in *Playwrights, Lyricists, Composers on Theater*, ed. Otis L. Guernsey (New York: Dodd, Mead, 1964), 65.

53. Bernstein, *Unanswered Question*, 359.

54. Debussy's "Essay in E Major," as Bernstein calls it, could well be the starting point for a section of the wedding vows, and Bernstein's own "Somewhere" could be read as an "Essay in E Major" about the difficulties of finding an idyllic place, much as Mallarmé's Faun does not know if he has dreamt or lived an experience. Indeed, Bernstein remarks on the ending of Mahler's Ninth Symphony ("vacillation is the final duality") suggests that a "Somewhere" is always out of reach.

55. Harold Shapero as quoted by Bernstein, *Unanswered Question*, 345.

56. Leonard Bernstein, *Unanswered Question,* 331.

57. Leonard Bernstein, *Unanswered Question,* 331.

58. Quoted in Secrest, *Sondheim,* 424.

59. Arthur Laurents, interview with author, June 3, 2008.

4

"Mambo!"

West Side Story *and the Hispanic*

"WHAT ABOUT DOING IT ABOUT THE CHICANOS?"

The quote[1] (and anecdote) is almost too good to be true: Robbins, Laurents, and Bernstein, struggling to find the perfect style, the right sound for *East Side Story,* have become discouraged and temporarily shelved the project. The initial premise—warring families of Catholics against Jews—has yielded few dramatic ideas, fewer musical ones. By coincidence, Laurents and Bernstein meet up at a Beverly Hills poolside and share their disappointment over the flagging project. Then Laurents notices a *Los Angeles Times* headline about gang warfare between Mexicans and whites. As Bernstein would later recall:

> In New York we had the Puerto Ricans, and at that time the papers were full of stories about juvenile delinquents and gangs. Arthur and I looked at one another and all I can say is that there are moments which are right for certain things and that moment seemed to have come.[2]

In that moment, stalled progress turns into renewed dedication. Bernstein puts continuing work on his troubled *Candide* on hold, director Jerome Robbins is "ecstatic" over the new concept. The composer confides excitedly to his diary, "Suddenly it all springs to life. I hear rhythms and pulses and—most of all—I can sort of feel the form."[3] The "form"—the shape and texture of the work—emerges from many styles and influences, but one element that pulls them together—and provides much of the flair that has made *West*

Side Story so popular—is the Hispanic.[4] It is neither integral to the underlying structure (which is widely recognized as hinging on the tritone motive) nor a purely exotic surface "gloss." Instead, the Hispanic element inhabits an area somewhere in between, suggesting both a familiarity with and absorption of a specific and by then highly stylized culture.[5] It appears, in fact, that the "rhythms and pulses" were, both for Bernstein and his audience, part of a lingua franca that already engaged in a convivial Spanish dialogue with concert and popular music styles. Although certainly one of *West Side Story*'s ultimate achievements lies in its successful synthesis of the larger traditions of Broadway, popular music, and art music, the adoption of a specific ethnic style in a serious and self-consciously "American" work has ultimately, and perhaps unexpectedly, earned for the Hispanic style a level of recognition in American culture it had never before achieved. And, in their own way, Bernstein, Laurents, Sondheim, and Robbins created an idea of Puerto Ricans that told passionately, if not entirely authentically, one of *West Side*'s many stories.

"IN NEW YORK WE HAD THE PUERTO RICANS . . . "

The connection between Mexican unrest on the West Coast and Puerto Rican gang warfare on the East was not a difficult one to make in the mid-1950s, and not just for Laurents and Bernstein. Juvenile delinquency, especially among minority groups, was a hot topic among both sociologists and the popular press. Almost daily, New York newspaper headlines reported dire stories such as "Hoodlum, 17, Seized as Slayer of Boy, 15" and "57.2% Rise in Delinquency Rate for Youths over 16," echoing a growing alarm about what appeared to be the largest and increasingly most problematic of New York's minority populations. Although the articles rarely blamed Puerto Ricans outright, newspaper accounts tended to emphasize the whiteness and good breeding of the victims and the seemingly unprovoked and cold-blooded behavior of their clearly brown-skinned Hispanic assailants.[6] Studies of the impact of Puerto Rican migration to the city surged during these years, raising concerns as to how this historically insular ethnic group was assimilating, in ever-increasing numbers, into American mainstream culture.[7] The consensus seemed to be that they were not. *Immigration*, which had been steadily flowing since the 1830s, became, in legal terms, *migration* after Puerto Rico became a U.S. possession in 1898. The Johnson Act of 1921, which restricted European immigration to the United States, made migration even easier and more lucrative. In many ways, the United States had initially encouraged the exodus: citing overpopulation as responsible for Puerto Rico's woes, the U.S. government had recommended bringing fifty thousand to one hundred thousand Puerto Ricans to work in the American agricultural industry as far back as 1917. On the surface, the move was meant to alleviate overpopulation, but the steady need for cheap labor would ensure a fairly constant flow of migration over the following decades, benefiting both parties. More and more Puerto Ricans came to the city after the war as New York garment and needlework industries faced increased competition. In the 1920s, starting wages in America had already been attractively higher than ending wages on the island; by the 1940s, Puerto Ricans could earn double what they had in their homeland for the same work.[8]

Inevitably, almost all migration to the United States was to New York City, where Puerto Ricans settled in "colonias" or communities. "El Barrio" (translating roughly as "the district") in East Harlem, also known as "Spanish Harlem," was by far the largest: the first and often last destination for hopeful newcomers. However, the same burdens of poverty, illness, and overpopulation that plagued migrants followed them to their new home, and New York was starting to take notice. Lawrence Chenault's *The Puerto Rican Migrant in New York City* addressed the problem as early as 1938, some eight years after social workers had expressed grave concerns over tensions in Puerto Rican family life.[9] Subsequent studies such as *Island in the City: Puerto Ricans in New York* and *The Puerto Rican Journey: New York's Newest Migrants* drew wider attention to the issues.[10] In 1948 the Migration Division of Puerto Rico's Department of Labor in New York City designed programs to educate Puerto Rican migrants about conditions in the metropolis, one of several attempts to quell the growing problem.[11] In the summer of 1955, the city hired a panel of Spanish-speaking legal-aid lawyers, and fifty school principals were sent to Puerto Rico to study the population and its culture. But no system could keep up with the growing number of migrants and their problems. With twenty-seven different airlines servicing the San Juan to New York route, and airfares between thirty dollars and fifty dollars, there was no sense of a long, arduous trek to a new world. Bernstein himself took one of those flights to do some primary research on Puerto Rican music; and although the collaborators wouldn't have spent much time in El Barrio, most had South American or Puerto Rican domestic help (Bernstein's maid was Rosalia, a name that found its way into *West Side Story*). There was no question, despite Sondheim's claims to the contrary, that the creators' awareness of Puerto Rican culture was, at least in a general sense, built on imagery and ideas prevalent in all levels of Manhattan society.

Although *West Side Story* partook in this same imagery creation, the authors were a little ahead of their time. It would take until the 1960s for sociologists to fully grasp the implications of mass Puerto Rican migration.[12] Clarence Senior's *The Puerto Ricans: Strangers—Then Neighbors* (published in cooperation with the Anti-Defamation League of B'nai Brith), Oscar Lewis's *La Vida: A Puerto Rican Family in the Culture of Poverty—San Juan and New York*,[13] and memoirs of growing up in New York by Bernardo Vega and, later, Piri Thomas heightened awareness of the problems.[14] But in the 1950s it just seemed to Americans that there were too many migrants and they were not assimilating; as Benjamin Nuñez, Costa Rican delegate to the United Nations, put it, "New Yorkers don't love Puerto Ricans and Puerto Ricans don't love New Yorkers."[15] Part of the problem was that the migrant population was not only growing but changing. Many Puerto Ricans already had college degrees by the time they reached New York and were moving into white-collar jobs and upper education. This increased earning power and numbers resulted in increased animosity from other minority neighbors, especially Italians on the East Side, the original locale for the *Romeo and Juliet* musical. Overpopulation was forcing Puerto Ricans out of El Barrio, first to Washington Heights and the West Side and eventually to all other areas of the city. In newspaper reports during mid-1955, the number of Puerto Ricans flowing into the city vacillated wildly. Some claimed migration was down 50 percent, others that numbers were up several hundred thousand, including a large and invisible invasion that was eluding researchers. Clearly, New Yorkers were worried, suddenly feeling that there was an entirely "new" community taking over their world.[16] Elena Padilla's ethnographic study *Up from Puerto Rico*[17] sensitively described the trials and tribulations of impoverished Puerto Ricans in a typical East Side neighborhood. In a similar attempt to replace fear with understanding, New York's secretary of state, Carmine DeSapio, publicly denounced talk of the "Puerto Rican problem" as prejudiced, malicious, and untruthful generalizations.[18] The problem, however, could not be ignored, especially when Puerto Rican gangs were continually implicated in youth crime.

Juvenile delinquency in general was on the rise. A Senate subcommittee was set up in 1957 to investigate juvenile delinquency in New York, and studies of gang violence such as Marjorie Rittwagen's *Sins of Their Fathers* soon followed.[19] Although statistically, delinquency rates were no higher among Puerto Ricans than among juveniles of other ethnic groups (nor was delinquency particularly prevalent in Puerto Rico),[20] Puerto Ricans were seen as part of an ever-increasing threat to the safety of white Americans. At exactly the same time, *West Side Story* opened on Broadway. Nothing could have been more topical or groundbreaking, and audiences ate it up.[21]

MAMBO ON BROADWAY

For all that New Yorkers may have resented the presence of their Latin American neighbors, one would never have known it from the pop charts. The "new" Hispanics brought with them musical styles and sounds that culminated in the biggest dance sensation of the decade: the mambo craze. The mambo was the most popular of many Latin dance styles current in the 1950s, some of which found their way into *West Side Story* in various guises. All were descendants of older dances, which, in turn, formed part of a long tradition of Latin American influence in popular music, starting with the tango craze of the second decade of the century. From the 1920s to the late 1950s, all became more and more assimilated into mainstream American music.[22]

Jelly Roll Morton goes down in history as the first non-Hispanic musician to extensively adopt the "Latin tinge,"[23] his term for the distinctive and pervasive syncopated rhythm that he felt was absolutely basic to the essence of jazz. Morton's "tinge" had been around since the earliest days of jazz, but entered the American popular mainstream in the 1930s in the form of the rumba. Two musicians were instrumental in the dissemination of the style: Don Azpiazú and Xavier Cugat. Both were among a growing number of dance band leaders regularly enlisting Latin American talent, especially musicians from Puerto Rico and Cuba. Juan Tizol, a Puerto Rican trombonist and composer who exemplified the Latin style in his recordings with Duke Ellington in the late 1930s, was one of the most successful soloists, combining South American elements with current North American musical practices. The eventual fusion of big band instrumentation and arrangement with Cuban percussion and musical structures became known as Afro-Cuban jazz. Born from

"Cubop," already a fusion of bop and traditional Cuban elements, the Afro-Cuban style was exploited most regularly by Dizzy Gillespie, who established an Afro-Cuban jazz orchestra in 1947.[24] Although Cuban percussionists such as Arnando Peraza (who recorded "Poodle Mambo" with George Shearing on the latter's *Latin Escapade* album of 1956) were very active during this period, strictly Cuban styles eventually gave way to more generically Latin ones by the late 1950s, when Afro-Cuban jazz was on the decline.[25]

The vogue of Latin American styles into which the movement fell, however, did not wane for twenty years, becoming so commonplace by the end of the 1950s as to be a standard part of the vernacular musical landscape, showing up in Bernstein's earlier *Wonderful Town* in "Conga" and in a more generic form in *Trouble in Tahiti*. The methods of dissemination were a large part of the style's success and Bernstein's familiarity. Xavier Cugat, although he led the resident band of Manhattan's Waldorf Hotel, gained most of his notoriety through his appearances in a large number of B-grade films of the 1930s, frequently alongside another icon of Latin Americanism, Carmen Miranda. Latin and Spanish themes had long been a feature of both Broadway musicals and film musicals, ranging from Latin numbers in Romberg's *Nina Rosa* (1929) to scenes in such films as Roders's and Astaire's *Flying Down to Rio* (1933). But now the Hispanic was growing from an occasional romantic or humorous character piece within a primarily "white" context into the subject of full-length films. The exposure coming from both the east and the west coasts ensured that Hispanic music would reach a wide audience across the continent.

One thing had not changed, though: for the most part, Hispanic culture and music were still portrayed inauthentically and humorously. At the same time, more non-Latins were playing Latin American music, notably Dizzy Gillespie, Woody Herman, and Stan Kenton. Eventually, white musicians and less prestigious ensembles began taking over the style, releasing "cover" versions of these tunes and new compositions in the same vein. Over the decades following *West Side Story*'s premiere, literally dozens of covers of the score by jazz musicians came out on the market, presumably reintegrating this "art Hispanic" into the jazz Hispanic. Perhaps Cugat's explanation for his own style best addresses the phenomenon: "Americans know nothing about Latin music. They neither understand nor feel it. So they have to be given music more for the eyes than the ears. Eighty percent visual, the rest aural . . . To succeed in America I gave the Americans a Latin music that had nothing authentic about it. Then I began to change the music and play more legitimately."[26]

Bernstein's own appropriation of the style in *Wonderful Town* frames it in purely comical terms: the conga number plays as a Carmen Miranda–like scene, with some sailors who interpolate the song with incongruous cries of "Conga!" There was no attempt at realism or at seeing the style as having anything to do with authentic feeling or representation. The American public, as well, seemed hardly concerned over the style's authenticity, judging by the proliferation of publications aimed at the amateur musician. By the early 1940s, one could find instructional publications teaching Latin American rhythms to white drummers and to amateur performers on many other instruments. In 1959 the Remick Music Corporation, in a series called "Music for Everyone," presented *37 Latin American Favorites, Including Examples and Explanations of Latin American Rhythms: Bossa Novas, Merengues, Cha-Cha-Chas, Rumbas, Mambos, Paso Dobles, Sambas*. Of those musicians who provided the Hispanic sound to the general population, the big band leaders were among the most popular, and they were behind the largest growth period for Latin music, the 1940s. Ironically, the young Bernstein was doing transcription work for the publisher Harms, Witmark in New York in that decade, transcribing jazz improvisations for publications, and therefore no doubt immersing himself even more deeply into a genre that he already knew quite well (although so embarrassed was he by his transcription and arrangement work for them, he published under the pseudonym Lenny Amber). Bernstein was in the big city during the era of the Mambo kings: first Azpiazú, then artists such as Tito Puente, Tito Rodriguez, and Perez Prado, gained in popularity during the late forties and fifties.[27] They also popularized what would become the three hottest dance styles of the time: the mambo, the merengue, and the cha-cha-cha. Prado is often credited with starting the mambo craze with his composition "Mambo No. 5," but, ironically, he was not part of the New York scene in which the mambo reached its zenith of popularity. Instead, he made his mark from touring with his orchestra and from recordings made for RCA. Although some claim that Prado "invented" the mambo, it was in fact like most other dance styles of the time: a permutation on what had come before, a kind of "melting pot" in which American dance tastes were combined with Latin styles.[28]

Prado himself was something of a musical hybrid: although his first success was within the Hispanic community, his tours and subsequent notoriety with white Americans led him into an ethnically suspect crossover realm that ultimately earned him the respect of neither group once the currency of the dance craze waned.[29] Until it did, though, Prado and bands such as his sold sexy Latin rhythms to an insatiable dance audience. Recordings of the mid-1950s, such as Tito Puente's *Mambo on Broadway* or Xavier Cugat's *Mambo at the Waldorf,* presented entire albums of strictly Latin American dances, however much watered down. Prado himself published some of his favorites arranged for solo piano.[30] But by far the most lucrative field for Latin music was in dance halls, many of them offering instruction. As John Storm Roberts relates, former bandleader Federico Pagani started "Latin nights" at the Alma Dance Studios on 53rd and Broadway in the early forties, a time when Latin dance bands were drawing crowds of five thousand.[31] Instructional dance records for home study abounded. The Arthur Murray dance empire offered an all-mambo record with cuts "personally recommended for dancing by Arthur Murray." The Fred Astaire Dance Studio Orchestra released a 1959 album, *Merengues and Mambos,* which included "dance instruction booklet and one studio dance lesson"; one of Tito Rodriguez's recordings bore the imposing title *Mambo Styles Strictly for Dancing.* Certainly, Latin dances were not new. But the 1950s provided the broadest consumer market yet for pleasure dancing and its attendant romance. Here is a chronology of the mambo during this period.

1950   Taylor: *Mambos and How to Play Them*
1952   Cugat: *Mambo at the Waldorf*
1953   Cugat: *Mamboland: A Folio of the Favorite Mambos So Successfully Recorded by Him* (music score) Royale Latin Orchestra: *Mambo*
1955   Prado: *Mambos for Piano* (music score)
1956   George Shearing: *Latin Escapade* featuring "Poodle Mambo"
1956   Cugat: *Mambo!* featuring "Mambo No. 5"
1956   Freddie Sateriale's Big Band: *Broadway Latin American Party*
1957   *West Side Story* premieres
1959   Fred Astaire Orchestra: *Merengues and Mambos*
1959   Remick Music Corporation: *37 Latin American Favorites, Including Examples and Explanations of Latin American Rhythms: Bossa Novas, Merengues, Cha-Cha-Chas, Rumbas, Mambos, Paso Dobles, Sambas.*
1961   Film release, *West Side Story*
1961   Stan Kenton's *West Side Story*
1964   Tito Puente: *My Fair Lady Goes Latin*

And here is a chronology of some important publications of the "Puerto Rican problem."

1957   New York University Graduate School of Public Administration and
        Social Service: *The Impact of Puerto Rican Migration on Governmental
        Services in New York City*
1958   New York Board of Education: *The Puerto Rican Study, 1953–1957; A
        Report on the Education and Adjustment of Puerto Rican Pupils in the
        Public Schools of the City of New York*; Elena Padilla: *Up From Puerto
        Rico*
1958   Christopher Rand: *The Puerto Ricans*

Although the mambo itself was not an overtly lascivious dance, its association with the sensual lent it much of its glamour.[32] Esy Morales's *Latin American Rhythms* was pressed on red vinyl to further its exotic appeal. And as an endless number of mambo compositions sprang up, they tended to focus on the alluring feminine: "Marilyn Monroe Mambo" and "Mambo Bardot" (the second from the soundtrack to *And God Created Woman*) venerated two stars who epitomized female voluptuousness in the 1950s. Hopeful males could find the appropriate date music on an album entitled *She Adores the Latin Type*, part of a series put out by Decca called Music for the Girl Friend. "Hot in Haiti" and "Penthouse Mambo" number among its cuts.

To be sure, the mambo was not an intellectual genre. Titles such as "Ya Ya Ya Cha Cha Cha" and "Merengue à la Mode" reveal their inspiration in the frivolous. And yet, the style was everywhere and combined with, seemingly, everything. Perhaps the most stunning example was a collection released by Freddie Sateriale's Big Band in 1956, entitled *Broadway Latin American Party*. This album consisted exclusively of Broadway show tunes adapted to cha-chas, merengues, and mambos. Selections included "Old Man River Cha Cha Cha," "On the Street Where You Live Cha Cha Cha," and "There's Nothing Like a Dame Cha Cha Cha."[33] The vogue of the Latin American even crossed religious and ethnic boundaries, with a bossa nova rendition of "Hava Nagila" appearing on a Columbia recording of 1962. All in all, unlikely candidates for Bernstein's tragic opera.[34]

"I'M SPANISH, I'M SUDDENLY SPANISH"

Indeed, music that could be considered "Hispanic" by the 1950s would have come from diverse sources and traditions, not least of which was the mainstream of Western art music, the other source of Bernstein's inspiration, but one not much more "tragically serious" than was evidenced by the mambo craze. Popular since the early nineteenth century, when composers in general started emulating what they considered the exotic (i.e., the non–Western European), the Spanish style rubbed elbows with music inspired by the Orient, the Middle East, and, in many cases, indigenous folk musics of other European countries. Certainly the melodic and harmonic style was unique, but Spain was also considered non-Western in the sense that it stood outside the mainstream of the more culturally elite and northern European countries (the "Viennese primacy within a tradition that united all Western nations," as James Parakilas identifies an Austrian's view of Spain).[35] Mikhail Glinka provides the perfect example of a composer swept up by another culture, identifying with it so strongly that he lived and composed in Spain for some time. After producing two important and imaginative Spanish-inspired pieces, including the much-loved *Jota aragonesa*, he used the same methods of fusing art and popular styles when turning his hand to his own Russian folk repertoire. The genre in which Glinka carried out his Spanish explorations, the orchestral showpiece, was particularly well suited to the Hispanic style. Indeed, much Hispanic-inspired music of the nineteenth century has the earmarks of the showstopper: fullness and brilliance of color, catchy tunes, rhythmic excitement, and orchestral luster. Works such as Lalo's *Symphonie espagnole*, Chabrier's *España*, and Rimsky-Korsakov's *Capriccio espagnol* have never lost their freshness and audience appeal. The vogue of the Hispanic that peaked in the 1880s found its ultimate vehicle in Bizet's *Carmen* (1875), a work fusing a French sensibility with melodies borrowed from real Spanish sources (whose publishers the composer, to some extent, credited in his score). Although Bizet did not adhere doggedly to any particular authentic style, the durability of his work has ensured the generalities of the "Spanish idiom" (as it is called by Gilbert Chase)[36] a place in the world of the best-known classical pieces. No one can hear the word *habanera* today without thinking of *Carmen*.

Although the Hispanic influence can be seen in music hailing from virtually all European nations, it was the French who took to it more readily and carried it most successfully into the twentieth century. Debussy, in his many

Spanish-inspired works, and especially Ravel,[37] who inherited much of his interest in Spain from his mother, downplayed the flamboyance and dance qualities of the Hispanic, and instead adapted its atmosphere and quiet exoticism to music that, as is often said of French music during this period, "suggests" rather than "depicts." Furthermore, works by Spanish composers, not just those inspired by them, began to see the light of day in Western concert programs; a production of Granados's *Goyescas* (in the original language) graced the 1915–1916 Met season, the first opera by a Spaniard to be performed there.[38] The popularity of the Hispanic, which prompted opportunities such as this, ensured that works such as Albeniz's *Tango in D* and parts of Falla's *El amor brujo* and *La vida breve* would be ushered into the realm of the concert gem. In addition, though, the relationship between Hispanic and pseudo-Hispanic composers, both in the classical and popular repertoires, showed a continuing cultural exchange between the old world and the new.[39] As the tango and habanera were the result of dances moving to Latin America and then back to Spain, so did Spanish composers take cues from their French counterparts. The style, as in popular music, became so standardized that classical works by indigenous composers such as Manuel de Falla sometimes reflected more on contemporary Spanish works by foreigners than on current music of their homelands.

In fact, by this time, there was no confusing the "Spanish idiom" in music worldwide, which incorporated a variety of almost stereotypical musical elements from this wide range of Hispanic traditions and influences. The opening of Ravel's short character piece *Alborada del gracioso* (originally for piano, later orchestrated) provides a perfect example of how the Hispanic was most typically represented in concert music of the early century (see example 4.1).

The first and most basic element is the distinctively Hispanic rhythm, based in a 3/4 or 3/8 time signature (the meter of the *jota*, one of the most widely known and borrowed of Spanish dance genres), particularly the alternation of 3/4 and 6/8 rhythms (as well as 6/8 and 9/8). In this example, the grouping of eighth notes and the accented offbeats in the pizzicato strings provide the initial "habanera" rhythm, and measure 6 regroups the eighths to simulate the switching of meters. Triplet turns are also a prominent feature (especially on or just after the first beat of the measure, as in the infamous genre of the bolero), and Ravel provides them in measure 12: chains of descending thirds, syncopations, and the ubiquitous lowered second scale degree (here melodi-

EXAMPLE 4.1

Ravel, *Alborada del gracioso*, mm. 1–13. Copyright © 1961 by Ernst Eulenburg Ltd., London. Rights renewed, all rights reserved. Used by permission of European American Music Distributors LLC, U.S. and Canadian agent for Ernst Eulenburg Ltd., London, a division of Schott Music, Ltd., London.

EXAMPLE 4.1 (*Continued*)

cally prominent in the descending scale of measure 6), often termed Phrygian in the literature, but frequently the third degree is major, producing a scale that matches no traditional church mode.[40] Melodies often span the interval of the sixth, with an insistence on one note (as in the melody presented at rehearsal 1 and then immediately repeated), and often the melodies and, subsequently, cadences tend to end on the fifth scale degree. In such cases, the sixth degree is often flat and the seventh natural, thereby reproducing—above the dominant—the augmented second degree frequently found above the tonic (as just noted).

In addition to purely melodic and rhythmic characteristics, a sense of instrumentation was essential to the Spanish idiom. The guitar, that paradigmatic Spanish stage prop, was usually present or at least alluded to. The pizzicato and *style brisé* nature of its performance was easily simulated with pizzicato strings, and the gradual build-up of chords to form a strumming sound was also readily reproducible in lieu of the real thing, as in Scarlatti's keyboard sonatas. Less easy to simulate on piano or strings were the distinctive sounds of the castanets and tambourine, but these instruments found their way into the orchestral and operatic repertoire, where much of the "Spanish idiom" found its life. And, of course, the Spanish idiom found its way into the Broadway musical. In Bernstein's own musicals, a humorous "Latin" number had become by this time standard: "Ya Got Me!" from *On the Town* (1944), the already mentioned "Conga!" from *Wonderful Town* (1953), and "I Am Easily Assimilated" from *Candide* (which will be discussed in more detail below). Jule Styne even included "Mu-Cha-Cha" in *Bells Are Ringing*, a year before *West Side Story* opened, and *Peter Pan* included "Captain Hook's Tango."[41] So for Bernstein, equally at home in both camps, the influence came from popular jazz, Broadway, and the art music tradition. Perhaps no other style could be seen to penetrate these different genres equally and contemporaneously.

"I WANT TO BE IN AMERICA"
This "Hispanicizing" orchestral repertoire was, of course, largely French, and was widely disseminated through the Western world. Bernstein would have been familiar with it through his conducting career. But, a more intimate and influential source of familiarity would come through his association with Aaron Copland, through Copland's early study in Paris, the compositional

center of the early century. Copland was one of the first in what was called the "Boulangerie," American composers who flocked to Paris to study with famed teacher Nadia Boulanger. Virgil Thomson, among that initial generation, later commented that "every town in the United States could boast two things: a five-and-ten-cent store and a Boulanger student."[42] The two most prominent "serious" composers of Copland's time there remained Stravinsky and Ravel, both using jazz, and the latter using the Spanish style. Copland was already considering jazz as the most likely source for forging an authentic American musical voice (an opinion to be shared by Bernstein, and propounded in his Harvard thesis, some years later).[43] The rhythmic complexity of his jazz-inspired compositions (Copland claimed not to be able to play jazz himself) intrigued his teacher, but they were also not unlike the rhythms and rhythmic alteration that were a regular part of Spanish works both in Europe and in the popular music of America.[44] Although Copland did not take up a Spanish style while in Paris, it was not many years after his return to America that another influence brought him in contact with the Hispanic, this time from Latin America.

"He conquered Mexico through Chávez" was how Virgil Thomson succinctly put Copland's relationship with his neighbors to the south. "Aaron was the president of young American music, and then middle-aged American music, because he had tact, good business sense about colleagues, and loyalty."[45] Copland was first invited to Mexico by composer and conductor Carlos Chávez in 1928, for performances of the *Piano Concerto*. Although Copland would not spend any extended time in Mexico until 1932, he found, both in Chávez and in the Mexican people, inspiration and motivation. In a letter to Thomson, Copland revealed, "The best is the people—there's nothing remotely like them in Europe. They are really the 'people'—nothing in them is striving to be bourgeois. In their overalls and bare feet they are not only poetic but positively 'émouvant.'"[46] His firsthand experience with Mexicans in overalls came when Chávez took him to a popular night spot called "El Salón México." The score eventually resulting from the experience was one of Copland's most popularly successful, even among the Mexican musicians who premiered it. It seems that Copland shared with the French an affinity for the musical style of a neighboring Hispanic culture. Indeed, he used many earmarks of the French musical world's "Spanish idiom" to reference Latin America.

"It took me three years in France to get as close a feeling to the country as I was able to get in these few months in Mexico," Copland wrote to Chávez near the end of his Latin American visit.[47] Boosey and Hawkes picked up publication of the work, with Ralph Hawkes nicknaming it an "American bolero." Hoping to further capitalize on the success of the piece, the company decided to commission a piano arrangement of the work by a young musician named Leonard Bernstein. One of the many substitute fathers who appeared throughout Bernstein's life, Copland represented everything that Bernstein could become as a composer. There seemed no limit to their shared sympathies and allegiances: both were gay (or bisexual) sons of Russian Jews, both were intellectual products of the East Coast, both were concerned with social issues, and both were tireless promoters of finding an "American" compositional voice in music. "I went to him as to a magnet because he was *the* American composer and he was the closest thing I ever had to a composition teacher."[48] Bernstein found in Copland a spiritual and musical role model and, although the Hispanic was well known to Bernstein from the standard repertoire and the popular music that surrounded him, the tradition of composition in this style was handed down to him not from Ravel or Rimsky-Korsakov, but from Copland. On an early 1940s trip to Havana, Copland bemoaned the fact that Bernstein was the only other composer who could understand the music. In a letter to Bernstein he writes:

> I wish you were here to share the music with me. I have a slightly frustrated feeling in not being able to discuss it with anyone; and a sinking feeling that no one but you and I would think it so much fun. Anyway, I'm bringing back a few records but they are only analogous to Guy Lombardo versions of the real thing. I've sat for hours on end in 5 cent a dance joints, listening. Finally the band in one place got the idea, and invited me up to the band platform. "Usted musico?" *Yes*, says I. What a music factory it is! Thirteen black men and me—quite a piquant scene. The thing I like most is the quality of voice when the Negroes sing down here. It does things to me—it's so sweet and moving. And just think, no serious Cuban composer is using any of this. It's awful tempting but I'll try to control myself.[49]

It was Copland's imprimatur that made the Latin American, the Hispanic, part of an "American" voice, and that allowed it to meld so comfortably with the many other influences that infuse *West Side Story*. Copland's fingerprints are all over this piece, not least in those numbers that are tinged (or utterly saturated) with the Hispanic.[50] Copland's *El Salón Mexico* was a work especially important to Bernstein; he actually made two different arrangements of it, one for piano solo, another for two pianos, the latter of which he performed on several occasions with Copland. Later, Bernstein stated that (apart from obvious employment reasons) he made the *Salón* arrangement because he was tired of American pianists using a Hungarian rhapsody for an encore. More than just an effective virtuosic turn, Bernstein's arrangement was intended also to contribute to American content in piano recital programming.[51] A letter of October 1938 from the Harvard senior to Copland reveals Bernstein's thoughts not just on the piece but also on the issues he would face in his own works for the musical theater:

> I saw the Group Theatre bunch today and they all asked for and about you. Odets, true to form, thinks the Salón Mexico "light," also Mozart except the G Minor Symphony. That angers me terrifically. I wish these people could see that a composer is just as *serious* when he writes a work, even if the piece is not defeatist (that Worker word again) and Weltschmerzy and misanthropic, and long. Light piece, indeed. I tremble when I think of producing something like the Salón.[52]

Twenty years later, Bernstein would compose just such a piece. The very obvious and striking similarities between *Salón* and the Hispanic aspects of *West Side Story* suggest that, although Bernstein was certainly exposed to this style through other works in the classical repertoire, the link with Copland was the closest to home and probably the most present in his mind when he sat down to write the Great American Opera.

In addition, Bernstein had even more direct contact with Latin-American culture. His wife, Chilean-born actress Felicia Monteleagre, accompanied him on a tour of Latin America in the early part of his career,[53] and he had this to say (publicly) about the music:

> The Latin American spirit has other ancestors besides "Latin" (Spanish and Portuguese) ones. First of all there are Indians—the original inhabitants of these countries, and in some cases very strong civilizations in themselves. And secondly, Africans, a tremendously important influence, at least as important as in our own country. It is the mingling of these different ancestors, influences,

and heritages which makes the Latin American spirit what it is, at least in music. The sweet, simple primitiveness of the Indian music mixes with the wild, syncopated, throbbing primitiveness of the African music; and both of these, mixed with the fiery flash of Spanish music and the sentimental sweetness of Portuguese songs, make up the music we know as Latin American.[54]

As Bernstein seems to suggest, the Latin American was in many ways analogous to the American musical world that Bernstein had recognized (and expounded on at length) in his Harvard senior thesis, "The Absorption of Race Elements into American Music." For Copland, *Salón* was only the first of a number of later works, such as *Billy the Kid* and *Appalachian Spring*, in which he sought a particularly American sound through the adoption of folk material into an art music context. It seems that, whereas Europe's fascination with the Hispanic provided (at the least) pleasantly distracting exotic color or (at most) a close embrace of the "other," once it was transplanted to America, the Latin American became similar to, if not outright part of, American music in general. Along with relating to the non-Hispanic composer of Hispanic music, however, the American composer shared with real Hispanic composers—in different time periods and geographical areas—the desire to forge a national identity while trying to get away from the European mainstream. Albéniz, Granados, Falla, Rodrigo, Ginastera, and Chávez served as good role models for how to do this while at the same time winning international acceptance. Copland's and Bernstein's interest in direct musical expression for everyday people—along with their interest in American musical identity—made them more interested than most in the possibilities of this "light" music.

"I AM SO EASILY ASSIMILATED"
Bernstein's first major attempt to meld these serious and popular elements in a theatrical context came in *Candide*. It was also Bernstein's first large-scale attempt at the Great American Opera of which he dreamed and that *West Side Story* would, in its own way, become.[55] Although commercially and artistically less successful than anticipated, *Candide* continued the vein of eclecticism most evident in *Trouble in Tahiti*. Among the parodies of different operatic and musical theater styles is Bernstein's caricature of the Hispanic, "I Am Easily Assimilated." Clearly this is a song Bernstein called his own; in a work notorious for the number of collaborative forces involved (five librettists in

the original version, not counting the much later additions by Wheeler and Sondheim), the composer wrote both text and music.

> I was not born in sunny Hispania.
> My father came from Rovno Gubernya
> But now I'm here, I'm dancing a tango:
> Di dee di!
> Dee di dee di!
> I am easily assimilated.
> I am so easily assimilated.
>
> I never learned a human language.
> My father spoke a High Middle Polish.
> In one half-hour I'm talking in Spanish:
> Por favor! Toreador!
> I am easily assimilated.
> I am so easily assimilated.
>
> It's easy, it's ever so easy!
> I'm Spanish, I'm suddenly Spanish!
>
> And you must be Spanish, too.
> Do like the natives do.
> These days you have to be
> In the majority.
>
> Tus labios rubí,
> Dos rosas que se abren a mí
> Conquistan mi corazón,
> Yo sólo con
> Una canción.
>
> Mis labios rubí,
> Drei viertel Takt,
> Mon très cher ami,
> Oui oui, sí sí,
> Ja ja ja, yes yes, da da,
> Je ne sais quoi!
>
> Me muero, me saleuna hernia!
> A long way from Rovno Gubernya!

Mis labios rubí,
Dos rosas qui se abren a tí,
Conquistan tu corazón,
Y sólo con
Una divina canción
De mis labios rubí

The lyric alone is typical of Bernstein in general and *Candide* in particular in its wit, humor, and breadth of allusion. The eclecticism of the language—switching between German, French, Spanish, Russian—defines not only the assimilation of the Old Lady, but also the phoniness that characterizes her. Faking her way through a number of situations and cultures, she has survived by her ability to assimilate into any milieu. Not disguising the political climate into which *Candide* fell (in either Hellmann's or Voltaire's time), her admonition that "These days you have to be in the majority" fits in perfectly with the comic-cynical mood of the work as a whole. The male chorus, a group of local natives, sings in Spanish about getting a hernia while trying to lift the Old Lady. In all, what would be a Carmen Miranda–style production number in which virile males deify a seductive female lead is made into an absurd parody of a peripatetic Jewish mother figure who constantly reminds us that she is endowed with only "one buttock." As Andrea Most has pointed out, musicals written by Jews from immigrant backgrounds from the 1920s and 1930s onwards had used the idea of changing identities (through changing costumes) to help navigate racial problems and deal with assimilation issues.[56] In musical terms, too, the number functions as a stereotypical example of the Hispanic à la Bernstein. The orchestration is full of Spanish-style features: the tambourine, the duet of English horn and piccolo, the heaviness and loudness of the brass and winds, the trombone glissandi, and the *pesante* string writing all point to the Hispanic. Also the mode, with raised fourth scale degree and flatted seventh, and the abundance of parallel chromatic major-third intervals are all stereotypical Spanish elements, as is the syncopated rhythm underlying the entire song (3 + 3 + 2 eighth notes in a 4/4 meter). It is, even in its comic context, a flashy dance number providing local color, and it obeys the form of the Broadway song, a reminder that we are still in America, not sunny Hispania. And yet, it is more sophisticated and more serious, musically, than

Bernstein's forays into a Latin style in his previous Broadway works. The style is, in an odd way, ironically more "assimilated."

However, on a musical and thematic level, the song can also be read as Jewish. The mode is not unlike the Hebraic formulas Bernstein employed in his Jewish works, notably the *Kaddish* and *Jeremiah* symphonies. The repeated note, often approached from above or below by an appoggiatura, is one of the features of Spanish music which, prominent scholars argued at the time, was inherited from Jewish chant.[57] And the orchestration, with the English horn and piccolo sounded together, is reminiscent of the instrumentation of a klezmer band. This similarity could not have been far from Bernstein's mind; although in the published score the number is simply entitled "I Am Easily Assimilated" with the tempo marking "Moderato," the composer's facsimile reads "Old Lady's Jewish Tango" with the marking "Moderato Hassidicamente" (see figure 4.1). Even the composer's sketched-in orchestration dictates those aspects of the piece that make it sound both Hispanic and, to use Bernstein's term, "Hassidic." Again, there was a precedent here, at least in musical comedy terms. In *Making Whoopee* (1928), a supposedly "Indian" melody sounded more like a Hassidic nigun—the characters were not supposed to hear it that way, but it was treated as an in-joke meant for the audience.[58]

The number sends up not just the Old Lady, but aspects of Bernstein's own image. The reference to "Rovno Gubernya" is no doubt an approximate allusion to the composer's father's roots, the "High Middle Polish" (a takeoff on the standard linguistic term "High Middle German") is likewise a reference to Bernstein's Jewish/Eastern European ancestry. That Bernstein has chosen such a multiethnic character to reflect his own background suggests the degree to which the composer was sensitive to these issues. Indeed, in his early letters while touring Europe as a young conductor, he constantly referenced his own Jewish identity as a foil to Europeans. The same may be said of the admonition, not just political but cultural, to fit in with a "majority." The constant shifting of languages, the ability to learn Spanish in "one half hour," both celebrates Bernstein's verbal and musical acuity and reflects his predicament of being constantly pulled from one kind of musical expression to another.

Although Jews were expelled from Spain in 1492, they took many Spanish songs with them, combining Jewish chant with originally Spanish material.

FIGURE 4.1

Bernstein: facsimile of manuscript, "I Am Easily Assimilated" from *Candide*, by Leonard Bernstein and Stephen Sondheim. Copyright © the Leonard Bernstein Estate. Courtesy of the Leonard Bernstein Music Publishing Company LLC, publisher. Boosey & Hawkes, Inc., sole agent. Reprinted by permission of Boosey & Hawkes, Inc.

Recordings from the early twentieth century document the fact that Sephardic Jews in New York were still performing Spanish songs, as well as sharing the Sephardic (Spanish) liturgy.[59] But even in the New World, the Latin and Hasidic were closely related. The Jewish theaters of East Harlem were intrigued by the Latin style and a large number of the audiences for Latin bands were Jewish.[60] As white bands had started taking over Latin music, many of the bandleaders and musicians were Jews, notably Alfredo Mendez, whose natal name was Mendelsohn, and Larry Harlow; a trend that would continue, not diminish.[61] Of course, "I Am Easily Assimilated" was not the only send-up Jewish number in this highly irreverent score.

"I WAS NOT BORN IN SUNNY HISPANIA . . . "

In retrospect, it seems odd that the Jewish tradition did not provide sufficient artistic inspiration for Bernstein to make some headway on a Jewish vs. Catholic score. Having grown up with a father devoted to his Hasidic ancestry (he traced his own lineage back to the tribe of Benjamin)[62] and actively involved in the Conservative Jewish congregation of Mishkan Tefila in suburban Roxbury, Massachusetts, Bernstein was surrounded by a rich and regular diet of Jewish liturgical music, from recordings of cantors on 78-rpm records to weekly meetings at the synagogue. The composer has credited his exposure to this tradition as one of the most important musical influences of his childhood. One arrangement by the temple's organist and choirmaster, Solomon G. Braslavsky, Bernstein describes as the first time he "discovered that there was such a thing as counterpoint: great obbligatos floating on high. 'Arrangement' is too small a word. It was a great composition. I knew every note of it because I heard it every year: it was like an opera."[63] Indeed, whether inspired by his own faith or as a gesture toward this heritage, Bernstein's compositional output is weighted heavily toward the Jewish. From a setting of Psalm 148 in 1932 (one of his first compositions) to "Oif Mayn Khas'neh" in his last work, *Arias and Barcarolles,* Bernstein eventually explored Jewish themes and musical styles in at least ten compositions, including two of his most substantial orchestral works, the first and third symphonies. By the mid-1950s, the works he had already written in this vein must have calmed any serious doubts that he may have held that he could employ Jewish material to communicate in a musically meaningful way. Nor was he unaware of the tremendous power born from the integration of current practices with a Jewish sensibility, so apparent (as he himself noted) in the creative works of his own hero, Mahler.[64] Still, although Mahler would influence *West Side Story* in other ways, he did not provide a good primary model for a work steeped in the violence and grittiness of working-class youth on New York City's East Side.[65]

It was probably more the timeliness of the theme and the influence of Robbins and Laurents than the result of an inner struggle that mitigated against Bernstein's following a Jewish/Catholic theme. "The East Side wasn't what it used to be, therefore the idea was old-fashioned—it would have been *Abie's Irish Rose* all over again and not very topical."[66] Although Robbins was the only choreographer ever to commission a work from Bernstein, it was not until *Dybbuk* (1974) that he set any of the composer's Jewish-inspired music to dance. Robbins commissioned *Fancy Free* (first performed in 1944) and *Facsimile* (1946) for his Ballet Theatre but had also found the composer's symphonic repertoire conducive to a dance treatment, setting the *Age of Anxiety* symphony for the New York City Ballet in 1950. These early works were set in the jazzy, urban style that Bernstein cultivated after his move to New York City in the 1940s and that was aptly suited to the subject material.[67] The story lines of the Robbins/Bernstein ballets were driven by the adventures and mores of modern-day urbanites, not conflict on a grand scale. It was clearly this urbane, sophisticated style that answered Robbins's desire for a youthful and, moreover, violent gang world, but the basic dichotomy necessary to tell the story was not an obvious outgrowth of jazz, itself a synthesis of a number of different elements. "I had a strong feeling of staleness of the East Side situation and I didn't like the too-angry, too-bitchy, too-vulgar tone of it," Bernstein recalled.[68] But, without religion, there was no essential difference left between these New York Montagues and Capulets, and, without a musical representation of difference, there would be no musical way to represent the conflict. The Hispanic element provided that difference, but how would Bernstein adapt the rather hackneyed and stereotypical aspects of the Hispanic—which are precisely what make *Candide*'s "I Am Easily Assimilated" work as a comic number—to suit the far more serious demands of a musical tragedy? How to integrate this element into the fabric of the score?

TEMPO DI HUAPANGO (FAST)

Joseph Swain's *The Broadway Musical: A Critical and Musical Survey*[69] and Jack Gottlieb's 1964 dissertation "The Music of Leonard Bernstein: A Study of Melodic Manipulations"[70] provide the most comprehensive and technical of musical analyses of *West Side Story*, and both naturally (though peripherally) address the issue of ethnicity. The authors focus less on harmonic or rhythmic aspects of the work than they do on Bernstein's use of motives, specifically the tritone interval, structuring the piece through both audible surface details and larger-scale harmonic motion.[71] Gottlieb, particularly, analyzes the entire musical based on Bernstein's variations of small motivic cells. For Swain, all musical elements that could be read as Hispanic (hemiola, the lowered seventh scale degree, dance rhythms) can be found in other of Bernstein's works, rendering them relatively insignificant here. Similarly, Gottlieb's analytical system "works" for virtually every one of Bernstein's compositions, making *West Side Story* no different in construction from his symphonies or chamber works. What both authors tend to ignore is the ways in which the music of the whites and Hispanics (Jets and Sharks) differs and the role that rhythm plays in this differentiation. The music generally associated with the Jets is "cool jazz," the best examples being the song (not surprisingly) "Cool," the signature tune "Jet Song," and the blues and jump music from the "Dance at the Gym." Although each contains rhythmic complexity to some degree, it is the combination of melodic awkwardness with metric shifting that creates the overall musical effect. Take, for instance, "Something's Coming," with the unwieldy repetition of a melodic idea made sensible by shifting accents between melody and accompaniment. Similarly, "Cool" is rendered more singable by rests, allowing the melody to be broken up into negotiable units. "Gee, Officer Krupke" and the "Jet Song" similarly contain modulatory passages that challenge the dancer/singer who intends to actually hit the notes.

The most overtly Hispanic number is the (rather ironically titled) song "America," in which Anita describes the Puerto Rican adaptation to American life. It is a kind of second-generation "I Am Easily Assimilated," treating the same subject matter in a way not dissimilar to its *Candide* predecessor. Here Bernstein keeps some of the more vital aspects of the Hispanic while toning down its triter ones, and seems to treat it more "seriously," at least to the extent that it is closer to an authentic model than any of the other Hispanic pieces in the score. Although the music of *West Side Story* has always been seen as being part of this watered-down version of real Latin music, Bernstein actually took time out of his busy schedule to fly down to Puerto Rico for a week during an intense working period, suggesting that his familiarity with at least some "authentic" genres was fresh.[72]

The number is an amalgam of two Latin American traditions: it combines the indigenous Mexican form, the *huapango*, with the Puerto Rican genre of the *seis*. The huapango was more than a dance for two people or groups of pairs; the term was also used to describe a genre: a type of dance party popular in South America. The essence of the huapango is its fast tempo and complex cross-rhythms: one instrument plays in 2/4, another 3/4, and a third 6/8.[73] This is precisely what Bernstein presents in the first bars of this number, adding as a tempo indication "Tempo di 'Seis.'" The seis was yet another form of Puerto Rican origin, although it also cropped up in Venezuela and Colombia. Apparently taking its name from the guitar ("six-string") which accompanies it, the seis is an accompanied vocal piece in several stanzas of varying numbers of six- or eight-syllable lines. The binary structure includes brief instrumental interludes performed usually by a guitar in strict V-I harmony with percussion accompaniment, followed by often unaccompanied, unmeasured text delivery. The seis is one of Puerto Rico's most popular, and most Spanish, song types.[74] Although there are no unaccompanied sections to Bernstein's seis, he does borrow a technique from the subcategory of the *seis de bomba* (a *bomba* being a verbal blow aimed at one of the singer's audience members). Rosalia's nostalgic reminiscences about her homeland are countered with Anita's bombas. Anita does not even allow Rosalia to finish her sixteen-bar vocal before jumping in two measures early with a sarcastic parody of Rosalia's sincere outpouring (Bernstein marks Anita's phrase "mockingly"). Anita then extends her own reportage of life in Puerto Rico with four extra bars of punctuated outcries (Bernstein marks them to be performed "rhythmically") about the downside of life in the old country. Although the vocal line is certainly set in notated rhythm, the "unmeasured" aspect of this slow prelude does resemble the spirit, if not the letter, of the seis. Bernstein has also scored the piece with an eye to authenticity: Spanish guitar, claves, and guiro (the latter two being essential to Latin American music, both in the form that would have been brought to the United States from Latin America and its North American counterparts). Even the piano/vocal score indicates the use of claves and guiro for the rhythmic "vamp" that precedes this number proper, an unusual indication considering that these instruments would likely not be part of the rehearsal pianist's percussion arsenal.[75]

The purpose of "America" is clearly to provide an opportunity for a dance number, and, although it obliquely addresses cultural problems, it would be difficult to imagine that it seriously attempts to address social ills any more than "I Am Easily Assimilated" is a commentary on the Diaspora. Indeed, the big comic number in this recurringly serious musical is "Officer Krupke," and it remains interesting that the cleverness of the lyric and the cynicism yet worldliness and insight presented in the song is the domain of the male, the white gang, not the Puerto Rican females. It also stops the show, long after we have forgotten the excitement of Anita's skirt-swirling dance display in "America."

The "Dance at the Gym," another ripe site of Latin American influence, is even more intriguing, in that it performs its dramatic and emotional function without the aid of the ubiquitous Broadway lyric. Here we see Bernstein and Robbins create a framing device within which the mystical meeting of the two lovers takes place. Although the dance scene begins in the "Puerto Rican" locale of the bridal shop, the musical segue (in the stage version, simulated through cinematic effects in the film version) takes us immediately into the "white" jazz world of the dance hall as heard in the "Blues."

From here on we see layers in which one Hispanic-tinged section gives way to one that is even more so; the emotions of the characters and their conflict become more intense as they become more Hispanic. The "Promenade" (marked "Tempo di Paso Doble") opens with a fanfare that seems clearly to mock the pompous attitude of the master of ceremonies, a character named (appropriately) Gladhand. The heavy, repetitive, monotonous nature of this vamp-like interlude (Bernstein has even marked it "pesante") seems to be almost "pseudo-Hispanic." It ends with the standard "cha-cha-cha" rhythm on the tonic note. Robbed of the rhythmic vitality and color of Latin jazz and Hispanic pop music, the drudgery of this section is clear from both the dull instrumentation and the plodding steps of the youths. It is Latin music as their parents might listen (or dance) to it. The decision to buck authority leads the two gangs suddenly into the "Mambo" section, and here we find the most vital and, in many ways, most Hispanic sections of the score (see figure 4.2).

The instrumentation (bongos, cowbells, trumpets) takes its inspiration from the Latin jazz band. The interpolated cries of "Mambo!" by the two gangs are a direct descendant of the flamenco tradition in which dancers are urged on by their enthusiastic onlookers. A cuadro flamenco is a kind of

FIGURE 4.2
Frenzied mambo from "Dance at the Gym," original Broadway production. Photo by
Fred Fehl.

dance party in which soloists take turns entertaining each other in semicir-
cular groups.[76] In fact, this is exactly what Robbins's dancers do; each gang
forms a semicircle around their own dance performers, who try to outdo the
other "team." Certainly the average amateur dance enthusiast would not be
able to execute Robbins's (and, specifically, Peter Gennaro's) choreography,
but the dance moves are based on conventions of Latin social dancing. Although the predominantly minor mode of the section has resonances in the
"Spanish idiom" scale, the Hispanic is most clearly embodied here through
the complex rhythm of the mambo.

When we reach the moment of the deepest, though also restrained, emotion, the cha-cha serves to represent the awakening feelings in the couple.
Although not by nature a refined dance, the cha-cha here is stylized to such an
extent that it has become almost a minuet. The spare orchestration, the peri-

odic phrase structure, and even a binary form with open and closed cadence points are mirrored in the courtly dance style adopted by the young lovers. The tune, of course, we will hear only minutes later as "Maria" (though we don't hear its vocal version, and words, yet). The dreamlike world of the cha-cha is soon crowded by the steadily increasing tempo and volume of the paso doble, the outside world, the world of the pseudo-Hispanic. Once we hear the sound of Gladhand's whistle, we are instantly brought back into the brightly lit everyday. All Hispanic influence is gone, and we suddenly hear a very laid-back, cool "Jump." Clearly, the world of the Hispanic can encompass not just the passion of the dance contest, but also the otherworldliness of the love relationship. As Tony reenters the dreamlike state of the initial meeting (and as the walls of the gym literally fly out of the scene), we hear the melody of the cha-cha, but now with the rhythmic underpinnings of the seis—the same type that underlies "America." In fact, the song "Maria," always referred to as a cha-cha, is not one at all, but a seis. The freely rhythmic opening section (even marked "slowly and freely" in the score) follows the same procedure that we later hear in "America," and the accompaniment to "Maria" is identical (although the scoring is completely different): dotted habanera rhythm in the bass, combination of duple and triple meters in the melody, and inner voices. At the same time, just as in "I Am Easily Assimilated," the song adheres to a fairly standard song form (with the exception that the orchestra takes over some of the inner repetitions from the singer). Why we don't hear this song as overtly Hispanic is mostly due to the scoring: the exotic percussion instrumentation and guitar of "America" are missing here; instead we get lush, soaring string sound. The whole combination of elements beautifully reflects the way in which Maria and her Hispanic world have infiltrated the predominantly "white" milieu into which Tony fits.

"THE BEST OF ALL POSSIBLE WORLDS"?

Although *Candide* failed for a number of different reasons, one thing that prevented it from being Bernstein's Great American Opera was that in many ways it was not American enough: the parodies of Gilbert and Sullivan, European operetta, and a number of other styles detracted from anything that seemed truly indigenous. *Candide* was American in its eclecticism and its worldly and cynical, yet hip, attitude, but not in its overall sound. (One problem was the locale, or plethora of locales, in *Candide*; *West Side Story* stays very firmly in one, uniformly American neighborhood.) Everyone could "understand it," as Bernstein had hoped, but not everyone could relate to it. The expansiveness, those open Copland-esque chords, the pioneering spirit of "Make Our Garden Grow," come too late. The "too bitchy, too vulgar" tone that put Bernstein off the original *East Side Story* was also what robbed *Candide* of its earnestness too early in the piece. And surely "earnestness" would seem a foremost requirement in the creation of a great American musical identity. With *West Side Story*, the eclecticism is just as pervasive, and the exoticism just as striking, but the absorption and dovetailing of these features into each other allows that ethnicity to seem less "quoted"—it sounds American while still allowing for "difference" between the warring factions. It also appears in a serious guise, not the "Conga!" of *Wonderful Town* or the comic turn of the Old Lady in *Candide*, comic moments that are foregrounded as standing out against the rest of the work. And no doubt, the reason the Hispanic works so well in this context is because it can represent unity and disunity at once. This effect could only be achieved if the Hispanic were part of a larger body of repertoires, part of in fact *all* repertoires within the American musical mainstream. In effect, the Hispanicism in all aspects of the work functions like an accent, albeit a fake one. The musical and verbal style do not represent the "real language" of Puerto Ricans, just as their lives are not portrayed accurately in other ways in this piece.

This results in two things: the "difference" of the Hispanic is less threatening to the audience, and it is more easily disguised within the other sources and styles that inform the work. In Benjamin Britten's opera *Paul Bunyan*, the use of a solo folk-song-style singer with guitar to narrate past events is a logical and authentic way of presenting the American legend it attempts to portray. The acoustic guitar is not the sole domain of the American folk artist, nor is the ballad style a foreign one to the composer's culture, and yet this whole number sticks out from the rest of the work and seems strained and somewhat unnatural. Even though this is an "ethnic" opera for Britten, there seems something too literal and realistic about that representation of "Americanness" that prevents that number from coming across to an audience who construct their own nostalgic and idealized version of themselves. In the same way, enlisting a more authentic Puerto Rican music, language, or culture might seem just as "obvious" and forced in *West Side Story*.

And yet at the same time, we need to ask whether the portrayal of Puerto Ricans, either dramatically or musically, is to some degree racist. Bernstein wrote to his brother, who was stationed at a military posting in Puerto Rico, "I wrote a spic song called 'Maria' which may finally bring me to the jukeboxes, who knows. And one called 'Cool' which will never see a jukebox. *Candide* is a certainty for next fall." Later in the letter he describes his research trip to Puerto Rico, referring to the island by the same dismissive initials used by Schrank and the Jets: "I'm going to try to get to PR for some local research on the Romeo show: an excuse, but I may get away with it. Let's hope."[77]

These musings can clearly be dismissed as the result of youth and intoxication—Bernstein was, if nothing else, a passionate and compassionate soul and defender of all humanity—they are simply the types of jokes one makes to one's intimates, not meant in any seriousness. But they point to a more culturally embedded sense of "othering" in which most Americans participated on some level at this time, even Americans as sensitive and educated as Bernstein. Although clearly he saw the Hispanic as a way to capitalize on the Latin dance craze (while at the same time realizing that the white, cool jazz was too highbrow for general popularity), one wonders whether his motivation in going to Puerto Rico was at least as much to have a vacation as to do serious musical research. That the Hispanic characters have less "serious" music, action, and personal voices may have been in part because the authors in their own way unintentionally bought into the racial stereotyping that surrounded them, accepting that "other" is always going to mean secondary. Only one cast member (Jamie Sanchez) in the original production was actually Puerto Rican, and part-Canadian, part-Scottish Allyn Ann McLerie, who took over the role of Anita, declared rather naively, "I know very few Spanish-speaking people and I haven't known many Puerto Ricans. But my husband knows a lot of Spanish people, so he gave me pointers. I feel much closer to Puerto Ricans now. I feel I understand them, how really disturbed they are."[78] Today no actor would say that to the press. What it shows is not American insensitivity but American naïveté, how little anyone had really considered ethnic diversity.

Although the Hispanicism of *West Side Story* grew out of varied sources, it in its own way served to perpetuate a style which was, by the late 1950s, starting to decline. Shortly after the release of the film version, an album called *Kenton's West Side Story* appeared on the Columbia label. Kenton, one of the big band leaders who had introduced the Latin style long before Bernstein, recorded an entire album of jazz reworkings of the songs, including the prologue. Kenton's nouveau *West Side* included the most obvious Spanish numbers, "America" and "Dance at the Gym." Not surprisingly, the remake of "America" was in some ways more authentic than Bernstein's original, a kind of second generation of the very Americanized Latin music that Kenton had originally promoted. In a similar vein, Copland's *Three Latin American Sketches*, which were really two sketches augmented by a third movement for publication in the 1970s, sounds more like Bernstein's score than Copland's earlier dabbling in this style. Perhaps both recognized in the composer's creation something that was more than just the "Latin tinge," something more—and perhaps, specifically white—American.

But there are other, more subtle resonances behind the adoption of the Hispanic. Take two accounts from the late 1950s. First, Gilbert Chase on Copland's music ("[Copland's *Salón*] has caught a bit of color and movement that strikes like a flash of lightning through the drab cerebralism of academic modernism")[79] and on the music of Spanish composer Mompou ("Mompou himself has defined his aesthetic ideal as tending toward an intimate type of musical expression, the cultivation of music in a state of purity, motivated by a purposeful reaction against the 'cerebralism' dominant in our epoch. He reacts against the 'music of the laboratory,' seeking a true form of expression in a lyrical feeling enriched by the musical experience of the past").[80]

Then consider the following by Aaron Copland: "My turn to a simpler style in *El Salón* and other pieces that followed puzzled some of my colleagues. Roger Sessions did not approve of my move to a 'popular' style, nor did Arthur Berger. After *El Salón*, I occasionally had the strange sensation of being divided in half—the austere, intellectual modernist on one side; the accessible, popular composer on the other."[81]

Purity, truth, cerebralism? It seems that the dichotomy drawn between "intellectual" modernism and "true" (indeed, "pure") feeling at midcentury finds an interesting outgrowth in the Hispanic. The popularity of the Spanish idiom was certainly felt in the concert hall, but its representative pieces would hardly have made it into the Western musical canon. Nor would its styles have been taught in composition classes. Copland's reception as a composer would have been quite different had he eschewed the "popular" in his oeuvre. We can see how Bernstein has incorporated the Hispanic elements, and yet *West Side Story* has not gone down in history as "that Spanish musical." Even Joseph Swain, in his survey of the best-known Broadway musicals, assigns *West Side Story* to the chapter "Tragedy as Musical" instead of "Ethnic Musical" (the chapter given to *Fiddler on the Roof*).[82] It seems that, in many ways, the dissonance of the score, the violence of the story, and the economy of the spoken dialogue and dance numbers mitigate the languid, emotional qualities that were deemed quintessentially Hispanic. The very quick cutting from Hispanic to non-Hispanic (take the segue from "America" to "Cool" and the close proximity of the subsections of "Dance at the Gym") keeps the Hispanic element in its place. It never escapes long enough to take over the score, and yet many of its rhythmic and harmonic aspects (the tritone as a melodic interval is, scholars have noted, a frequent feature of Spanish idiom music) allow a sense of continuity throughout the work. The universal appeal of this Hispanic "Americanism" is perhaps best explained by Chávez, himself deeply interested in this issue: "The feeling of universality is not new in history. Localism also has existed always, but with the limitations of fear, or poverty of spirit. For this reason, it has been an error to seek the originality of American art by way of nationalism inspired in localisms and limitations. No. The American is as universal as the rest."[83]

If, however, we consider *West Side Story* symbolic of the mambo craze, part of a larger popular music culture of which it is only one aspect, whose *West Side Story* do we imagine it to be? Certainly, for composers like Bernstein and Copland, an American voice suggested a white, middle-class, and perhaps Jewish ethos built on the music of predominantly East Coast composers. Bernstein clearly sees the Latin American as outside his own milieu, and yet at the same time his appropriation of it and absorption of it into his own music creates a tension within his composition that cannot be explained away as simply local color. The universality that Mompou names, and to which *West Side Story* seems to aspire through its amalgamation of different styles, lies somewhere between a colonial empiricism and a fraught Jewish identity at the American midcentury. Perhaps not surprisingly, it was Bernstein's last Hispanic work, not because it was a corollary of Gershwin's "final amalgamation," but because Bernstein could take it no further.

In the 2008–2009 season Arthur Laurents, after revisiting his own *Gypsy* as a director, took on a major revival on Broadway of *West Side Story*. Now, with

Robbins and Bernstein gone, it was time for Laurents as a playwright to come to the fore, for a different story to be told. (Laurents had always prided himself on the fact that it was racism that precipitated the tragedy in *West Side*, not just a misconstrued message, as in Shakespeare.) He saw no reason for reviving a musical simply for the sake of reviving it; it had to say something new. With *Gypsy*, that newness came as a more direct look at the underlying psychology, the sexuality, and the toughness of that show and its characters— elements that would have been downplayed for a 1957 Broadway audience.[84] For *West Side Story*, it was bringing the show into the twenty-first century, which for Laurents meant redressing the attitude toward Puerto Ricans that informed the original work. His longtime partner, Tom Hatcher, had seen an all-Spanish production and had reported to Laurents how differently the work played, and would play, if the Sharks were the indigenous, "American" gang and the Jets the outsiders. How to change the musical to give the Sharks more emphasis, more authenticity, and more respect? Laurents could not realistically change the music, but he changed the parts over which the playwright has control: the language. Scenes between Shark members that were originally played in English were now played in Spanish. The most frothy number in the score and one of the more Hispanic, "I Feel Pretty" was now translated into Spanish, with the benediction of Sondheim, who never liked his lyric for that number to begin with. The show still takes place in the 1950s (Laurents could have presumably updated it to make the gang more twenty-first-century in its costumes, setting, or lingo), but a 1950s that never actually existed: an America where the Hispanic characters spoke and acted in their own language, not in the "accent" that was handed to them by the creators in the only way they realistically could—not through the appropriated mambo craze, the translated social justice, and the Americanized Latin dance styles. The Washington previews in 2008 included subtitles to assist audience members in understanding the language, but audience reaction was much more positive when they were removed, partial proof that the authenticity that was perhaps always lurking under the surface was one Americans were now ready to hear (or that the work is so well known that line-by-line understanding is no longer necessary). Audience reaction to "I Feel Pretty" was even warmer than at most other productions I have witnessed—the audience celebrated the diversity, reveled in the ethnicity, and recognized the work for what it could (and, some would argue, perhaps should) be. Whether Laurents's changes will become the standard way to present this musical remains to be seen; for Puerto Ricans who resent the original work for its stereotyping of their culture (an issue that has cropped up more frequently in recent years), it may not be enough. That these changes beautifully deepen the complexity of this work and its relationship to the Hispanic in our own time is undeniable. Alexander Bernstein, the composer's son, remarked on the opening night in Washington that his father would have loved to have shared the stage that night with Arthur Laurents. If Bernstein had seen how much farther *West Side Story* had come and how much more passionately it argued for acceptance and understanding, I have no doubt that he would.

NOTES

1. Leonard Bernstein to Arthur Laurents, quoted in Otis L. Guernsey, *Broadway Song and Story: Playwrights/Lyricists/Composers Discuss Their Hits* (New York: Dodd, Mead, 1985), 42.

2. Quoted in Guernsey, *Broadway*, 42; and Craig Zadan, *Sondheim & Company* (New York: Da Capo, 1994), 15.

3. Quoted in "Excerpts from a *West Side Story* Log" in *Findings* (New York: Simon & Schuster, 1982), 145. The original sketches for this diary are in the Leonard Bernstein Collection, writings series, box 75, folder 7, Library of Congress, Washington, DC.

4. For the purposes of the general discussion, I will use the more wide-ranging "Hispanic," a political term adopted by Spanish-speaking people to unify against white domination, but which also refers more generically to the people, language, and culture of Spain, Portugal, and Latin America, as opposed to the more limiting "Spanish," "Latino," "Chicano," or "South American," although these other terms will appear where appropriate.

5. For a discussion of the tritone motive in *West Side Story*, see chapter 3.

6. A front-page *New York Times* story of May 1955 juxtaposed the victim, a "good student" at Mount St. Michael Academy and son of a prominent member of the community, with his accused murderer, Mark Santana. Although gang rivalry was in general blamed for the murder, Santana and the Hispanic names of his gang friends were documented, along with Santana's inexplicable lack of remorse over the incident. The story followed one in which the mayor urged an overhaul of the police force to deal with youth crime (*New York Times*, May 2, 1955, section 1, 1).

7. New York Board of Education, The Puerto Rican Study, 1953–1957; A Report on the Education and Adjustment of Puerto Rican Pupils in the Public Schools of the City of New York (New York Board of Education, 1958); New York University Graduate School of Public Administration and Social Service, The Impact of Puerto Rican Migration on Governmental Services in New York City (New York: New York University Press, 1957); Office of the Coordinator of Spanish-American Catholic Action at the Chancery Office of the New York Archdiocese. Conference on the Spiritual Care of Puerto Rican Migrants, San Juan, Puerto Rico, 11–16, April 11–16, 1955; Beatrice Bishop Berle, *80 Puerto Rican Families in New York City: Health and Disease Studied in Context* (New York: Columbia University Press, 1958).

8. Virginia E. Sánchez Korrol, *From Colonia to Community: The History of Puerto Ricans in New York City, 1917–1948* (Westport, CT: Greenwood Press, 1983), 35.

9. Lawrence Chenault, *The Puerto Rican Migrant in New York City* (New York: Columbia University Press, 1938).

10. Dan Wakefield, *Island in the City: Puerto Ricans in New York* (New York: Corinth, 1959). Numerous general studies of Hispanic groups in the United States emerged during this period, for instance: John H. Burma, *Spanish-Speaking Groups in the United States*, Duke University Press Sociological Series 9 (Durham, NC: Duke University Press, 1954); Benjamin Malzberg, *Mental Disease among the Puerto Rican Population of New York State, 1960–61* (Albany, NY: Research Foundation for Mental Hygiene, 1965); Joseph Fitzpatrick, *Puerto Rican Americans: The Meaning of Migration to the Mainland* (Englewood Cliffs, NJ: Prentice Hall, 1971).

11. Korrol, *From Colonia to Community*, 35; Luis A. Cardona, *The Coming of the Puerto Ricans* (Washington, DC: Unidos, 1974); Edward B. Lockett, *The Puerto Rico Problem* (New York: Exposition Press, 1964); Nathan Glazer, *Beyond the Melting Pot: The Negroes, Puerto Ricans, Jews, Italians, and Irish of New York City* (Cambridge, MA: MIT Press, 1963).

12. For instance, José Hernández Álvarez, "The Movement and Settlement of Puerto Rican Migrants within the United States, 1950–1960," *International Migration Review* 2, no. 2 (1968): 40–51; and Lockett, *The Puerto Rico Problem*.

13. Oscar Lewis, *La Vida: A Puerto Rican Family in the Culture of Poverty—San Juan and New York* (New York: Random House, 1966); Clarence Senior, *The Puerto Ricans: Strangers—Then Neighbors* (New York: Random House, 1966, reprinted 1968 and 1969).

14. Piri Thomas, *Down These Mean Streets* (New York: Knopf, 1967) and *Memoirs of Bernardo Vega: A Contribution to the History of the Puerto Rican Community in New York* (New York: Monthly Review Press, 1984). Other English-language memoirs on growing up Puerto Rican emerged from the 1960s on.

15. Nuñez made this statement at a luncheon attended by five hundred people in 1955, quoted in the *New York Times*, April 17, 1955, section 1, 77.

16. Most literature emphasized the cultural differences between white America and Puerto Rican, but also fostered a false sense of the "newness" of the migrant population. For example, see Oscar Handlin, *The Newcomers: Negroes and Puerto Ricans in a Changing Metropolis* (Cambridge, MA: Harvard University Press, 1959); and C. Wright Mills, *New York's Newest Migrants* (New York: Harper, 1950).

17. Elena Padilla, *Up From Puerto Rico* (New York: Columbia University Press, 1958); Christopher Rand, *The Puerto Ricans* (New York: Oxford University Press, 1958).

18. Carmine G. DeSapio at a dinner honoring Antonio Mendez, the first Puerto Rican to become a democratic leader in Manhattan, quoted in the *New York Times*, June 12, 1955, section 1, 15.

19. United States Congress Senate Committee on the Judiciary, Subcommittee to Investigate Juvenile Delinquency, *Juvenile Delinquency: New York Programs for the Prevention and Treatment of Juvenile Delinquency. Hearing before the Subcommittee to Investigate Juvenile Delinquency of the Committee on the Judiciary*, December 4, 1957; Marjorie Rittwagen, *Sins of Their Fathers* (Boston: Houghton Mifflin, 1958).

20. All fears were manifested in the "Capeman" case of 1959, in which Salvador Agron, a sixteen-year-old member of the Vampires gang, stabbed two white teenagers in Hell's Kitchen. Earning his nickname for the black cape he sported, Agron was arrested and eventually became the youngest criminal in New York state history to be given the death penalty (later commuted) (Stephen J. Dubner, "The Pop Perfectionist," *New York Times Magazine*, November 9, 1997, 45). Almost forty years later, the Capeman case became the inspiration for a musical by the same name composed by pop artist Paul Simon. Attempting to integrate Latin American music with his own style, Simon spent seven years on the project, approximately the same amount of time that collaborators took to create *West Side Story*. *The Capeman* opened on Broadway in January 1998 to generally horrendous reviews and closed two months later, losing eleven million dollars for its investors.

136

CHAPTER 4

21. In fact, both the problems but also the ethnic identities of Puerto Ricans and African-Americans were often conflated during this period, factoring into a larger racial picture in both New York City and the entire United States to which *West Side Story* (in both musical and cultural ways) spoke.

22. The early stages of this development are chronicled in Ruth Glasser's *My Music Is My Flag: Puerto Rican Musicians and Their New York Communities, 1917–1940* (Berkeley: University of California Press, 1995).

23. Sometimes referred to as the "Spanish tinge," this style appears in Morton's works from the 1920s on.

24. Machito established the "Afro-Cubans" in the early 1940s in New York City, the first big band of this kind, but the style was associated with Gillespie throughout his career.

25. Gunther Schuller, "Afro-Cuban Jazz," in *New Grove Dictionary of Jazz*, vol. 1 (London: Macmillan, 1988), 7.

26. Quoted in John Storm Roberts, *The Latin Tinge* (Oxford: Oxford University Press, 1979), 87.

27. Steven Loza, *Tito Puente and the Making of Latin Music* (Urbana: University of Illinois Press, 1999).

28. The mambo was a variation on the rumba, and the cha-cha-cha was a further development of the mambo. The merengue was actually a dance hailing from Venezuela, Haiti, and the Dominican Republic, but was influenced by Afro-Cuban dance styles.

29. Prado's release of *Rockambo* in 1961 probably signaled the demise of the genre, along with its success in fusing with newer pop music styles.

30. Perez Prado, *Mambos for Piano* (New York: Southern Music Publishing Company, 1955).

31. Roberts, *Latin Tinge*, 113.

32. The mambo is a couples dance in which the partners either stand completely apart or in an embrace with space between their bodies. It is characterized by forward and backward motion and a dance step which begins, rather unusually, on the fourth beat of a 4/4 measure. Contrast this with the style of and furor over the later lambada.

33. Freddie Sateriale's Big Band, *Broadway Latin American Party: Cha chas, Merengues and Mambos*, Pirouette Records, 1956. Other titles from this album include "Smoke Gets in Your Eyes Cha Cha Cha" and "I Love Paris Cha Cha Cha."

34. Perhaps there is another connection with Stravinsky, who includes the cancan and other popular dance styles in his *Oedipus Rex*.

35. In a discussion of Artur Schnabel's view of the "Spanish" tradition as opposed to the Viennese, James Parakilas writes, "He could not erase the difference in his listeners' ways of thinking about the two musical traditions. The waltz was a dance they danced, and the well-known claim of Viennese musicians to a distinctive way of playing the waltz beat (Schnabel's 'corruption of the three-quarter measure') was a claim of Viennese primacy within a tradition that united all Western nations. Spanish dances did not belong to his listeners—to non-Spaniards—in the same sense; they were dances to watch others dance, on stage or on screen, signifying 'Spain.'" James Parakilas, "How Spain Got a Soul," in *The Exotic in Western Music*, ed. Jonathan Bellman (Boston: Northeastern University Press, 1998), 137.

36. Gilbert Chase, *The Music of Spain*, 2nd rev. ed. (New York: Dover, 1959).

37. Debussy's "Soirée dans Grenade" from *Estampes* and "Ibéria" from *Images*; Ravel's *Habanera, Rapsodie espagnole, L'Heure espagnole, Bolero, Alborada del Gracioso*, and others.

38. For a contemporary view of the popularity of the Hispanic in music of the early century, see Carl Van Vechten's *The Music of Spain* (New York: Knopf, 1918).

39. The "pseudo-Hispanic" is another colorful but apt description coined by Gilbert Chase.

40. Notable examples include the first movement of Albeniz's *Cantos de España* (also known as "Asturias") and the entr'acte to act 4 of Bizet's *Carmen*, based on a *polo* for voice and piano by Manuel Garcia, Sr.

41. David Van Leer, "What Lola Got," in *The Other Fifties: Interrogating Midcentury American Icons*, ed. Joel Freeman (Urbana: University of Illinois Press, 1997), 179.

42. Quoted in Aaron Copland and Vivian Perlis, *Copland: 1900 through 1942* (London: Faber and Faber, 1984), 62.

43. Reprinted in its entirety in Bernstein, *Findings*, 36–99.

44. In describing the finale from his ballet *Grohg*, excerpts of which were later adapted into his *Dance Symphony*, Copland refers to rapid alternations of 5/4, 3/4,

and 3/8, not unlike those of Latin American music. His *Short Symphony* was also noted for its rhythmic complexity, mostly the result of the same kinds of metric shifts; it was dedicated to Latin American composer Carlos Chávez.

45. Virgil Thomson, interview by Vivian Perlis, quoted in Perlis, *Copland*, 200.

46. Copland to Virgil Thomson, 5 December 1932, quoted in Perlis, *Copland*, 214.

47. Copland to Chávez, 2 January 1933, quoted in Perlis, *Copland*, 216.

48. Bernstein, interview by Susan Lacy, date unknown, *Reaching for the Note*, DVD, directed by Susan Lacy (New York: Winstar, 1998).

49. Excerpt of a letter from Aaron Copland to Leonard Bernstein, April 1941, reproduced by permission of The Aaron Copland Fund for Music, Inc., copyright owner.

50. For more on the other musical influences on *West Side Story*, see chapter 3.

51. John Gruen, recording notes, *Bernstein: Complete Works for Solo Piano*, Pro Arte PAD 109, 1983.

52. Bernstein to Copland, 20 October 1938. The reference is to the Communist party newspaper *The Daily Worker*.

53. Among Latin American compositions Bernstein recorded were Fernández's *Batuque*, Guarnieri's *Dansa brasileira*, Revueltas's *Sensemayá*, and Chávez's *Sinfonía India*, all recently reissued in Sony's "Bernstein Century" series as *Latin American Fiesta*.

54. Leonard Bernstein, recording notes, *Latin American Fiesta*, reissued as Sony Classical SMK 60571.

55. Bernstein wrote on the creation of the Great American Opera in 1948, reproduced in *Findings*, 129.

56. Andrea Most, "'Big Chief Izzy Horowitz': Theatricality and Jewish Identity in the Wild West," *American Jewish History* 87, no. 4 (1999): 314.

57. Chase, *Spain*, 224.

58. Most, "Theatricality," 319.

59. Chase, *Spain*, 36.

60. Roberts, *Latin Tinge*, 88.

61. Roberts, *Latin Tinge*, 91–92.

62. Secrest, *Leonard Bernstein*, 5.

63. Humphrey Burton, *Leonard Bernstein*, 9, quoted in "Childhood," a BBC-TV/ Unitel film. Also on Bernstein's early experiences with Jewish music, see Peyser, *Bernstein: A Biography* and Secrest, *Leonard Bernstein*.

64. Bernstein discusses this in an essay on Mahler, reproduced in *Findings*, 255–64. For more on Mahler, see Christopher Jarrett Page, "Leonard Bernstein and the Resurrection of Gustav Mahler" (PhD diss., University of California at Los Angeles, 2000).

65. For more on the influence of composers in the classical tradition, see chapter 3.

66. Quoted in Zadan, *Sondheim & Company*, 14.

67. Indeed, Bernstein's most jazz-inspired compositions have received the most frequent dance settings over his career—at least six choreographed versions of *Prelude, Fugue, and Riffs* alone. For a more complete list of Bernstein works adapted for dance, see Jack Gottlieb's *Leonard Bernstein: A Complete Catalog of His Works: Celebrating His 70th Birthday* (New York: Jalni, 1988).

68. Zadan, *Sondheim & Company*, 15.

69. Swain, *Broadway Musical*.

70. Jack Gottlieb, "The Music of Leonard Bernstein."

71. Swain, *Broadway Musical*, 208–11.

72. Bernstein Collection, date book series, box 322, folder 1.

73. Pan American Union, *Music of Latin America* (Washington, DC: General Secretariat of the Organization of American States, 1963), 13; and William Gradante, "Seis," in *New Grove Dictionary of Music and Musicians*, 2001.

74. Jorge Duany, "Popular Music in Puerto Rico: Toward an Anthropology of *Salsa*," *Latin American Music Review* 5, no. 2 (1984): 190.

75. Very few instrumentation cues are provided in the piano/vocal score, published by Boosey and Hawkes.

76. Chase, *Spain*, 336n10.

77. Leonard Bernstein to Burton Bernstein, October 1955, Bernstein collection, box 5, folder 33. There were other concerns, too. In March of 1955, U.S. Secretary of

State Dulles stated publicly that the United States might use atomic warfare against China over the communist takeover of Quemoy-Matsu. Bernstein, in a drunken letter from Italy, writes to his brother: "There you are in tropical grandeur on Spic-Isle, recovering from the bivouac period, roaring with rum. Then I keep reading with trepidation the Quemoy-type items in the daily press, and I go queer with apprehension about the duration of your stay on Spic-Isle." (Leonard Bernstein in Milan to Burton Bernstein, 19 March 1955, Bernstein collection, box 5, folder 33.)

78. Bea Smith, "No Type Casting," *New York Sunday News,* May 22, 1960. See also Henderson Cleaves, "Redhead Plays a Puerto Rican," *New York World-Telegram and Sun,* April 27, 1960. Apparently it took an hour in makeup, using a substance called "Texas Dirt," to make McLerie look Latin; a friend remarked that she would be the only Puerto Rican on stage with a plaid mantilla (David Stewart, "Dream Street," *New York Daily News,* April 30, 1960).

79. Chase, *Spain,* 304.

80. Chase, *Spain,* 320.

81. Aaron Copland, quoted in Copland and Perlis, *Copland: 1900 through 1942,* 245–51.

82. Swain, *Broadway Musical.*

83. Carlos Chávez, 1952, quoted in Ann Livermore, *A Short History of Spanish Music* (London: Duckworth, 1972), 244.

84. Arthur Laurents, interview with the author, June 3, 2008.

"I and Velma Ain't Dumb"

The Women of West Side Story

To tell you the truth, they wouldn't even understand it, I don't think—I mean this business about the gang war, they wouldn't understand it.

Your girlfriend's stupid, Charlie, she don't understand nothin' anyway.

—*Juvenile delinquents from the University Settlement House on Rivington Street on the Lower East Side interviewed by social workers after a matinee performance in 1958, on what their girlfriends would think of* West Side Story. *John McClain, "Story Acts as JD Deterrent," New York Journal-American, November 2, 1958*

What are we poopin' around with dumb broads?

—*Action, act 1, scene 6,* West Side Story

In musical theater, who gets music, how much, and of what kind helps to define the importance of each character's role. Traditional musical comedy convention during this time period usually revolved around a romantic plot in which lovers are thwarted by various hurdles, often of their own making, and eventually—often suddenly—the couple is happily united for a joyful finale. The female lead in this situation is often an assertive and daring individual: consider the heroines of *South Pacific, The Sound of Music, Oklahoma!,* or *Annie Get Your Gun.* Even the more traditional *The Music Man,* produced the same year as *West Side Story,* presents its female protagonist as a quiet and conservative librarian who nevertheless has the tenacity and verve to change the world around her. This often intrepid Broadway heroine traditionally had several solo turns, not infrequently the showstopping eleven o'clock number that comes in a more or less penultimate position in the performance ("Let Me Entertain You" from *Gypsy* or "The Saga of Jenny" from *Lady in the Dark* offer archetypal examples).[1] In short, female characters shared the stage with their male counterparts more equally than we might expect in mainstream American culture at midcentury, often dominating it. Indeed, the "star system" of Broadway theater was ruled at this time by female performers.[2] Just a year before *West Side Story* opened, Robbins, Bob Fosse, and Comden and Green created *Bells Are Ringing*, a vehicle for new Hollywood star Judy Holliday. Nothing new, this kind of show was part of a long tradition, in which a series of blockbuster musicals showcased talents such as Ethel Merman (*Annie Get Your Gun, Anything Goes, Gypsy,* etc.), Mary Martin (*Peter Pan, South Pacific*), and Gwen Verdon (*Damn Yankees, Sweet Charity*). Indeed, critics often reviewed the star herself instead of the theatrical work, given that the show was simply an extension of her particular talents as revealed against a backdrop of music, lyrics, and choreography.[3]

Since the days of burlesque, the power of the female star also brought with it the all-important box office return, epitomized in the Ziegfeld Follies tradition and its emphasis on the body spectacle provided by the barely clothed and ubiquitous chorus girl.[4] In order to achieve *West Side Story*'s smooth flow from song to dance to speech, the creators downplayed the structure of song and dance typical of the traditional musical to achieve a more seamless effect. A star turn, no matter how theatrically spectacular, would interfere with the pacing and flow of the musical and consequently detract from the seriousness of and attention to the tragic drama. It would also shift the emphasis to the female, something which would not work in this show primarily about male conflict.

Given this context, the role of women in *West Side Story* is curious and rather unorthodox. The authors negotiated a territory between female stars and female characters, struggling to situate them comfortably in a show about male gangs and in the end downplaying their roles in rather unexpected ways. Why is this? One of the most obvious reasons lies in the creators' determined attempts to invert or disable the stereotypical characters and situations of traditional musical comedy. They wanted to avoid the inevitable song lead-up; the disjunction between speech, song, and dance; large production numbers;

and spectacle for its own sake (not to mention a happy ending). As part of this agenda, they opted to cast relative unknowns in the lead roles, thus undermining the star system and its attendant strictures, a star system which would normally have placed a strong female performer at the center of the show. Although Chita Rivera was the closest to a "star" (she had formerly danced to Peter Gennaro's choreography in the 1955 *Seventh Heaven*, show-doctored by Robbins), and Carol Lawrence was certainly made a star by the show, the musical managed in general to dismantle the conventional spectacle of the female body (although we shall see that this changed somewhat through its initial run). Moreover, *West Side Story* is structured heavily through its dances, and although such works are designed in general to showcase both male and female talents and physiques rather equally, the overwhelming influence of classical dance that Robbins brought to the show and its attendant emphasis on athleticism brought male dancers to the fore to balance the traditional emphasis on the female dancer and the distracting allure of her body. Obviously, this stems from the subject matter itself, in which gang members (more certainly male in this era than female, although more will be said about this later), pitted against each other in a battle of life or death, provided the fulcrum for the drama. But there seem to be other, more subtle reasons for this emphasis. *West Side Story* is, among other things, an unabashed celebration of the male dancer and male singing actor. The large set pieces, like the famous all-danced "Prologue" and the "Rumble," are ritualistic tableaux in which male energy, male behaviors, and male street values are reified. *West Side Story* is a glorious celebration of men, created by a team of men, and something very different from what Broadway was accustomed to. Indeed, this celebration of the male dancer was prominent, especially after the visit of Moscow's Moiseyev Dance Company in 1958. "The men—possibly the most masculine male dancers ever to kick a leg in Manhattan—performed their muscle-twisting feats with a pure animal joy of movement rarely seen on the stage," wrote critic Harold Clurman. "The qualities these dancers possess are those we [Americans] like to claim as our own when we feel ourselves to be at our best."[5] So, at the root of ideal Americanism, at least for some at that time, was "pure animal joy" and masculinity. This comes as no surprise from middle America at midcentury; certainly feminist scholars have remarked on this aspect of the period for decades. However, where did it leave the creators, who were attempting to navigate this new male emphasis while still making the female protagonists vital and appealing? How did audience expectations about the female body play out in the work? The ultimate result is fascinating: in this musical, female characters wend their way in and out of power and agency, both musically and narratively, in a way that shows the collaborative process at work. The way women are portrayed and treated musically and dramatically, then, does not so much evince a garden-variety misogyny but instead shows some of the tensions within both the theater and culture between male and female roles and how these dovetail with ethnicity, voice, and the demands of a story unlike any told in musical theater before. Fascinatingly, it is the ostensibly minor character of Anybodys who emerges from this web as a perfect distillation of this tension, and it is ultimately she who has more to do in this musical than we might ever have expected.

ANITA AND THE GIRLS

"Back home, women know their place."

—*Bernardo to Chino, act 1, scene 5*

Where are the women of *West Side Story*, and who are they? For the most part, they are Hispanic. And, ultimately, the worlds of the Hispanic and the feminine are inextricably combined in this drama. The musical traverses the familiar ground of the exotic opera or operetta repertoire in which the female lead, especially the romantic lead, is an exotic, ethnically differentiated character who woos—or despite her chaste passivity, attracts—a white male tenor, often to his demise (like Leila, the priestess in *The Pearl Fishers*, or the protagonist of *Lakmé*). This ethnic tension, made at times more explicitly racial in *West Side Story* (thus hinting at America's black-white divide) adds a layer to the musical that is a new departure from Shakespeare.[6] Romeo and Juliet are from rival families, but both are assumed equal in status. Neither family is the newcomer, the outsider to an already established social order, as the Puerto Rican Sharks are to the mostly "white" Jets. The decision to make Tony Caucasian and Maria Hispanic follows the operetta convention but also serves to lower Maria's value, as she is part of a more stifled Hispanic world.[7]

It is hard to imagine the work with Maria a white Jet girl and Tony a Hispanic Shark. Maria would not only lose her exotic appeal, but would also outclass Tony through her whiteness, inverting the power dynamic between

male and "other" that—here and in the various exotic operas and operettas—
drives the romantic situation. It follows, then, that Anita, the nurse character
in Shakespeare's play, must be from the same "family" or ethnic group. Both
women are therefore identified strongly with the exotic, and their music reflects this.

"Ai! Here comes the whole commercial!"

—Anita, act 1, scene 5

Anita is one of the most ethnically inflected of all the characters, and her song
"America" addresses her role as an outsider. Although this flashy dance number reveals a spicy character (at least compared to the milder Maria), Anita's
strength is expressed primarily in terms of her relationship to her male counterparts in the Sharks. "America" doesn't allow her to break out of her role
as simply local color. Indeed, this number was intended, and still remains, a
showstopping production number, the entertainment climax of the first act.
Yet, it neither advances plot (like the other major dance numbers, "Prologue,"
"Rumble," "Dance at the Gym" or the "Taunting Scene") or develops her
character, as does Tony's "Something's Coming." In Anita's "America," her
lyrics pit her against detractors of her support of the American way, forcing
her to "sell" her idea to a playful yet obstreperous Puerto Rican gathering.
The interruptions and interjections to Anita's song (sometimes line by line)
by Rosalia (and in the film version, the men) serve to problematize, even
undermine, her unabashed optimism, an attempt to subtly silence her voice.
When we look at the original conception of the song (in which the Shark men
were involved), we see that even this much of a voice was not intended.[8] In
his previously unpublished notes to fellow creators, the director laid out the
ground rules.

The Puerto Ricans are at home, relaxed, at ease without any outside pressures
. . . not on guard. The Scene should have a feeling of warm, relaxed affection
. . . should bring out the warmth and kidding qualities of the humor of the
song of "America." If possible, the material should serve as some cue and hint
to the Balcony Scene (which comes after it—now) and that is a variation on
"love feelings." It is also one of the few scenes in which we get a chance to see
Bernardo other than in his "chip on the shoulder" attitude and in this Scene,

we can possibly see his sensitivity, hurt, longings and his early dreams which were slapped out of him.[9]

The note suggests the players in the song thus: Anita presents the pro-American side; Rosalia (and Bernardo, in Robbins's conception and the film version) opposes her with anti-American sentiments. However, there is no indication as to how the song is meant to reveal anything about Anita, the character who actually sings it; she is not mentioned at all except as a foil to the "sensitive, hurt, and longing" Bernardo. Clearly the song was intended to develop Bernardo more fully as a character, to provide him with the depth that ultimately remains missing from the portrayal of his character in the finished work. The fact that the original stage version finally included only women suggests a number of different possibilities. Rivera's considerable performing talents may have inspired the choreographers to use the number as a showcase for her, thus adding a complexity to a reading of the work along strictly gendered and ethnic lines. Clearly there were practical reasons for these decisions beyond the demands of the story itself. Perhaps it also seemed unwise to burden the already overextended male dancers between the dance-intensive "Dance at the Gym" and "Rumble" numbers. Or perhaps the song was considered too light and entertainment-oriented to involve the "serious" main plot: the tragic love duo and the male gang members. If this was indeed the reason, it would explain the tendency to segregate women's and men's numbers (consider the tone and style of "I Feel Pretty" and "America" as opposed to the "Jet Song" and "Cool") as representing "art" and "entertainment." Why Robbins reintegrated men (featuring Bernardo in particular) into this number for the film version remains equally open to question. Perhaps the director realized that it would be more effective as a dance production number using male and female couples. Perhaps he rethought the piece and reverted to the original concept. Or perhaps including the dissenting male voice served to further contain the female characters, a trend that seems to underlie the entire work. In this mixed-gender rendition, Anita does not simply fool around with her female friends, she has to lock horns with Bernardo in a male-female showdown. To her credit, Anita ends up having the last word: The final stanzas of the song present her final triumphant conclusion on Puerto Rico, that despite the "better" things in her homeland, "Everyone there will have moved here." For the moment, Anita seems to have won. However, she is not able to, in the ensuing dialogue, stop Bernardo from attending the war council meeting. Despite her new status as "American," Bernardo reminds her that he is in charge of the domestic sphere.

Other aspects of the number suggest that it held less importance to the "art" aspects of the show: "America" was choreographed by assistant choreographer Peter Gennaro. Robbins, who is credited with both choreography and direction, did not spend his time on frivolous entertainment numbers such as this one, but focused his energy on the large male dance pieces ("Prologue," "Rumble," and the humorous but sharply pointed "Gee, Officer Krupke"). The reasons for this are not entirely, however, inherently either misogynist or racist: Robbins apparently wanted to focus more on directing than creating the choreography, threatening to back out of the project if he had to take on the burden of choreographing the entire show.[10] Also, Gennaro was renowned for his expertise in Latin dance, an area which Robbins did not feel as comfortable in as in traditional styles. Still, the fact remains that Robbins kept for himself the male, and ultimately, the "white" numbers, those that advanced the plot as opposed to those that provided the audience with some relief from the plot. This "relief" function of "America" and "I Feel Pretty" is heightened by the placement of the two numbers: each immediately succeeds one of the most crucial and serious plot events in the story (the "Balcony Scene" and the "Rumble," respectively). As the work is considered a serious tragedy, it seems unusual that the scenes that ostensibly portray the private lives of the Shark women are the most lighthearted of the entire musical. That they specifically concern the women and not the male gang members leads to an inevitable gendering of this particular ethnic group as a whole.[11] It appears that, consciously or not, the creators have portrayed the Jets (read white, male) as more sophisticated and serious and the Sharks (primarily female and Hispanic) as simple and perhaps even rustic. In the most primitivist sense, "they have rhythm."

While the female Hispanic numbers in *West Side Story* are musically and aesthetically attractive, they are also more "entertaining," bowing somewhat to the audience expectation of female body spectacle. Indeed, an early reviewer described Rivera as a "throbbing bundle of vivacious Latin femininity."[12] On the other hand, the music for the white male Jets is cool, angular, and indebted to certain "modern" strands of jazz—it contains the most sophisticated and progressive musical techniques in the score, which are never shared with the Hispanic characters and certainly not with the women. Indeed, the drive to become American, non-Hispanic, is the major focus of Maria's and Anita's roles, their way out of a restrictive society. "I'm an American girl now," Anita tells Bernardo as he goes off to the rumble: "I don't wait." For Maria, too, an aspiration to be "American," to be more white, is the road out of her poor Puerto Rican background. In "I Feel Pretty," Maria's immigrant friends urge her to dress up, not as a bride, but as Miss America, the highest pinnacle that she could reach, presumably.

MARIA VS. TONY

"I pity any girl who isn't me tonight."

—*Maria, act 2, scene 1*

Looking at the two solo (and only solo) expressions of our two lovers highlights the differences in how they are portrayed. Richard Kislan, in his survey of the American musical, defines songs according to type: the ballad, the production number, the aforementioned showstopping eleven o'clock number, the "I am" song, and so on. Numerous examples of each kind can be found in the Broadway literature from this period, and it is easy to assume that the creators, no matter how invested in subverting theatrical stereotypes, still worked within a system in which a particular type of song would be appropriate at a particular point in the drama. Maria's "I Feel Pretty" might fall into two of Kislan's categories: the "I am" song, in which a character presents himself or herself to other characters and the audience simultaneously ("I'm Just a Girl Who Cain't Say No"—*Oklahoma!*—is a perfect example) and a "charm song," meant to win over the audience by presenting a life-affirming positive view of the world that makes the audience feel relaxed, happy, and secure (i.e., "Mister Snow" in *Carousel*).[13]

One of the most popular numbers from the score, "I Feel Pretty" highlights Maria's naïveté and sweetness, but also her weakness and her role in the drama as musical comedy relief. The guitar sound and cha-cha rhythm carried over from "America" return in spades here; this song provides the most deliberately light utterances of the entire work (sent up perfectly by Little Richard in a cover of this song for the 1994 recording *The Songs of West Side Story*).[14] A lingering sexism finds resonance with the authors. Maria's "I

Feel Pretty" remains the most problematic and embarrassing song for Sondheim, who felt the rhymes were too sophisticated for the character of Maria. He wrote a simplified version that was subsequently rejected by the other collaborators. Sondheim explains, "When rhyme goes against character, out it should go, and rhyme always implies education and mind working, and the more rhymes, the sharper the mind."[15] As he saw it, there is no way a girl just off the boat from Puerto Rico would be able to put together the sentence "It's alarming how charming I feel."[16] But, Sondheim's analysis is deeply problematic. Although Maria is young, there is no reason to believe that she is any more naive or sophisticated than Tony, or, for that matter, any of the other characters in this drama of the teenage street. We hear the Shark women utter such lines as "I like the shores of America!/ Comfort is yours in America!/ Knobs on the doors in America,/Wall-to-wall floors in America!" and Action delivers, "Dear kindly judge your honor,/My parents treat me rough/With all their marijuana/They won't give me a puff./They didn't wanna have me,/But somehow I was had./ Leapin' lizards! That's why I'm so bad."[17] In an early draft of the song, Diesel (playing the part of the bailiff) actually says,

> Whereas and howsoever, inasmuch as you was caught in the fact of purloinin'
> a parked convertible with malice forethought which belonged to another party
> what they didn't give you ipso facto permission, how do you plead?[18]

The idea that the Jet gang members would have been more "sharp" and educated than their Puerto Rican counterparts imagines that the audience believes that the white characters, with similar educational backgrounds to the Puerto Ricans, will naturally be smarter. As for Maria being "fresh off the boat," this seems a highly literalist objection that suggests Sondheim's position may be ingenuous: suspension of disbelief allows us to understand that Maria's commentary is Spanish translated into an English idiom for the stage (as is suggested by a few words of inserted Spanish: "You go, *querida*. I will lock up."). In the same way, we would not believe that the dialogue between the Sharks would have occurred in English.[19] Or, more likely, we simply suspend our disbelief about how "well" immigrants can speak English, since the lyrics, and even some of the dialogue, transcend the purely naturalistic, giving us a glimpse instead into the characters' unfettered feelings, whether or not they could express such feelings in words. It is surely for this reason that

Maria's lyrics don't sound all that different from what we hear from the other characters. Indeed, if she spoke in the somewhat stilted language that characterizes the performers in "America"—one of the few spots where the Puerto Ricans seem to be struggling with their new language—it might be more difficult for the audience to take her seriously as the romantic lead (as opposed to a secondary character). She needs to speak the audience's language fluently in order for them to differentiate her from the rest of the cast and relate to her emotionally (or perhaps allow her to "rate" on the same class level as the white Tony).

Maria's song is pure, unadulterated fluff, summing up her character's image of herself in visual terms: she is pretty. Although clearly meant to be lighthearted relief for the audience, the song still presents this character as somewhat vacuous—there is no action associated with her expression, simply unexamined reflection on *her* reflection in a proverbial mirror, a mirror created and held up by others. To undercut Maria are the interjections of her Puerto Rican friends (Rosalia and Consuelo), not unlike the interruptions that Anita faces in her number, "America." Clearly not meant to be truly derogatory, this framing device provided by the other women nevertheless sends up Maria and our ability to take her entirely seriously.[20] Indeed, Bernstein's music supports this reading, but with strikingly racial implications. Maria's song begins with an upbeat allegro opening that could be taken from any musical theater song of this period. The castanets that are subtly alluded to in the sixteenth-note figure place the song vaguely in a Hispanic world, but the audience would not specifically read these in this way were this song presented in another musical and a different context. After Maria's outpouring of pure joy, she is suddenly interrupted by the two girls, who introduce a new, heavily Hispanic theme, replete with the musical characteristics of the Spanish style.[21] Particularly striking is the sudden change to A minor from Maria's opening F major, inflected with a lowered second scale degree, descending Spanish flourishes, and a triplet sixteenth rhythm reflective of the more Hispanic numbers in the work and elsewhere in the repertoire. The girls' playful teasing focuses on Maria's delusion of being both "pretty" and Spanish. "She thinks she's in love./She thinks she's in Spain./She isn't in love,/ She's merely insane." They hearken back to the same kind of language Anita uses in "America" to describe the plight of the Puerto Rican "savage," even to the point of paralleling, sometimes line-by-line, the same image or concern (bad weather, etc.). Consuelo and Rosalia's lines in "I Feel Pretty" are similar to Anita's lines in "America."

It must be the heat	→	Always the hurricanes blowing
Or some rare disease	→	Island of tropic diseases
Or too much to eat	→	Always the population growing
Or maybe it's fleas	→	Hundreds of people in each room

In effect, the girls remind Maria of her place, the Puerto Rican identity that undermines her ability to be free. The creators have a hand in undercutting Maria's song. It opens act 2 and, although certainly an upbeat opening provides some relief after the violence and tragedy of the "Rumble," the rumble also makes Maria's attitude seem even less serious. Not so much adding to the tragedy, Maria's ignorance of the events of the rumble shuts her out of the world in which the "real" and serious drama unfolds, the world of the men. Granted, Maria has not yet heard about the rumble, but for the audience this is the last image burned into their minds from act 1.[22] More telling perhaps is a comparison of the main establishing numbers for the romantic leads. Unlike "I Feel Pretty," Tony's signature song, "Something's Coming," is an "I want" song—a type that has been characterized as going beyond the sentiments expressed in an "I am" song, emphasizing action rather than reflection, plot rather than character.[23] (Both songs' lyrics appear in appendix A at the end of this volume).

Tony's number follows, musically, from the macho establishing number of the musical, the "Jet Song." However Tony may claim to eschew the lifestyle and values of the gang members, his role as Riff's best friend and the placement of this song early in the drama and right after the "Jet Song" allow Tony a certain primacy and strong association with this male world. Clearly, the creators saw a need for this. The song was added later in the production, judging from Leonard Bernstein's correspondence with his wife, as late as August 1957: "We wrote a new song for Tony that's a killer, & it just wasn't the same not playing it first for you. It's really going to save his character—a driving 2/4 in the great tradition (but of course fucked up by me with 3/4s and what not)—but it gives Tony balls—so that he doesn't emerge as just a euphoric dreamer"[24] (see chapter 4 for further discussion of this song). Maria's number, similarly, is a perfect example of a "euphoric dreamer" utterance, and yet the creators saw no apparent problem with that. Indeed, Sondheim's criticism of the song suggests that it is not dreamy *enough*, but instead too intellectual. The fact that Tony's character needed to be "saved" from the fate of Maria's portrayal suggests that the male lead had to have more to him than simply emotional appeal. Perhaps, in a very practical sense, the creators believed that in order for Tony to be a credible vengeance murderer in the rumble, he needed to show more "balls" than the rather pacifist character portrayed in his dialogue up to this point. Bernstein's characterization of the song as "driving," and indeed the obsessive, repetitive motive that characterizes Tony's song, present him as a force to be reckoned with. The action-oriented and sharply inflected language ("click," "shock," "knock," "cannonballin'" down through the sky," etc.), gives Tony a kind of intensity and forward motion that is missing from Maria's lyrics. He takes much longer to intone each of his words (in general, two to three bars of long tones are sustained at the end of each line) instead of throwing them off as Maria does. The rhythmic complexity (obviously important to Bernstein, judging from his comments) makes Tony "smarter" than the popular-music appropriations of Maria's flashy Latin number. As Sondheim says, giving intricate rhyme shows intelligence. She also "gives in" to the popular music convention of jacking up the number in each verse to a progressively higher key—starting in F major and working up to G major through the simple insert of a short section (sung by the other girls) in a secondary dominant—surely the most obvious and least sophisticated way to effect such a harmonic change. This allows her to show off an extended high note at the end of the song, but her note is sustained on the text "boy"—the subject matter, ultimately, of her song, his love and acceptance the only reason why she is able to feel "pretty." Tony's long notes are entirely existential and immediate, focusing on verbs: "be," "knows," "tonight," and so on. He does not pin his fate on a "girl," per se, but on something larger and more important than simply "feeling pretty." He reaches out for some kind of mystical, even spiritual experience. Maria, in contrast, tries on a dress and demands alterations. In addition, Tony's song is one of the most sophisticated, harmonically, of the score, remaining tonally ambiguous, a kind of D minor with a raised fourth degree (to provide the tritone relationship) that flirts with a number of key areas over a repeating and tonally unclear bass ostinato before ending on the flatted seventh scale degree of the original key.

Granted, the music perfectly encapsulates the searching, longing sentiment of the lyrics and adds further to the song's restlessness and forward propulsion. But, it also leaves Tony as a much more musically sophisticated, "arty" character—less tonal, more modern. Furthermore, and more importantly, the song is presented to the audience as a solo number with no one else on stage. Normal convention would suggest that after Riff's comment that what Tony wants may be found "twitching at the gym" tonight, he would then listen to Tony's response, presenting the desires and longings that grew out of their conversation. Strangely, Riff leaves the stage immediately upon delivering his line to let Tony fantasize alone. Because Riff is such a strong and charismatic character, perhaps the creators felt that his presence would undermine Tony's prominence in the scene. At the same time, Tony is given the theatrical space and uninterrupted solo opportunity that is not afforded Maria. Her identity is provided by her group; Tony is self-made, self-actualized.

And yet, despite the obvious drive in the lyrics and Bernstein and Sondheim's intent, the song fails to get across the most important aspect of an "I want" song—what it is the character actually wants. There is, in fact, neither an "I am" component, nor any suggested course of action. The same could be said for his next number, "Maria." The razor-sharp Robbins immediately sensed a problem theatrically with this aspect. Upon hearing "Maria" for the first time, he asked the composer and lyricist what action the song was supposed to suggest. "Well, you know, he is standing outside her house and, you know, he senses that she's going to appear on the balcony," explained Sondheim. "Yeah, but what is he doing?" prodded Robbins. "Oh, he's standing there and singing a song." Robbins persisted: "*What is he doing?*" Sondheim: "Well, he sings 'Maria, Maria, I just met a girl named Maria and suddenly that name will never be the same to me.'" Robbins: "And then what happens?" Sondheim: "Then he sings . . . " Finally, Robbins asked: "You mean he just stands looking at the audience?" Sondheim: "Well, yes." Robbins: "You stage it!"[25]

Although Tony's initial song similarly does not indicate the next action (or any action at all), it does in its own way presage what comes next: the "Dance at the Gym" scene in which the lovers meet (and where his iteration of "Maria" becomes the underscoring for their dance). So, ultimately *more* power is given to Tony's expression, as he seems to both predict and make happen—not least, musically—the most powerful and important moment in the drama. Maria, by contrast, is "set up" by the preceding rumble to look naive and superficial. Similarly, her "presence" in "I Feel Pretty" is immediately overshadowed by the arrival of Tony, whose tragic message completely obliterates the carefree atmosphere she had just created (her song is also reduced by the ensuing "Somewhere" ballet, one of the largest set pieces in the musical). Perhaps ironically, though, it is Maria who has more insight into the inevitabilities of the relationship than Tony or Bernardo. And it is she and Anita, in "A Boy Like That/I Have a Love," who provide the only successful and rational mediation of conflict in the entire work.

ANITA VS. MARIA

"Tony is one of them!"

—*Anita to Maria, act 2, scene 3*

The duet between Maria and Anita, the famous "A Boy Like That/I Have a Love," provides an elegant example, in fact, of how the two musical styles (Hispanic and non-Hispanic) of *West Side Story* fit into not only the drama but the ethnic and gender associations of these styles and how a move from the Hispanic to the classical means not only a change of expression but of language. There is a clear progression musically and dramatically from Hispanic (female) to European (male). The fiery and Latin-tinged music that opens the number finds Anita berating Maria about "A Boy Like That"—in essence, a Caucasian boy.[26] The song follows a predictable AABA pattern for two verses, when Maria interrupts Anita and the expected resolution of her final line with a completely different musical style, more operatic *and* more European. This middle section, sung by Maria, begins in the same Hispanic style as Anita's opening, although employing a new melody. The turning point in musical style is the line "I Have a Love"—here the style of the music, not just its tempo or mood, changes to a more "classical" operatic style. Through this calm, controlled, well-thought-out response, she eventually wins over Anita and extinguishes the fire, and they finish singing the same—that is, Maria's—music. The scene has been singled out by commentators as the show's most "operatic" moment in that it is an ensemble, plot actions occur within the song, and musical material is shared in a dramatically meaningful way between two characters.[27] However, the number doesn't start out that way—it's a typical Broadway Latin number with possible overtones of "blackness" from Gershwin's *Porgy and Bess*, which transmogrifies through Maria's intervention into a European operatic duet.[28] Does this song demonstrate the gradual change from irrationality to rationality, from Hispanic to white, from female to male? The possibilities for interpretation are myriad, but the musical and dramatic result is the same: both women have shed their ethnic identity by the end of the number. "We need female solidarity to get through this," suggests Maria with her *music*, "but it can't be our old ways. Become white with me." Anita's "American" aspirations can only be achieved if she accepts Tony, through Maria's love. The triumph, the increasing centrality in this show, of the women and their insight into events is clear, but so is the price that they pay to become so all-wise. Women—widows, really—convey the horror of a men's world, but they also must abjure their ethnic allegiances, a primary source of their spirit and group identity (and fun for the audience). Must womanly wisdom triumph through the denial of the distinctive voice, envy, and playfulness of Hispanic culture, so well conveyed earlier in the show? Apart from a dialogue scene that follows, this is the last real expression by either of these women. Anita is raped both physically and psychologically in the drug store; Maria is devastated and destroyed by Tony's death. Their responses to these atrocities are the loss of faith, the loss of compassion, and the loss of the redemptive feminine. "I can kill now, because I hate, too," claims Maria, taking Chino's gun into her own hand. Her love (she once believed that love was enough) can't save Tony, any more than Anita's attempt at reconciliation can. This is no longer the Anita of "America"—this is no longer the Maria of "I Feel Pretty." They have both died in the violent world of the male.

ROBBINS VS. MARIA AND ANITA

"Is Maria too strong?"

—*Jerome Robbins to Arthur Laurents, notes*

It seems that Maria's character was intended originally to be stronger than the innocent girl we meet in the musical. Judging from Robbins's extensive planning documents of *West Side Story* and in a version of the book dated winter 1956 (Arthur Laurents does not believe he wrote this scene, although it appears in a bound typescript), Maria was planned as a much more assertive character. In a police interrogation scene very similar to act 2, scene 3 (in which Schrank questions Maria about the rumble), an officer named Magill reports Bernardo's murder. Consider the end of the final stage version: Maria and Anita are alone, with only each other for support or comfort. Schrank arrives and is immediately overbearing, even raising his voice at the women, and they are forced to lie in order to get around him.

SCHRANK: There are just a coupla questions—

MARIA: Afterward, please. Later.

SCHRANK: It'll only take a minute.

ANITA: Couldn't you wait until—

SCHRANK: (*sharply*) No! (*a smile to Maria*) You were at the dance at the gym last night.

MARIA: Yes.

SCHRANK: Your brother got in a heavy argument because you danced with the wrong boy.

MARIA: Oh?

SCHRANK: Who was the boy?

MARIA: Excuse me. Anita, my head is worse. Will you go to the drugstore and tell them what I need?

SCHRANK: Don't you keep aspirin around?

MARIA: This is something special. Will you go for me, Anita?

ANITA: (*hesitates, looks at Maria, then nods*) Shall I tell him to hold it for you till you come?

MARIA: (*to Schrank*) Will I be long?

SCHRANK: As long as it takes.

MARIA: (*to Anita*) Yes. Tell him I will pick it up myself. (*Anita goes out.*) I'm sorry. Now you asked?

SCHRANK: (*as the lights dim*) I didn't ask, I told you. There was an argument over a boy. Who was that boy?

MARIA: Another from my country.

SCHRANK: And his name?

MARIA: José.

In this version of 1956, both of Maria's parents are in the apartment, with her father "singing in Spanish a few fragments to her mother."[29] Rosalia and Consuelo are helping Maria to get dressed for her date, and they break into "I Feel Pretty." News of Bernardo's death is brought by Magill, a police character who resembles Krupke.[30] After Maria's parents run out in a panic, this exchange ensues.

MARIA: (*lighting a match: she is in front of the Shrine of the Virgin*) He is really dead, Bernardo?

MAGILL: (*nodding*) I'm sorry.

MARIA: (*lighting the candle*) Well . . . well (*turning with a cry*) What is going on here? Rosalia . . . Rosalia . . . (*cups Rosalia's face in her hands and kisses her*) There is nothing for you to say. Really. Nothing. Nothing. So go. Please (*opening the door*). Thank you. (*to Magill*) Thank you, sir.

MAGILL: (*embarrassed*) Look . . . you both—have to go over to the police station.

ROSALIA: Why?

MAGILL: They're rounding up all you kids for questioning.

ROSALIA: But Bernardo was her brother!

MAGILL: Then they'll certainly want to question her.

MARIA: About what?

MAGILL: Who maybe had it in for your brother. Who he had it in for. (*The two girls look at each other.*)

MARIA: (*to Magill*) Would you please wait outside one moment?

MAGILL: Well—I don't mind myself—but I got my orders—

MARIA: (*sharply*) Wait outside! (*Magill looks at her, then goes out.*)[31]

In this version, Maria and Rosalia practically dominate the sheepish police officer, and it becomes Maria who "sharply" orders him to leave (which he promptly does). The intimacy between the two females further establishes their connection as fellow Puerto Ricans, alienating the officer. The lighting of the candle in the Shrine to the Virgin becomes an act that separates Maria culturally and emotionally from the world of Magill; in the final version this same praying moment comes between Chino's report of the rumble and the appearance of Tony, almost an apparition through her window. And it is Tony who is portrayed as weaker. Robbins worries in his notes:

> Too high flying all the way thru? When does he come down to earth—are all his dreams with Maria essentially unrealistic & impractical? Does he ever plot & plan truly so that his *need* for her is more than just in love with love?[32]

In Robbins's planning notes, this is how he describes Maria, especially in act I, scene 3 (The Bridal Shop) her first scene with Anita:

> Maria begs—cajoles
> To enjoy herself before its too late
> To experience fully—
> Tears—threatens—blackmails—
> To *get* her *way*
> Determined
> Keeps at it—bull-dog like—insistent
> Refuses to be blocked
> Constantly seeks the way
> Never overcome by obstacles
> Maria's expectancy
> Loving
> Helps thru her love—
> Achieves thru her love[33]

Although her portrayal here *seems* active, her methods are manipulative, like a child or a pet. Robbins is wary of her appearing too strong and guards her purity. In a note to Arthur Laurents on the same scene, he muses:

> Does Anita's "kneeling" line hurt Maria's innocence? [referring to Anita's warning "With those boys you can start in dancing and end up kneeling."] Is Maria too strong? In meeting scene.[34]

Perhaps Jerome Robbins's quip to a New York newspaper during women's auditions—"It does not take long to find the good ones. There are so few."[35]—evinces a certain misogynist backdrop against which the piece was conceived or at least rehearsed. Indeed, Robbins's harsh and often cruel treatment of female dancers was a signature of his operating style. That being said, so was his attitude toward male dancers. In particular, Robbins usually chose a scapegoat in each production on whom he would inflict his frustration with the production as a whole. In *West Side Story*, he chose Mickey Calin, who was the first Riff.[36] At the same time he assured Carole D'Andrea, who played the role of Velma, that she would be spared his caustic criticism. Indeed, Chita Rivera remembers Robbins as a father figure adored by both male and female cast members alike.[37] Robbins's complex psychology has been discussed by his friends and collaborators, but there is no reason to believe that he went into this project with any preconceived partiality for his female characters or dancers.

There are other ways in which the female characters have essentially died before the tragedy has completely unfolded. Highly significant is the fact that Maria, the female romantic lead, is not really given a satisfactory ending. Although Juliet has a great dying speech in Shakespeare's original, Maria doesn't kill herself either before or after Tony's death (although early typescript versions of the book have her impaling herself on dressmaker's shears, among other things). The conceit that Tony *believes* her dead remains from Shakespeare, but Maria is left at the end of the musical simply to walk away with the rival gangs. Here, the composer obviously had an appropriate but daunting operatic model: the "Liebestod." Ultimately, at the end of *Tristan und Isolde*, it is Isolde who has the last word, the center stage, the moment of transcendence that Tristan does not get to express. What we remember when we walk away from *Tristan* (and which, certainly, audiences took with them in the nineteenth century) is the "Liebestod," the musical and philosophical summation of the entire work. Bernstein seemed not up to the challenge: he tried different things, but was never able to write a convincing final number for Maria to sing, and so she is left with no musical material to differentiate her from anyone else, nor to give her the final apotheosis. In terms of the spoken drama, Maria is certainly the one who brings a glimpse of reality and ultimately hope to the rival gangs. But she must do so with Laurents's words, not Bernstein's music. In the composer's eyes, this was his greatest failing with the piece. Bernstein still held on to this regret when reflecting on the show at the time of his "definitive" version of *West Side Story* in the 1980s: "It cries out for music. I tried to set it very bitterly, understated, swift. I tried giving all the material to the orchestra and having her sing an *obbligato* throughout. I tried a version that sounded just like a Puccini aria, which we really did not need. I never got past six bars with it. I never had an experience like that. Everything sounded wrong. I made a difficult, painful but surgically clean decision not to set it at all."[38] Was Bernstein's inability to conceive of the right music for this character simply because she was dead already? Was it simply that the creators had no voice for a woman who has failed to redeem with her love? For a woman who, severed from the male from whom she takes her meaning, has no other source of identity? As a character, Maria has had moments of some power and agency. But she isn't "pretty" anymore, and perhaps for the 1950s there was really no language for that.

Although the female characters are silenced in subtle ways, there is also an increased sense of violence and animosity toward women that characterizes the work, and that is certainly a departure from the tone of Shakespeare's original. Anita, when she tries to warn Tony that Maria is waiting for him, is waylaid by the Jet gang and raped on stage. This is a radical departure from Shakespeare's play and a shocking one. Like most of the important moments in the drama, this scene is also told entirely through dance, and so again music comes to the forefront in the absence of words. The creators chose for this scene a sonic backdrop of the mambo from "Dance at the Gym," prerecorded and played as though coming from a jukebox on stage. That they chose the music that stood for gang rivalry, instead of the more violent and presumably more apt music of the rumble, suggests that perhaps the attack on Anita is an attack on race, on Hispanicism, instead of simply another continuing conflict in the drama. And yet there is a distancing effect by having it come from an onstage, mechanized source.[39] The actual attack on Anita segues from this prerecorded music to a rendition of the music of "America," reduced to a kind of carnivalesque version that becomes increasingly louder (climaxing at *ffff*) and *marcatissimo* until Doc interrupts the assault. It is not just Anita as a character, but her signature music (both Hispanic but also the moment—in "America"—in which she showed the most impudence and spark) that is battered by the Jets. Robbins, in his planning documents, dictated the mood for this scene:

The rape of Anita
Fake spanishy[40]

It also seems to be a suggestion that in fact the America that Anita envisions is not to be. Instead it is the oppressive, manipulative system that she argues against in her number. Anita's attempts to break out of her role have serious consequences, as we can see, and it is her bitterness over the attack that causes her to lie to the Jets and tell them Maria is in fact dead; this in turn precipitates the tragedy. It is not just her disillusionment with the Jets, but with "America." Her bid to become white, at Maria's urging, fails. As Laurents recalls, "The thing I'm proudest of in telling the story is why she can't get the message through: because of prejudice. I think it's better than the original story."[41]

COOL WHITE GIRLS

"I and Velma ain't kid stuff, neither. Are we, Vel?"

—*Graziella, act 1, scene 6*

What about the other female characters in *West Side Story*—the Jet girlfriends? Although they get to dance along with the men in the big "Cool" and "Dance at the Gym" numbers, they never get to do anything else. Anita can have her big "America" dance number because she is part of a larger, ethnically different femininity that exists for entertainment purposes. But the Jet girls have absolutely nothing to do, no plot function. Unlike in traditional musical comedy, they don't fulfill a female pulchritude function, nor do they present their own world in relation to the men. Their perfunctory existence shows us that the Jet gang members are normal, red-blooded (i.e., heterosexual) American boys, but little more.[42] For the important gang war council meeting in the candy store and anything else of dramatic import, the Jet girlfriends are summarily dismissed because they are "chicks" and are too stupid to understand what is going on (the stage direction indicates that Riff "pats Velma on her behind. Followed by Graziella, she runs out, slithering past the Sharks.") Graziella utters the deathless comeback "I and Velma ain't dumb." Clearly, they are dumb—literally, too: they have almost no dialogue, and no music in the entire show (see figure 5.1).

ANYBODYS

"I ain't like any other girl on earth."

—*Anybodys, cut number from act 1, scene 6*

One very unusual female character has a lot to say and a special role to play and fits into no category, Jets nor Sharks: Anybodys. In a drama that shows few deviations from Shakespeare's original, the character of Anybodys provides the greatest departure. She is the only significant character who has no counterpart in *Romeo and Juliet*, she is the only character in *West Side Story* who doesn't get her own song or dance number (although she joins in on chorus numbers), and yet it is this character who expedites the tragedy. It is she who understands the ramifications of events unfolding in the drama and warns everyone that Chino has a gun and is trying to kill Tony. She is the only character who appears neither male nor female. Who is this woman in blue jeans and close-cropped hair, and where does she come from?

Anybodys is played as a tomboy who is almost genderless, rejected by the Jet girls as too unfeminine and by the Jet boys as a kind of freak. She can't be a Shark, she doesn't get to take part in the fights, and she is even kicked out of the dance scene at the gym (here she tries to join in with the line of men in their ensemble dance number, not with the girls). It is she who seems to magically appear after the gangs have their rumble to save Tony from arrest, bringing down the act 1 curtain. It is she who is sent out to find the lovers at the end of the musical. And it is she who was also added to the musical only a few months before it opened, for no apparent reason. In a typescript manuscript of the show marked "Winter of 1956 version," the character of Anybodys

FIGURE 5.1
Jet Girls, from original Broadway production. Photo by Fred Fehl.

doesn't exist, nor is any other character provided to fulfill the dramatic function she eventually takes on in the show. By this time an August 1957 opening
was probably already planned, judging from the markings on the front page
in Sondheim's hand that count out the weeks between February and August
26, 1957.[43] A revised version dated April 15, 1957, falls less than a week before
Cheryl Crawford decided to drop the project (in the preproduction period,
although she had already started looking for cast members) and features the
first appearance of Anybodys.[44]

> Scene 6: Drugstore
> ACTION is doing push-ups, counting aloud; BABY JOHN is reading a comic
> book; A-RAB is playing the pinball machine. Leaning against the juke box
> expertly flipping a yo-yo is a scrawny girl wearing jeans and a jacket which is
> obviously an attempt to imitate the Jets. Her name: ANYBODYS.[45]

This scene is the locale for the war council, a heated event early in act 1 that
excludes the women (including Anybodys) and by which Baby John and A-
Rab clearly feel a little intimidated. On the most basic level, Anybodys represents the juvenile delinquency problem that was ostensibly the central focus
of the work. Although viewed as an updated version of the Romeo and Juliet
story, at the time *West Side Story* struck its audience more directly as a piece
of social commentary (see chapter 6). Juvenile delinquency was a new and
shocking problem emerging in postwar America, and it spoke directly to the
concerns of an increasingly socially and ethnically diverse society that could
not fully identify where and why the problem was out of control. Following
on the heels of such film dramas as *The Blackboard Jungle*, the musical was
only one of many presentations on the theme of juvenile delinquency and
its attendant issues. And books like *All the Way Down*, written by a Manhattan social worker, revealed, to a much wider audience than ever before, the
drug-ridden and violent street life of an increasing proportion of America's
youth. More often than not, the teenagers were presented as being a tragic
result of a failed social system. Although a large number of studies emerged
during the late 1950s addressing the Puerto Rican problem in New York City
and its relationship to youth crime, there was an even more disturbing and
unprecedented trend: the emergence of "girl gangs." Latino youths from the
Spanish ghetto and unemployed white males with no education and too much

time on their hands were one thing; young women involved in violence was quite another.

Enter the character of Anybodys. Perhaps the creators were trying to find plot solutions that Anybodys ultimately solved—she does act as the messenger, but any of the Jet gang members could have done that. Perhaps her status as an outsider, as different, as not fitting in, reflected the feelings of the show's authors, mostly gay Jewish men in a very white and straight 1950s.[46] The central song of the musical, "Somewhere," seems to address this yearning for normalcy and acceptance that Anybodys seems to embody perfectly. As the lyric reads, "There's a place for us./Somewhere, a place for us./Peace and quiet and open air." Even the ballet over which this song is initially sung suggests the feeling of escape. The city landscape flies up and reveals a clear stage with a suggestion of open fields and blue skies. Although we can clearly see what is required for the other characters to escape—for Puerto Ricans and whites to stop fighting, for Tony and Maria to run away—the metaphor of an incomplete or impossible escape suits Anybodys more closely. There is, in fact, no solution to her dilemma of not fitting in with anyone, anywhere.

It seems likely that in one way or another her creation had something to do with the show's original producer, Cheryl Crawford. Crawford was a powerful player on Broadway in her time, a time when the theatrical world was completely dominated by men. She produced a number of successful shows, and she agreed to take on *West Side Story* in its preliminary phase. But she was also distrusted, perhaps because she was a lesbian in the 1950s and one of a handful of women in her very competitive and high-powered field. At the last minute, after not being able to raise the money needed to produce the show, Crawford got cold feet and pulled out. It was a decision she was later to regret when the show went on to great success. But it seems that there were more problems than simply trying to sell a highbrow, long-haired tragic musical to middle-aged New York investors. Crawford also had criticisms of the show that directly related to its portrayal of juvenile delinquency (again, see chapter 6). What she thought the show lacked (among other things) was an adequate explanation as to *why* the characters in *West Side Story* were delinquent. The creators argued that they did not want to make the piece one primarily about social conscience, although certainly that was a major theme. Crawford pushed them to address the social problems more directly. However, it is tempting to imagine that the character of Anybodys was a suggestion—or echo—of Crawford herself. The character was up-to-the-minute, representing the girl gang member who was so prominent in the *New York Times*. Or maybe the creators modeled Anybodys indirectly and subconsciously on Crawford herself and her anomalous place in the theater world, in part as a way of appeasing her, or perhaps resisting her. Although the character is not portrayed as a comic lead (except as the butt of the Jet members' merciless, plainly sexist teasing), her musical numbers were excised shortly after Crawford withdrew from the production. Perhaps her material was removed as an embittered response from the creators, perhaps they were freed up to pursue different angles not insisted upon by Crawford, or perhaps the cuts were made for the more standard theatrical reasons (such as pacing). As of this writing, neither Laurents nor Sondheim remember the impetus or thinking behind the creation of the character, perhaps not surprising fifty years on, but perhaps also telling.

Though I mentioned earlier that the white female characters don't get their own song, this was not entirely true during the compositional process. In the full, original concept of the piece, Anybodys sings a trio with two of the Jet gang members—A-Rab and Baby John. Each of the kids gets his or her own verse in which each bemoans the particular problem that prevents social acceptance. It was called "Like Everybody Else." The boys want to be older or bigger, but Anybodys puts it succinctly: "Why can't I be male?" In her lyric she complains bitterly about other girls who wiggle, giggle, and flirt, squeal hysterically, and so on. What really appeals to her are the freedoms that her male counterparts enjoy: "*I* swear and *I* smoke and *I* even inhale" professes part of her lyric. She goes so far as to claim that girls are not good for anything and that those who are not "clobbered" should be drowned.

It seems that the dramatic function of the song was not an "I am" but rather an "I am not" for the three teenagers. A-Rab complains of being short, Baby John of having a too-youthful appearance, and Anybodys of not fitting into either male or female worlds. All of these limitations result in the exclusion of the three characters from the more adult pleasures ("shaving or driving or necking" for Baby John, "youknowwhat" for A-Rab, "swearing or smoking or spitting" for Anybodys). Although each character takes a turn decrying his or her particular fate, it is Anybodys who sings first and establishes the problem. For all that her differences seem to be a certain badge of courage, Anybodys' "faults" are that she is indeed too male to fit in "with everybody else" of her own gender. In a misogynist way, the shortcomings of the other characters are explicitly female traits: Baby John is "no good for nothing but sounding like girls when they speak" and A-Rab is emasculated by, "No broad respects you who has to bend down for a kiss." The fact that all three characters share the song and consequently its music means that for all of them the ultimate goal of being "like everybody else" is to be male, men being the only people who matter, either in the narrative or in terms of stage power. At the same time, Anybodys describes her alienation from her peers in the most disparaging of terms, almost as though she is disfigured: "I'm an accident of birth! It's revolting." The song falls into the same scene as "Cool," and it seems likely that this was the outcasts' response to the "cool" that they could never achieve because of their inadequacies. By expressing an inverse relationship to the "being in" sentiment suggested by coolness, the song further removes these characters from the mainstream of which they so want to be a part.

This song's manuscript is dated "August 23rd, 1957, Washington, D.C." Considering that the show opened in Washington on August 19, presumably the song was written *after* the opening but must have been a very late addition and certainly did not make it to the New York premiere approximately a month later. Laurents mentions in the roundtable discussions some decades later that the song threw the balance of the show into musical comedy and that was the primary reason it was cut. Although clearly the song's misogyny might have made it problematic even in 1957, one wonders how the anomalous and somewhat aberrant character of Anybodys earned such a prominent song in a tragedy where very few of the chorus members are that clearly differentiated. It is intended to be funny, but it also packed a very large gender message. When we look back on those strong women of *The Music Man* or *The King and I*, *My Fair Lady* or *South Pacific*, however, are they so different from Anybodys? Do not the plots of those musicals often revolve around the taming of those independent women, through love or possession or both?[47]

To a certain extent, the other women in *West Side Story* fill some standard Broadway expectations for the mid-1950s. Anita's "America" was one of the showstopping numbers and certainly was designed for its flashy dance appeal. Still, Chita Rivera, the only performer who would have rated any kind of star status among the newcomer cast, did not claim the eleven o'clock number. For plot reasons, this would have been difficult: the killing of Bernardo prevents her from presenting any kind of entertainment front after the rumble. But it is interesting that this pivotal point in the Broadway musical is made into a number that features none of the principals, but instead the male chorus. Almost a way of reifying the chorus concept of the show, these almost nameless male performers win over the audience and stop the show just before the tragic ending unfolds.

In the famous number "Gee, Officer Krupke," the boys carry out a number of skits in which they send up a psychiatrist, a judge, and a social worker. The score indicates that the social worker should be sung as though imitating a female, which is what happens in any standard performance, often with the addition of a kerchief or other prop. But the original line was written for Anybodys, since her name is in early drafts of the song. Whereas "Like Everybody Else" was cut before the show opened, the "Officer Krupke" change leaves Anybodys out of an otherwise *retained* number, and effectively removes any female influence in that—again—male song-and-dance tour de force. All we have left is a boy's insulting imitation of a female. And so Anybodys' independent singing voice is removed entirely from the final version of *West Side Story*.

Further to this is a telling document from the late 1950s. This is an excerpt from an interview conducted with real juvenile delinquents who were taken to see a matinee performance of *West Side Story*. Among the topics they discuss are the depiction of youth gangs, the merits of the show from a musical and dance perspective (according to their own experience), and especially how the show addresses the racial/ethnic tensions inherent in Manhattan during this period. The following excerpt comes out of a discussion of dances at gyms. The "Dance at the Gym" scene in *West Side Story* is one of the most important musically and dramatically, as that is where the rival gangs are seen competing choreographically, and that is where the lovers meet for the first time.

In this short excerpt, we get a lot of racial, sociological, and gender information in a very short period of time, even from the interviewers themselves.

INT: I wonder—somebody said something about the girls. Um, when you dance with a Puerto Rican girl, uh do you respect her as you respect a Puerto Rican—

KID: Sure.

KID: Yeah.

KID: It depends on how the girl dances with you, that's what I say.

KID: Allright, let's talk about this.

KID: No, I'm serious.

INT: Yeah, allright.

KID: Here's the truth. Most of these, how do I say, regular girls, right—

INT: The girls.

KID: The girls.

KID: When they dance with you, they wouldn't do as much as most—most of the Puerto Rican girls—

KID: They hold you

KID: as the Puerto Ricans would. If you try to get a little close to them, nine out of ten times they stop you, but the Puerto Rican girls, seems like they—they come closer to you, so you—you wouldn't have much respect for them.

KID: They want to be friendly.

ALL: [Laugh]

KID: So if they come to you, if they don't come to you, I mean you ain't going to run go away, dance. So if they come on top of you, you're gonna

KID: Yeah.

KID: Then you start all over again.

KID: [Laughs]

INT2: What about the dancin' in the show? I hadn't seen it.

KID: Was terrific.

KID: The music was terrific, the chorus—everything was terrific,

KID: Good

KID: as far as acting and singing, as musical. The band was terrific. As far as music, was, it was—everything was very good.

KID: Yeah, they had good

KID: The only part that I think ruined the play, not exactly ruined the play, but was the part when they were tryin' to make it a comedy, when they kept knocking that kid on the head: "bam, bam."

KIDS: [Laugh]

KID: The story, the acting was very good.

KID: But that kid was

KID: The story was a little exaggerated

INT2: Uh, you know, there are some people say that uh, this isn't a show for fellows your age, that don't—a show for

KID: Adults?

INT2: for adults. How do you feel about that?

KID: I don't think so.

KID: No, I think that to see what you're actually doing, as a whole.

KID: Uh, most of the people who see that show, don't even know the inside story, 'cause they've never seen that action.

KID: That's right.

KID: But people not our age, even the people who live around here who see it could tell if it's a good story or not.

KID: You see people from our neighborhood who saw that—

KID: They would think it was disgusting.

KID: They wouldn't know.

KID: No, just the opposite.

KID: I think they would under—

KID: They see *worse* around here. So it would be like nothin' to them, you know?

KID: But they don't find it—

KID: I think—I think the people around *here* should be the critics. I mean, the people who live *in* it. Not the people who live on 5th Avenue and just see it.

KID: That's right.

KID: They don't know what it is.

KID: That's right.

KID: I think people from around here would understand the story better.

KID: And another thing, like when they come to a joke,

KID: And you know some of the words: "boppin'" and "Daddy-O" and

KID: You see, they overdid that.

KID: They overdid.

KID: And another thing, like, when they come to a joke, like we'd understand they don't know. We would be the only ones laughing. The other people were not even laughing at the joke.

INT: who laughed in the whole thing. You know what it was? And this was the one that hurt. It was when uh the candy store operator said to the kids when they were pushin' the girl around, he said, "What a lousy place." And the kid turned back and he said "That's the way we found it."

KID: Yeah.

KID: That's right.

INT: That hit every single one of us.

KID: That's right.

INT: I wanted to applaud, you know? And not another person did. Because I thought that was the crux of the whole thing.

KID: And a—and another thing, when when the guy says, when the guy says you come here with your heart open, And another guy says, With your pants open. Everybody else, Only us were laughing. We understand, the other ones didn't understand. I mean, not that we are smarter, just that we know.

KID: But we understand what it means.

INT: [Laughs]

KID: The only part when they started laughing was the part when uh the guy tell when uh the guy called her a schmuck

KID: Oh, yeah.

KID: and that means. uh

KID: In Jewish . . .

INT: This was a very Jewish audience. This was a matinée and there uh

KID: That's what I mean.

KID: were many ladies from the bridge clubs, you know, bar stools, and everything. And that shocked them. It really shocked them.

INT2: What, the schmuck stuff?

INT: Yeah, the schmuck really shocked them.

KID: They almost jumped out of their seats.

ALL: [Laugh]

KID: Schmuck, what did he say? [Laughs]

KID: when somebody told the Puerto Rican girl, they came with their panties open, with their bloomers open.

INT: Yeah, but you guys remember that very clearly.

KID: [Laughs]

KID: There was something else, but I can't remember what it was.

INT2: But, do you think this would be a good thing for fellows your age to see?

KID: I think they would.

KID: Yeah.

KID: I think so.

INT2: What about your girlfriends, what would you think about that?

KID: I, I wouldn't think of—

KID: To tell you the truth, they wouldn't even understand it, I don't think.

KID: No, I think they *would.*

KID: It's propaganda, let's face it.

KID: No, I mean they'll understand it but—

KID: Yeah, Charlie, eh.

KID: —I mean this business about the gang war, they wouldn't understand it.

KID: Your girlfriend's stupid, Charlie, she don't understand nothin' anyway.

KID: I don't think so, because actually, these girls from here don't butt in when there's a gang war, they wouldn't come over to you and tell you "don't fight" or anything like that.

KID: Yeah.

INT2: But do you think they'd like the show?

KID: Yeah, I think so.

KID: Yeah, I think they'd enjoy the dancing.

KID: They would enjoy the story.

KID: They'd like the dancing and singing.

It is notable that no females were taken to see the show or interviewed about it, nor do the boys—presumably "white" though perhaps ethnically mixed—comment on the rather odd character of Anybodys in their discussion of female characters in the musical. It would seem then, that in fact in the boy's mind, Velma *is* dumb and maybe Anita, too, along with the middle-class Jewish "ladies" who attended the matinee and failed to get the jokes that the kids picked up on so readily. Although the creation of a unique female character like Anybodys was probably a step forward in some ways, it was also a step back to the extent that she did not earn equal dramatic representation with her male counterparts.

When rehearsing *West Side Story*, director and choreographer Jerome Robbins wanted to make the cast identify as completely as possible with the juvenile delinquents they were playing. He played the dancers of the rival gangs off each other so that by opening night the actors really disliked each other. True to character, Lee Becker, who created the role of Anybodys, could not find anyone to eat lunch with during the rehearsal period (see figure 5.2). She was shunned by both the male and female dancers.[48] But it was Lee Becker who took over from Jerome Robbins to stage the Israeli production of *West Side Story*, the first leg of the international tour and reportedly the first musical to be staged in that country. Whereas most of the Jet girls did not ascend to Broadway stardom, nor make it into the film cast a few years later (even the principals, Chita Rivera and Carol Lawrence, were replaced with younger,

FIGURE 5.2
Lee Becker as "Anybodys," original Broadway production. Photo by Fred Fehl.

more marketable "stars"), Lee Becker went on to establish the American Dance Machine, an organization dedicated to the preservation of American dance works. So perhaps, even for Anybodys, the scrawny girl who survives and even makes it into the pack, life imitates art after all.

MARIA AND TONY: THE "GOOD GIRL"

"It isn't a man that's up there, Doc. It's a girl, a lady."

—*Tony, act 1, scene 6*

Although *West Side Story* did not rely on the power of the star for its draw, it made famous the female performers who took on the roles of Anita and Maria. It certainly launched Carol Lawrence's career, and early press coverage on the musical tended to highlight Lawrence's personal life, style, and television appearances, leaving her male counterparts relatively unnoticed.[49] She was even interviewed for a public opinion piece in the *New York Journal American* that reported on the scandalous appearance of a woman in court sporting trousers. Judge Edward D. Caiazzo reprimanded a twenty-eight-year-old woman for wearing slacks into the courtroom, complaining of the inherent "loss of femininity" that this entailed. Among other New Yorkers, Carol Lawrence was asked her opinion: "If you go to court and you're a woman, you should look like one." She used pants in rehearsals, but felt they were out of place in court. "I think most girls will agree with me," concludes her statement.[50] But *West Side Story*, for all its aspirations to high art, ended up capitulating to some of the more mainstream (and sexist) tendencies of 1950s America. Consider the poster art for the opening, highlighting the love relationship between Tony and Maria in which her love seems to pull him, staggering, from his delinquent way of life to an idyllic future (figure 5.3). As Jerome Robbins described her, "Maria to drive her thru it for what she wants. Not to let it prevent her from reaching the hand of her loved one. To run between the gunshots to meet her love to safeground."[51]

In subsequent advertising, this transcendent vision was replaced by an illustration of Anita and her dancing partner performing a Hispanic dance number (figure 5.4), where Anita's sexuality and exoticism are highlighted as a Spanish-style skirt is lifted to reveal her leg. Here, the purity and romance of Tony and Maria's relationship (they join hands but look into the future) is

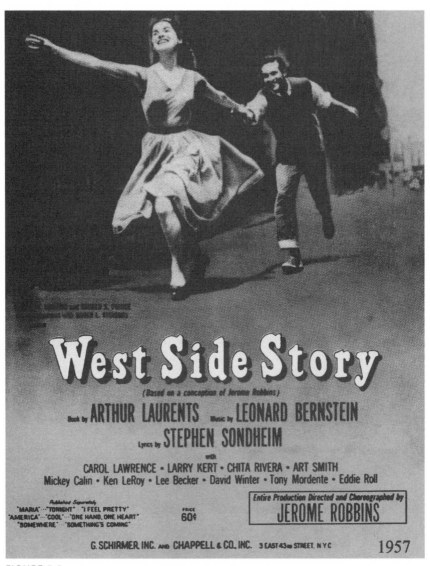

FIGURE 5.3
Poster art, original Broadway production. Courtesy of Harold Prince.

FIGURE 5.4
Poster art, revival of *West Side Story*. Courtesy of Will Rapport Photography. Copyright © Harvard Theatre Collection and Billy Rose Theatre Division, New York Public Library for the Performing Arts, Astor, Lenox and Tilden Foundations.

replaced with Allyn Ann McLerie's leg with hiked-up skirt and her sexualized relationship with Bernardo (played by George Marcy). The "wiggle, giggle, and flirt" about which Anybodys complains in her cut number, "Like Everybody Else," seems exemplified by the seductive Anita. Although certainly exploitive in some ways, this started to push the musical back into the mainstream of musical theater and audience expectations, away from the high-art aspirations that accompanied its opening.

Perhaps the real power of women in *West Side Story* surrounds their ability to offer redemptive love in a troubled world, making them kind of *Ewig Weibliche* figures for the mid-1950s. In the world of the juvenile delinquent, Vincent Riccio, a streetworker with troubled kids in 1950s Manhattan, wrote a memoir of his experiences called *All the Way Down: The Violent Underworld of Street Gangs*. In it he, like "Gee, Officer Krupke," blames the social workers, police, and parents who have let these kids down. But he also argues that there is one thing alone that has saved more of these children from tragic lives than all social programs combined: love and marriage. For most of the delinquent boys, rumbles ensued less from struggles over property or money than from an insult to a gang member's girlfriend. Defending the honor of women was a huge issue for many of these kids. Even the juvenile delinquents who were taken to *West Side Story* echo this sentiment.

KID: But we used to have a lot of girls, here, you remember. Plenty of girls used to come here.

KID: Plenty of guys.

KID: Like, if a guy fools around with a girl, right? Her and her friends are going to come. So we got to sort of like protect those girls, you know what I mean? And that's how maybe it will start.

KID: In other words, we're still obligated to them. Is that what you're trying to say?

KID: Wait, notice at the dance tonight, when we dance with the Spanish girls, their guys give us dirty looks. But they won't *say* nothin'. But yet they won't touch none of our girls, because they respect us. They figure we're going to break their backs.

INT: They respect you, how about the girls?

KID: They respect the girls because they respect the guys.

As Riccio says, "the 'good girl' is fantastically important to the gang kid from the very second he realizes he is in love. Instinctively he knows that she is his best chance to escape from a future he sees all too clearly." The playwright Arthur Miller echoed the same sentiment in a magazine article: "To date the only known cure for delinquency is marriage."[52] The redemptive (if regressive) female is certainly familiar to us all (not least from the operatic repertoire), but think of the end of "Dance at the Gym" in *West Side Story*: Tony and Maria see each other "across a crowded room" (as in Hammerstein's lyric in *South Pacific*) and fall instantly in love (again, a dramatic convention that we accept). As the other gang members discuss the imminent rumble, they fade away offstage and the scenery flies up and away, revealing Tony in a dreamlike state, consumed only by the thought of Maria, the name repeated twenty-six times in the ensuing song. The meeting of course changes Tony's approach to his gang past. Although he has already told Riff that gang life is no longer for him, he never gave a particularly convincing reason why: "Riff, I've had it," is his only pronouncement on the subject of continuing involvement with the gang.[53] He explains then that he wakes up from a dream, reaching out for something unknown. This of course leads into one of his most important solo songs, "Something's Coming." When we reach the "Dance at the Gym," the appearance of Maria answers his (and the audience's) question as to what it is that will prove the turning point in Tony's life. As Robbins summarizes it: "Maria is that magical answer that transfigures life & living into real & utter happiness. No problems with her. She is the reason to exist."[54]

The fact that Maria is pure (as indicated by her line at the dance at the gym, "I have not yet learned to joke that way. I think now I never will," in response to Tony's questions about her sincerity) allows her to become what Riccio calls the "good girl," who can save Tony. That this very tender and important moment is interrupted by Bernardo, who claims "I told you; there's only one thing they want from a Puerto Rican girl!" reflects the defending of a woman's honor that was a corollary of the true love experience. Presumably the influence of popular culture, especially film, would engender in Riccio's teenagers the expectation of, or at least belief in, a redemptive true love experience. In the interview with juvenile delinquents who were interviewed about *West Side Story*, they confirm this worldview when asked whether Maria should have disavowed Tony after the killing of Bernardo.

KID: —uh, 'cause she could have gone out with somebody else, find somebody else as good as him, maybe better than *him*. That's the way I would take it.

KID: Sure.

KID: But she was so crazy about him she couldn't just drop him like that, no matter what he did.

Redemptive, innocent, powerful, undercut? In these many perspectives on the women of *West Side Story*, we are left with some questions unanswered, some conclusions unmade, some portrayals competing. It is almost as if the work is in conflict with itself, as though the creators were not, as they always claimed, "writing the same work." Indeed, they weren't. Some of the early book scenes, like the one featuring the policeman Magill as discussed above, show Maria much stronger and in control. Those were written by playwright Arthur Laurents, who asserts that he was interested in exploring feminism in this musical, in the same way that the social message was uppermost in his mind.

AL: Maria was too strong to die. She's *not* an ingénue. She is a passionate girl— and death makes her a young woman . . .

EW: I was curious as to whether you had a feminist bent in the 1950s when you were conceiving these characters.

AL: Yes, I did.

EW: That was different than the typical—

AL: I did, very much so.

EW: Do you think that was shared by the other creators, or was that more you?

AL: That it was felt by them?

EW: Yes.

AL: No. I wrote a play, for example, about three years later where the heroine was an unmarried mother, and that's a little early for that, and I didn't think I was doing anything extraordinary.[55]

When Laurents revived *West Side Story* for Broadway in 2009, his major change to the text was to translate many of the dialogue sections and "I Feel

Pretty" into Spanish (for more on this, see chapter 4). The primary impetus for this was to bring the Sharks up to the level of respect and attention that the Jets had formerly enjoyed. However, through this process he also by extension raises the characters of the women to where he believed they should be. Now, Maria's clever rhymes in "I Feel Pretty" are in Spanish—she speaks with her own voice and with her own cleverness. Anita and Bernardo's arguments seem more equal when they bicker in Spanish. Sexuality, which was an important aspect for Laurents ("That's what young love is all about," he reminds us), comes to the fore so that the scenes between the lovers are more equal and more passionate. Maria partakes in the banter with Anita in the bridal shop scene in a more knowing, more open way. Laurents, like Bernstein and Robbins before him, recreated *West Side Story* in his own image, free from the collaborative process. The tensions within that process, the different ways each of these collaborators saw their culture, emerge in the complexity of this work, and the story of women in *West Side* is one of its most fraught and fascinating.

When we then revisit the creative process in the late 1950s, a look at the end of act 1 and the editorial decisions made about it poignantly sums up these paradoxes. At the moment of greatest crisis, the end of the rumble, Tony, abandoned by his fleeing gang cohorts, realizes that he has just killed Bernardo. Like the juvenile delinquents Riccio describes, Tony calls out for the only thing that can save him: "Maria!" Here, in Bernstein's non-texted score, we see perhaps the most telling removal of the female voice. In an early version of this scene (example 5.1), not only does Tony call out Maria's name, but we hear the Maria theme, slower, and fortissimo, ending in a held note that extends for twelve entire measures, to the very end of the act. In the final version (example 5.2), this important leitmotif, this very encapsulation in music of the idea of "Maria," is omitted, and we are left only with the stark, pizzicato, tonally unstable, and rhythmically faltering music of the broken Jets (based on the dance music before the "Jet Song" in act 1). In a score that prides itself on integration and unity, motivicism and organicism, the end of act 1 cuts the emotion and connection between Maria's love and the scene of destruction by omitting her leitmotif. All we are left with is one high tremolo note and the distant chimes of the clock. Ironically, the only character left onstage to save Tony, to bring him to his senses, is Anybodys.

EXAMPLE 5.1

Sketch for ending to Act I (final pages of the "Rumble"). Bernstein prominently foregrounds the "Maria" leitmotif. Leonard Bernstein Collection, Library of Congress, West Side Story materials: Box 1, Folder 11. Courtesy of the Leonard Bernstein Foundation.

EXAMPLE 5.2
Final version of ending of Act I, *West Side Story*, fortissimo statement of "Maria" leitmotif conspicuously absent, leaving only wisps of "Jet" music. Leonard Bernstein through Boosey.

NOTES

1. Eleven o'clock numbers, because they are often production numbers including chorus, are also perfect vehicles to showcase the star. Judy Holliday is alleged to have boycotted the opening of *Bells Are Ringing* three days in advance if not given an eleven o'clock number to outshine her costar, Sydney Chaplin. Cited in Greg Lawrence, *Dance with Demons: The Life of Jerome Robbins* (New York: G. P. Putnam, 2001), 244. An account of this event by Jule Styne is reprinted in Stephen Citron, *The Musical from the Inside Out* (Chicago: Ivan R. Dee, 1992), 156–57.

2. This has changed to a certain extent, in that in the late twentieth century such male stars as Michael Burgess, Michael Crawford, Nathan Lane, and Mandy Patinkin have taken their places alongside Bernadette Peters, Sarah Brightman, and Patti LuPone.

3. Take, for instance, this review of *Annie Get Your Gun* by William Hawkins: "Ethel Merman shot a bull's eye last night with *Annie Get Your Gun*. For verve and buoyancy, unslackening, there has seldom if ever been a show like it. It would not be a bad idea to declare an annual Merman Day of all May 16ths in the future." Quoted in Steven Suskin, *Opening Night on Broadway: A Critical Quotebook of the Golden Era of the Musical Theatre* (New York: Schirmer, 1990), 55.

4. Ironically, Carol Lawrence, who created the role of Maria, was discovered by the producers while she was performing in the revue "*Ziegfeld Follies of 1957*" at the Winter Garden Theatre in the spring of 1957. She was so demure and almost homespun at her audition that "it wasn't until they passed the theatre some days later and saw a picture of her undressed in two sequins and a pearl necklace that they realized she was the kid they'd been watching the night they caught the show." John McClain, "Griffith and Prince Steal Early Lead," *New York Journal-American*, July 14, 1957, 17.

5. Music, "O.K.!" *Time*, May 12, 1958, 40.

6. See Ralph P. Locke, "Constructing the Oriental 'Other': Saint-Saëns's *Samson et Dalila*," *Cambridge Opera Journal* 3 (1991): 261–302 and his "The Border Territory between Classical and Broadway."

7. See Locke, "Border Territory," as well as chapter 4 of the present study on class associations with the Hispanic.

8. This typescript song synopsis may have been either Laurents's or Robbins's creation. In my interview with Arthur Laurents, he could not recall if it was he or Robbins who created the document.

9. Jerome Robbins, undated typescript memo (untitled), circa 1956–1957. Stephen Sondheim Archive, box 18, folder 1, University of Wisconsin at Madison.

10. Lawrence, *Demons*, 249.

11. Locke, "Border Territory."

12. Morton Shulman, "Dynamic! That's My Word for 'West Side'," *London Evening Standard*, December 1959.

13. Richard Kislan, *The Musical: A Look at the American Musical Theater* (Englewood Cliffs, NJ: Prentice Hall, 1980). Kislan outlines the different types on pp. 196 passim. Kislan credits Bob Fosse for being the first to recognize the categories of "I am" and "I want" songs.

14. *The Songs of West Side Story*, RCA Victor 09026-62707-2.

15. Quoted in Zadan, *Sondheim & Company*, 2nd ed., 22.

16. Sondheim also discusses this lyric in "Theatre Lyrics," in *Playwrights, Lyricists, Composers on Theater*, ed. Guernsey, 85.

17. "Leapin' lizards" and "gloryoski" may well be references to the Orphan Annie comics.

18. Lyric sketches, Sondheim Archive.

19. In the novelization of the film version by Irving Shulman, he presents the language dichotomy this way: "'Now will you please hold still?' Anita cautioned in Spanish.
   'Talk with me in English,' Maria replied.
   'If you want to speak English you have to think in English.'
   'But I like to think in Spanish,' she rolled her eyes expressively, 'because that's the nicest language for thinking about love.'" Irving Shulman, *West Side Story*. (New York: Simon & Schuster, 1961), 57.

20. It is strikingly like the *Verfremdungseffekt* of Brechtian theater that the Shark women provide kinds of musical and verbal placards to Maria's performance, although here their intention is clearly humorous.

21. For more on this style, see chapter 4.

22. Bernstein recalls, "Well, the idea of a musical the first act of which ends with two corpses on the stage was reprehensible." "Landmark," 17.

23. Kislan, *The Musical*, 228.

24. Bernstein to Felicia Bernstein, 8 August 1957, while she was in Chile, Leonard Bernstein Collection, correspondence series, box 5, folder 33, Library of Congress. Also quoted in Burton, *Leonard Bernstein*, 272. Indeed, actor Paul Nolan, who played the part of Tony in a recent lauded production at the Stratford Shakespeare Festival, commented on the need to make Tony believable as a gang member. As he says, "It was very important to me to portray Tony so that he was believable as the alpha—to go so far as to think of Tony as the leader of the gang, the older brother

figure to Riff. I wanted him to be tough; to have enough grit inside him that an audience would believe he *could* snap, leading him to kill Bernardo." Paul Nolan, interview with the author, August 21, 2009.

25. Guernsey, *Broadway Song & Story.*

26. For more on *West Side Story* and the Hispanic, see chapter 4.

27. Swain, *The Broadway Musical,* 4–6; and Larry Stempel, "A Mozart in America," in *Sennets and Tuckets: A Bernstein Celebration,* ed. Steven Ledbetter (Boston: BSO Association, 1988).

28. See Locke, "Border Territory."

29. Typescript manuscript, Stephen Sondheim Collection, University of Wisconsin, Madison.

30. This character, called "McGill" in Cheryl Crawford's planning notes, existed along with Krupke and Schrank as one of twenty-two named characters in early plans for the musical. Handwritten notes, Cheryl Crawford Collection, "Series V: Unproduced Works," box 83, folder 4, New York Public Library Theatre Division.

31. Typescript manuscript, Sondheim Collection, U Mss 66AN, box 17, folder 5, pp. 2-1-4, 2-1-5.

32. Handwritten notes, Jerome Robbins Archive, box 2, folder 11, New York Public Library Dance Collection.

33. Handwritten notes, Jerome Robbins Archive, box 2, folder 11, New York Public Library Dance Collection.

34. Handwritten notes, undated, Jerome Robbins Archive, box 2, folder 9.

35. The comment captioned a photo in the *Newark Sun News,* May 1, 1960, E2.

36. Lawrence, *Demons,* 252. Lawrence's biography catalogs numerous instances of animosity and outright cruelty to which Robbins's dancers were subjected.

37. Lawrence, *Demons,* 255–56. Although those he worked with generally considered Robbins a genius, there were mixed reactions to the choreographer as a person. Rivera clearly is on the pro-Robbins side, perhaps as a result of her positive experiences with him in *West Side Story.*

38. Quoted in Burton, *Leonard Bernstein,* 275. See also Laurents, *Original Story By.*

39. It also accurately reflects white America's embrace of commercialized Hispanic musical styles on their jukeboxes, while fearing and excluding Hispanics.

40. Handwritten notes, undated, Robbins Archive, box 2, folder 11.

41. "Landmark," 18.

42. In reality, gang culture was understood at the time by social scientists, at least, as more homosocial than hetero: "Contrary to the popular, yet erroneous, images created by *The West Side Story* and other glamorized 'fictional' versions of violent-gang activity, the sociopathic gang youth maintains a type of 'homosexual' relationship system in the gang that reflects his personality. The youth who tends toward a more compassionate female relationship is generally a more marginal violent-gang member. The most sociopathic core gang members will ridicule the youth who attempts to relate to a girl on a human level beyond a simple sexual 'trick' or as an object for exploitation." Lewis Yablonsky, *The Violent Gang* (New York: Macmillan, 1963), 200. For more on "*West Side Story* Syndrome," see chapter 6.

43. Sondheim Archive, box 17, folder 5.

44. Cheryl Crawford to John A. Commy, 26 April 1957, Crawford Collection, box 83, folder 4. Looking for "mostly boys and girls who look around 17 to 20. Do you have any talents out there you could recommend? I need a tenor, baritone, and [for Maria] lyric soprano of the type of Maria Alberghetti."

45. Sondheim Archive, box 17, folder 6.

46. Certainly Jews were "white" by American standards, but not Western European. See Karen Brodkin, *How Jews Became White Folks and What That Says about Race in America* (New Brunswick, NJ: Rutgers University Press, 1998).

47. I thank Jennie Wood for this trenchant observation.

48. Peyser, *Bernstein*, 276.

49. Larry Kert eventually received a fair amount of press, but mostly due to his longevity in the role rather than the further development of his own career.

50. "Public Look at Slacks Backs Up Judge . . . Well, Almost," *New York Journal-American*, August 11, 1960, 8.

51. Robbins Archive, box 2, folder 15.

52. Arthur Miller, "The Bored and the Violent," *Harper's*, November 1962, 50–52.

53. Tony also, of course, is conspicuously absent from the gang's bonding number, the "Jet Song."

54. Robbins Archive, box 2, folder 15.

55. Arthur Laurents, interview with the author, June 3, 2008.

6

"A Boy Like That"

The Gangs of West Side Story

[Cheryl Crawford] said the essential reason she was withdrawing from the show was, she wanted us to explain why these kids were the way they were. We are making a poetic interpretation of a social situation, but she wanted it to be more realistic.

—*Stephen Sondheim*

It was all about juvenile delinquency then.

—*Arthur Laurents, interview with the author, June 3, 2008*

INT: Well, what about the story? I would be interested in knowing, was it phoney, or was it real?
KID 1: It was very real, coming from life itself.
INT: You say it was real?
KID 2: Yeah.

—*Juvenile delinquents, interviewed in 1958 after seeing* West Side Story

Central to the lore of *West Side Story*'s early, tortured history lies a distinct and overarching issue that provided both the heart of the show and its biggest liability in terms of commercial potential: the message. Although Arthur Laurents claims that it was this added element of racial prejudice that made his version superior to Shakespeare's,[1] trying to adapt that message and the wider issues of social conscience within the conventions of Broadway "musical comedy" was challenging. To do so without coming across as preachy, overly sentimental, and overtly political would be even more difficult. As Bernstein wrote in his *West Side Story* log: "Avoid being 'messagy.' The line is there, but it's very fine, and sometimes takes a lot of peering around to discern it."[2] Producer Cheryl Crawford saw this challenge as potentially insurmountable, and it was at least partly behind her decision to drop the project late in the game. However, her reasons were not just artistic, but practical. In trying to sell the show to potential investors, she identified a double issue: the musical was considered too dark and ugly to be commercially viable, yet at the same time that darkness and ugliness needed a raison d'être, and that justification seemed most plausibly to come from a strong social message. As she wrote to Arthur Laurents in June of 1956:

> We both feel that exciting as the show can be, it is no cinch and I think all of you realize that too. It has very few of the customary Broadway values of comedy and splash with three killings and music leaning to opera and it must be cast brilliantly with no names which means the chance of big out of town losses and difficulty in getting benefits and a theatre.[3]

Even Harold Prince and Robert Griffith, who took over the show in the eleventh hour, faced similar problems in their attempt to raise funds. "It took us a week to raise the $300,000 for the show. Some of the investors told us frankly they thought it was too arty and serious to be popular but that they would put money in it just so we would keep them in mind for our next."[4] This "artiness," of course, was exemplified by the stylized music and dance, the dissonance and rhythmic and textual complexity of the score, and the absence of any recognized stars, as Crawford (and every other Broadway producer who had rejected the show) had already identified. But, it had equally as much to do with the subject matter and the way the creators chose to address it. In short, *West Side Story* attempted to treat in a serious manner serious contemporary subject matter for a particular audience.

When Jerome Robbins posed the vital question "What is it about?" to his creative team, they answered it in different ways.[5] Sondheim goes on record with his assessment that *West Side Story* was *about* theater; this seems the remark of a theater professional who cringes at the suggestion that the play might convey a social message primarily.[6] There is certainly truth in his assertion: the show is fueled in large part by the interaction of the various elements of music theater, each energized yet taking care to serve the whole. But in the show's time, there seemed to be a larger message that we often ignore today: that of social commentary. As Arthur Laurents writes, "if *West Side Story* influenced the musical theatre, it was in content, not form. Serious subjects—bigotry, race, rape, murder, death—were dealt with for the first time in a musical and as seriously as they would be in a play. That was innovative; style and technique were not."[7] *West Side Story* accurately and stunningly portrayed juvenile delinquency in a more direct way than Broadway had seen before and in a way that it is hard now for us to entirely appreciate—and it was not alone.

CRIME IN THE STREETS

Although the authors of *West Side Story* claim not to have done specific primary research on the habits of New York city gang members, many aspects of the production bear striking resemblances to *New York Times* reportage on recent crime waves: for instance, candy stores (such as Doc's) were featured in one story as the locale for gang war-council meetings, and there was rising anxiety about the new anomaly within youth culture: girl gangs and young female criminals. The character of Anybodys in *West Side Story* fits perfectly into this mold, and her character was added fairly late in the creative process (see chapter 5 for more on Anybodys and the other women of *West Side Story*). She is also the only character who has no parallel in the original Shakespeare drama. But it is not just these details of local color that make the piece of its time: it is the deep concern with the issues and how they were handled in society and a sensitive and determined method for bringing those issues to life on stage. Further, it is more than mere coincidence that there are so many resonances between *West Side Story*'s particular realism and trends in the depiction of juvenile delinquency. Jerome Robbins, in early planning documents for the work, listed at the bottom of one page a number of gang movies currently out:

Blackboard Jungle
Crime in the Streets
On the Bowery—55th St. Playhouse[8]

Leonard Bernstein, in his date book entry for March 14, 1956, marks an 8:30 p.m. screening of *Crime in the Streets*, all the days surrounding it heavily scheduled with *West Side Story* working sessions with Robbins, Laurents, and Sondheim.[9] *Crime in the Streets*, an Allied Artists Hollywood treatment of gang life, starred Sal Mineo, John Cassavetes, and James Whitmore. The plot surrounds two rival gangs and a plot to murder one of the boys as a vengeance killing. Directed by Don Siegel (who was later to direct *Dirty Harry*), the film centers on the street violence and the toughness of the kids and the futile attempts of law enforcement to stem the problem. *On the Bowery* was a joint project by a number of independent filmmakers, shot on location in New York's Bowery district, presenting a portrait of down-and-out men as seen through the eyes of a street social worker. Juvenile delinquency and social unrest in the newspapers clearly provided creative inspiration, but, portrayed in film, they raised other issues. One important aspect of Crawford's concern was not simply that the musical should be timely, but that in fact it might be *too* timely. Correspondence to Arthur Laurents in 1956 outlines the problem:

> I just discovered that there is a new play called The Seventh Day by the author of The Blackboard Jungle which Jose Quintero is supposed to be directing this fall. I read a synopsis of it. It is about teen-age Puerto Rican gangs in Harlem who wear purple jackets and under the leadership of a tough boy are planning to kill one of their young neighbors. There is also a love story that happens in a split second between a young Puerto Rican girl and a sailor. They use expressions like "cool," "Rumble." Essentially the story is a slice of life which I find rather pedantic. But it is somewhat worrisome to think that the milieu may be covered before WEST SIDE STORY gets on.[10]

Crawford's concerns were certainly valid, since by the time *West Side Story* was in production, juvenile delinquency was already getting coverage on film but also in literature, specifically through Evan Hunter's novel *The Blackboard Jungle*, which was published four years earlier and reached a more general audience than the rather more arty film *On the Bowery* or even *Crime in the Streets*. The novel was adapted for film in 1955, starring Sidney Poitier as the leader of an unruly high school class. It was certainly more in the minds of the population by the time *West Side Story* came out, judging by the reaction of teenagers who saw the show (and perhaps studied *The Blackboard Jungle* in school).

INT: Did anybody see, did anyone ever read a play or a book that reminded them of it?

KID: *Blackboard Jungle.*

KID: *Blackboard Jungle*—no that doesn't remind you of the book.

KID: *Blackboard Dukes.*

INT: Did anybody know the story of *Romeo and Juliet?*

KID: No.

KID: You read that from the book.

INT: No in advance. The—

KID: Well, the only part of it that would remind you of *Romeo and Juliet* was when she was on the balcony singing and he was down there singing and climbing up to her.

KID: Yeah.

INT: That would—

KID: [sings] Meeeee.

KID: I don't know if it is true, but I heard Romeo and Juliet were pretty young.

INT: That's right, yeah.

KID: yeah, that reminded me of it.

INT: —and they came from different families—

KID: Yeah, like—

INT: —who hated each other.

KID: Maybe they were—

INT: —Like these were different groups. And they they fought it out because of a couple of hotheads, one on each side. And it ended up that the two people who were really in love, who were good kids, ended up getting in trouble, which was the boy and the girl, and they both died.[11]

"THE BORED AND THE VIOLENT"

Juvenile delinquency was not just a popular topic for West-Coast filmmakers or the New York City press. It was an overwhelming and terrifying unknown, on par only with communism as a threat to the very fabric of American society. Between the late 1940s and the opening of *West Side Story* in 1957, youth crime had doubled. Delinquency had of course always existed, especially in the Depression era, but postwar Americans had never experienced this problem on such a large scale.[12] And even though poverty, unemployment, and overcrowding in city slums were blamed for the problem, the *real* fear for most Americans came not from the Spanish barrio, but from primarily white, middle-class, and suburban areas. Books such as *Other People's Children*, by a juvenile court judge, and *Delinquency in our Democracy* warned adults of the dangers of crime creeping into *everyone's* life.[13] Playwright Arthur Miller summed up this line of thinking in an article for *Harper's* entitled "The Bored and the Violent"—he argued that not poverty, but overindulgence, prosperity, and ennui sparked gang violence in the affluent suburbs of Greenwich, Connecticut. As he explained,

> The boredom of the delinquent is remarkable mainly because it is so little compensated for, as it may be among the middle classes and the rich who can fly down to the Caribbean or to Europe, or refurbish the house, or have an affair, or at least go shopping. My own view is that delinquency is related to this dreamworld from two opposing sides. There are the deprived who cannot take part in the dream; poverty bars them. There are the oversated who are caught in its indefiniteness, its unreality, its boring hum, and strike for the real now and then—they rob, they hurt, they kill. In flight from the nothingness of this comfort they have inherited, they butt against its rubber walls in order to feel a real pain, a genuine consequence. For the world in which comfort rules is a delusion, whether one is within it or deprived of it.[14]

"You've got trouble, my friends, right here in River City," sings the protagonist of *The Music Man*, which opened on Broadway the same year as *West Side Story*. Although the two shows are generally considered quite disparate in style and content, the song "Trouble" brings the same message as Bernstein's musical, warning parents teasingly of the dangers of juvenile delinquency even in a sleepy little town. Further, consider this striking passage from a contemporary book.

Let's pretend that you are Joe. It is spring, and you are sixteen, a tall lad, half-boy and half-man, full of the uncertainties of youth and the desires of manhood. There is a restlessness in your bones, a restlessness built of desire and fear and adventure. In your mouth you can almost taste the sweetness of excitement. A full moon is out tonight, throwing silver against the window of your apartment. Dad has already fallen asleep on the sofa with the paper over his face, and Mom is hurrying around the kitchen, clearing the table. Your kid brother is taking up the only bedroom with his model plane. You think it must be tough to grow old and to feel the marrow of excitement dry up in your bones. It's a spring night, and you are sixteen. Hank and Billy stop by. They, too, are restless. There's nothing to do at home, no place to be alone with your friends. And you want them to remain your friends. The folks have moved so many times you're always meeting new kids in new towns and new states. It gets a fellow sometimes, this moving around. That Hank's a smart one, too. Knows all the angles. While Hank and Billy wait at the door, you change your shirt, tell Mom that you're going for a walk, and start down the apartment stairs with the boys. Hank knows a place where you can buy beer, even though you're under-age. You get outside with the boys, and the excitement becomes an urge. So you head for the beer joint. And you drink a few beers and begin to feel all safe inside. Maybe before the night is over you even "lift" a car and go for a joy ride or pick up a couple of girls and have some fun . . . But maybe your name isn't Joe. Maybe it's George, and you live on the "right" side of town.[15]

The excerpt is taken from a thin volume entitled *Pillars of Support*, published by the Hogg Foundation for Mental Hygiene. It was aimed not at a teenage audience, but at their parents and neighbors. Based on the latest research, it was a how-to manual for the average American to help identify and, ultimately, confront the nation's most difficult social problem: juvenile delinquency. The book was aimed at Texans but seemed to reflect the overall American concerns about juvenile delinquency in middle-class life. The excerpt goes on to explain that even George, from "the right side of town," is a delinquent. The Hogg family included Ima Hogg, who became one of America's most generous patrons of classical music. This is no coincidence: both social science research (or propaganda) and the support of high culture had a certain appeal to the sense of civic duty of the nation's financial and political elites in the 1950s and 1960s. This book, and dozens like it, appeared just a year before the premiere of *West Side Story*.

The mainstream propaganda material of the time treats delinquency as both a disease that needed to be cured and prevented and a scourge as insidious as communism. One book exhorts, "we need to penetrate into the home, as though a plague were raging, all the adults dead and the children moaning in their cribs for help."[16] And, in case this didn't scare you enough, *Pillars of Support* gave this reminder:

> But what can you do? One citizen in all this huge state. You're busy with your own family and your business and trying to pay your income tax. You don't have time to worry about other people's kids—unless, that is, this juvenile delinquency reaches into your own front yard and grabs your son or daughter or snatches money from your wallet.[17]

Starting in the late 1940s and peaking in the mid-1950s, senate subcommittee after senate subcommittee heard testimony from witnesses on the crisis. Studies targeting different urban areas, using a myriad of different theories and testing systems, attempted to answer the question of why children indulged in criminal behavior and how they could be stopped.[18] This kind of research had begun as early as the 1920s, when theories of the "subnormal" mind attempted to explain in some physiological sense why children became criminals. Early testing methods were less sociological and more physiological; "biological psychiatry" was popular and the investigation of somatotypes (varieties of the human physique, codified in the 1930s as a collaborative research venture) attempted to find physical reasons for negative behaviors. At least seven widely used prediction devices were employed to diagnose the delinquents and administer prevention, including the Minnesota Multiphasic Personality Inventory, the Porteus Maze Test, the Washburne Social Adjustment Inventory, and the Stogdill Behavior Cards.[19] One expert from Tufts University, William Kvaraceus, developed the KD Proneness Scale and Check List. Based on his sociological studies, a watered-down version was published for school teachers. Like *Pillars of Support*, it hoped to guide the white middle class in stemming the rampant growth of youthful offenses, through an easily administered questionnaire (see figure 6.1).

DELINQUENCY PRONENESS CHECK LIST

Yes	No	Not Sure	
✓	—	—	1. Shows marked dislike for school.
✓	—	—	2. Resents school routine and restriction.
✓	—	—	3. Disinterested in school program.
—	—	—	4. Is failing in a number of subjects.
—	—	—	5. Has repeated one or more grades.
—	—	—	6. Attends special class for retarded pupils.
—	—	—	7. Has attended many different schools.
—	—	—	8. Intends to leave school as soon as the law allows.
—	—	—	9. Has only vague academic or vocational plans.
—	—	—	10. Has limited academic ability.
—	—	—	11. Is a child who seriously or persistently misbehaves.
—	—	—	12. Destroys school materials or property.
—	—	—	13. Is cruel and bullying on the playground.
—	—	—	14. Has temper tantrums in the classroom.
—	—	—	15. Wants to stop schooling at once.
—	—	—	16. Truants from school.
—	—	—	17. Does not participate in organized extracurricular programs.
—	—	—	18. Feels he does not "belong" in the classroom.

FIGURE 6.1

"Delinquency Proneness Check List" from William C. Kvaraceus. *Juvenile Delinquency.* Series: What Research Says to the Teacher, Volume 15 (Department of Classroom Teachers, American Research Association, 1958), 17.

UNRAVELING JUVENILE DELINQUENCY

At the forefront of this research were the Gluecks, a husband-and-wife team of Harvard professors who authored twenty books on criminal behavior. They were the primary experts for the subcommittee hearings, and their research was widely used to educate the public and governmental agencies. Their major work, *Unraveling Juvenile Delinquency*, was an exhaustive study of one thousand boys, five hundred delinquent and five hundred nondelinquent.[20] They compared every imaginable variable, from family structure to the physical shape and size of the children's bodies and whether they were nail-biters, used coffee or tea excessively, or were sleepwalkers; they even compared the size and shape of their teeth and submitted the juveniles to Rorschach tests.[21] In the end, their worst fears were realized: they found no physiological differences between delinquents and nondelinquents. They couldn't predict the behavior. The only thing they could say with any certainty was that delinquents tended to be more muscular and energetic and less emotionally complex but also more intelligent than their nondelinquent counterparts. So, stronger, faster, and smarter.

Ultimately, the Gluecks developed and tested a Glueck Prediction Table. But it would take ten years, following young children through their teenage years, before they could tell if it worked. By 1964, they discovered they could predict with 85–97 percent accuracy who would become delinquent.[22] By that time, the *film* version of *West Side Story* was in the theaters. By then they blamed parents' lack of affection for their children, broken homes, and the working mother. But in the mid-fifties, the only solution to this mysterious problem seemed to be more police, more psychiatrists, and more social programs. Among reform solutions was the Highfields Project run on Charles Lindbergh's estate in New Jersey, an alternative to the violent reformatory school model, where a small number of mild offenders lived, working during the day to foster a sense of responsibility and attending group therapy with the other boys at night.[23] Psychology, especially Freudian psychology, was seen as another treatment method: the concept of the "delinquent ego" was a popular one, differentiating the offender from people with plain ordinary egos.[24] Even an economist got on the scene, trying to explain the phenomenon as one of supply and demand: a steady supply of delinquents serviced a demand for delinquent activity.[25]

"The one funny song was added later . . . "

—*Cheryl Crawford*

Arthur Laurents claims that the impetus for *West Side Story* grew more out of this context than that of the mambo craze or the "Puerto Rican Problem."[26] If we look at the song "Gee, Officer Krupke," from *West Side Story* in this light, we see not only a very funny song by a bunch of boys, but also biting social commentary on each of the ways in which society attempted to solve these problems (see figure 6.2). The boys run through a series of "skits" in which the gang members imitate authority figures: judge, social worker, psychiatrist. However, early lyric drafts by Sondheim and Bernstein were even more sharply satirical and political. One early and the most overriding theme of writings on delinquency was the breakdown of the family—in other words, blame the parents.

Composer and lyricist had tried and discarded lyrics which put the parents as the progenitors of the delinquents' unrest, some of which ended up in the final published lyrics. On the medical/physiological approach that was most

FIGURE 6.2
"Gee, Officer Krupke" from the original Broadway production. Photo by Fred Fehl.

prevalent in the late 1940s and informed the Gluecks' work, sketches of discarded lyrics reference injections and social welfare and a desire for society to take on responsibility for the delinquents. Some versions were more specific about social programs and the intervention of law enforcement, suggesting that the army and police were ready and waiting to either enlist or arrest the young offenders, and in one version reform schools are even invoked. Other sketches are even more pointedly Freudian, referencing the id, paranoia, and the Oedipus complex. The different social programs that are described in the final, published version are sketched much more broadly in the working drafts, which go on for a number of pages. At one point, they turn the paradigm of sickness around and project it on the audience, which reads about the youths in the media.[27]

Although Bernstein and Sondheim may have discarded these lyrics for artistic reasons, they may well have been rejected for reasons of tone, being both more pointed than the final version that we now know but also more self-pitying and self-reflexive. In the final version, the kids completely own their delinquency. This song, the showstopping number, was particularly popular in London even before the show opened there. One of the reasons was that Britain was experiencing similar social problems.[28] In premiere-night coverage in the *London Daily Sketch*, one of the most prominent photos was of Justice Salmon, a judge who had recently sentenced nine juvenile offenders to four years imprisonment for their involvement in race riots. He understandably declined to comment to reporters on the message of tolerance and sympathy that the show put forward (see chapter 7 for a further discussion of *West Side Story*'s British and other international receptions).[29]

But even at home, responses to social reform sounded much like "Officer Krupke." This from an underprivileged citizen who was a guinea pig of the new social programs:

> Once upon a time we thought that if we could only get our problem families out of those dreadful slums then papa would stop taking dope, mama would stop chasing around and Junior would stop carrying a knife. Well, we've got them in a nice apartment with modern kitchens and a recreation center. And they're the same bunch of bastards they always were.[30]

Not just the content of the show but its production seemed fuelled by awareness of the psychological and sociological realities of gang life. Jerome Robbins, as director and choreographer, conceived and even rehearsed the work to instill in the cast members a sense of immediacy, reality, and psychological truth. Parental figures, who play definite roles in the Shakespeare play, are removed. At one time, there was a sung part for Maria's father in "I Feel Pretty" and a song intended to be sung to both parents by Tony and Maria. All that is left in the final version is one offstage line, when Maria's father calls to her during the balcony scene (using a Spanish nickname). The only other adults, Doc (the candy store owner) and the police, never sing or dance, only speak, creating a greater sense of isolation for the teenagers. Much like the white characters in *Porgy and Bess*, they stand outside, almost extra-theatrically, from the teenage protagonists. The warring gangs of Sharks and Jets not only had separate cultural identities but, for the first time in a Broadway musical, the chorus members were shaped as individual characters with their own names—not just male and female chorus. Playwright Arthur Laurents even rearranged lines and wrote different dialogue to help the actors to differentiate the characters from each other.[31] As Stephen Sondheim recalls:

> It helped that Jerry kept the Jets and the Sharks apart as groups separate during rehearsals, even having their meals as separate gangs. I thought it was pretentious, but of course it was perfect, because, without any animosity or hostility, there was a sense of each gang having its own individuality, so that you had two giant personalities onstage. And I believe this is the first show whose chorus had individual characterizations. Maybe one or two people would be characterized, like Agnes de Mille's The Girl Who Falls Down in *Oklahoma!*, but in *West Side Story* each of the members of the chorus had a name and a personality and was cast accordingly. Everybody takes that for granted now, but in those days it was a startling notion.[32]

Jerome Robbins, in an attempt to deepen the sense of rivalry, of identification as gangs, played the two groups of dancers off against each other emotionally and made them sit separately at meals. By the time of the initial tryouts in Washington, the animosity between the actors was palpable. As one of the orchestra members recalled, in some of the knife fighting the dancers were actually taking jabs at each other and drawing a little blood.[33]

For us as an audience, much of this does not read: very few people can identify the Jet members Tiger or Gee-Tar. True, we remember Riff, Tony, A-Rab, and Baby John, and Action and Diesel have slight but real prominence.

But, aside from Bernardo and Chino, not one of the Shark members—Pepe, Luis, Nibbles, Juano, Toro, or Moose—is ever addressed by name in the dialogue. Audiences tend to see the gangs and especially the Sharks as fairly undifferentiated kids, to them a chorus. Sondheim actually attributes part of the show's success (or at least its status as a theatrical rather than social statement) to the fact that Arthur Laurents created one-dimensional archetypes, not real characters.[34] However, it was the inner workings of Robbins's method and the identification that the actors had with these characters that simulated the gang environment. At one point in the rehearsal period, the cast appeared on stage in their own chosen gang colors. This was outside of the dictates of the designer or costumer—they just did it on their own as a way of identifying themselves.[35]

Aspects of gang life, at least how it was portrayed and discussed in both fiction and nonfiction, seem to have struck a chord with both performers and authors and ultimately, audiences. A study in the 1960s, by Martin E. Wolfgang, on the delinquency problem conflates delinquents not with common criminals, but with people just like Robbins, Laurents, Sondheim, and Bernstein: "The thoughtful wit, the easy verbalizer, even the striving musician and artist are, in the dominant culture, equivalents of male assertiveness where broad shoulders and fighting fists were once the major symbols. The young culture heroes may range from Van Cliburn to the Beatles, but Billy the Kid is a fantasy figure from an earlier history."[36] Ultimately, the delinquents were seen as somehow linked to positive aspects of American culture. Wolfgang continues, "The Glueck delinquents also sound much like our nineteenth century captains of industry, our twentieth century political leaders and corporation executives. The freedom to be assertive, to defy authority and orthodoxy may sometimes have such consequences as crime and delinquency. But it is well to remember that many aspects of American ethos, our freedom, our benevolent attitude toward rapid social change, our heritage of revolution, our encouragement of massive migrations, our desire to be in or near large urban centers, and many other values that we cherish may produce the delinquency we deplore as well as the many things we desire."[37] Ultimately, the creators sympathized with the protagonists on this level, as the world of the delinquents is shown, although tragic, as authentic. Otherwise, we as an audience would not be able to identify with their plight. But it was also the "equivalents of male assertiveness" that must have been, for primarily closeted gay or bisexual men (as the creators were), a point of identification with the Jets and Sharks. The idea of not fitting in, exemplified by the gang members in general and by the character of Anybodys in particular, makes the existence of a "Somewhere" more imperative.

But juvenile delinquency did not just mean being different—it also had to do precisely *with* fitting in. As Joseph Sorrentino writes, "it was a decade in which a conformist culture predominated: the emphasis was on loyalty oaths, the organization man, being well adjusted, 'fitting in.'"[38] If the 1950s were indeed a period of conformity (and Arthur Miller likewise argued that the juvenile delinquent was a conformist, not a deviant), then the audience identified with the juvenile delinquent precisely because the idea of bowing to peer pressure reflected aspects of American culture. Greg Lawrence, in his biography of Jerome Robbins, suggests that Robbins was manipulated into informing to the House Un-American Activities Committee (HUAC) under the pressure of being exposed as gay.[39] Laurents, for whom this was also a large issue, remembers that his relationship with Robbins before *West Side Story* was a relationship of friends. After was a different story: "No one becomes an informer at the moment he informs," he writes. "He's always been an informer, he's just been waiting for the opportunity. And that man is a man who goes on to betray friends and coworkers in other ways . . . I worked with him [Robbins] and I worked with Kazan knowing they were informers; I crossed that line knowing what it meant that they both were."[40] Laurents's bitterness about this period and Robbins's involvement still remains strong in his autobiography, written over forty years later.

The prevalent social consciousness of the show would have especially appealed to *West Side Story*'s original audience, a heavily Jewish, middle-class, postwar demographic who identified with the ideas of racial tolerance that the musical espoused. As Andrea Most has pointed out about the musicals of Rodgers and Hammerstein, the authors' involvement in political activism found a voice in their artistic creations. Musicals such as *South Pacific* and *The King and I* covered much of the same area: tolerance of difference and the serious consequences of intolerance.[41] *West Side Story* fell into an era (followed by other politically conscious musicals such as *Cabaret* and *Fiddler on the Roof*) that was already established by the Rodgers and Hammerstein musicals. As Most has argued, the problems of difference that pervade *South Pacific* relate to the same sentiments resonating through the culture during the cold war and the HUAC's suspicion of Jewish theater as part of a pro-communist wing. *West Side Story*'s similar subject matter (at least in terms of a mixed-race love relationship and promotion of tolerance) and use of an ethnic "other" (in this case Puerto Rican; for Rodgers and Hammerstein, Asian) to play off "white" characters suggests that Laurents's assertion that *West Side Story* broke new ground in terms of content may have been optimistic. The stage was certainly set—in the public's mind—for the socially conscious musical.

"DEAR KINDLY SERGEANT KRUPKE"

A perfect example of this new social awareness and sensitivity at work came in 1959, when (as we have seen in earlier chapters) seven juvenile delinquents were taken to see performances of *West Side Story*, accompanied by a social worker. Perhaps the initiative came from the New York Youth Board, the official body set up by the mayor in the 1950s to provide full-time social support to the growing number of gang members in the city and to distract them as much as possible from the delinquent activities that were their almost full-time occupation. Perhaps it came from Harold Prince's office, who supplied a block of tickets free of charge to Wednesday matinee performances. The teenagers were from the University Settlement House in Rivington Street on the Lower East Side, accompanied by the house director, Charles Cook, who felt that this was probably the first time the kids had ever been in a theater at all (rather than a movie house).

The purpose of the outing seemed to be twofold: the social work model attempted to entertain the kids and keep them off the streets as well as to provide an outlet for them to explore the issues surrounding their troubled lives. The teenagers were a mixture of ethnicities—Italian, Jewish, Puerto Rican, and Irish—and most had criminal records.[42] The interview, conducted by what appears to be Charles Cook and the social worker who attended, concerns turf protection, dances at gyms, and the realities of gang life on the streets. The sounds of the voices, the inflection, and, at times, the content of the interview could easily be taken from a rehearsal or a working session with the actors; in fact, sometimes it is hard to differentiate this recording from parts of *West Side Story*'s script. Gym dances, referenced here, were seen as an appropriate reform outlet for teenagers, providing them with a wholesome outlet for coed interaction.[43]

JD#1: no, but that's individual. But I mean like a gang, they don't go and say—

JD#2: but to start like I said they went to the same dance.

INT: Mm hm.

JD#1: Yeah, but there's no neutral—like when he says, "tonight when we go to the dance" and all that, he says "we'll talk" and remember he says it's a neutral spot. I don't think there's no neutral spot.

JD#3: No.

JD#1: —You can hang around in this certain area and you're not allowed to—to mix with each other.

JD#2: They meant by neutral anybody could come there.

JD#3: They did.

JD#1: No, that's a neutral spot, they couldn't fight each other there.

INT: Well, they said it was neutral. But suppose, for instance, there was a big dance here on the Lower East Side at Chateau Gardens like we went to last year, remember the uh, the Youth Board dance.

JD#3: Yeah.

INT: Now there must have been some guys there that didn't like other guys—

JD#2: That's right.

JD#1: *This* year, they were all guys from Fort Worth.

INT: Yeah. You mean, last Friday, there was guys there who might have started trouble? Was there any trouble?

JD#1: No, no there was no trouble. You see all these guys from Fort Worth, I used to go to school about them, you know what I mean? As soon as they come in, I let this kid Joel speak, and I told him listen: 'Case my friends and your friends have a fight, we break it up right away. So he agreed on it and he told his friends, 'cause when we stay—go some place we always stay in one spot.

JD#2: That's right.

JD#1: I told him, then he told all his friends in that spot "I know them." Don't bother them in other words, you know what I mean?

INT: Yeah.

JD#1: So—but, if he wanted to have a talk with me, that's my neighborhood he's around. He ain't gonna come in there and tell *me*, "don't bother my friends." You see I go over and tell him because its my neighborhood. It's not like they'd come up there and right away; we dance with their girl they're gonna fight us. They ain't. If they dance with our girls, we could fight them because it's our neighborhood. We expect to get more guys than they do.

INT: Uh huh?

JD#1: In other words, in that picture either the Spanish guys or the white guys own that . . .

Despite the obvious assumption that these outings, and their reportage, were part of a large publicity stunt (after all, a report and photo appeared in the daily newspaper), the Prince/Griffith office asserted that the project was a social, not commercial one. They stated that they felt that the show should be seen by contemporary gangs. No publicity was released prior to the newspaper story, but by that time 250 street kids had seen the show (suggesting that this had gone on for over six months). The program was intended to continue indefinitely, at least till the Broadway closing in the summer of 1959.[44]

"You was never my age, none a you!"

—Action, act 1, scene 6

The creators understood one very important aspect to accurately representing a youth culture: the invention of a kind of slang, of a street argot. The creators claimed that Arthur Laurents created his own made-up street language so as not to date the piece or make it *too* authentic. However, there were so many street words in use at the time that making up one's own was not that original an idea. *The Shook-Up Generation* includes an entire glossary of street gang argot that includes *rumble* and *cool*, and other lists appeared in magazines.[45] For all that *West Side Story* attempted to simulate a real youth culture, it ended up making an "other" of it as well. The world of the teenage gangs was not seen through the eyes and ears of the gang members, but through those of its creators: teenagers became the "other" onto which both the fantasies and fears of the predominant (adult) culture projected themselves. Although dances at gyms were seen to be wholesome activities that provided an alternative to gang fighting, the music that was generally played at them in the 1950s was not Latin jazz, but the burgeoning style of rock and roll. The main dance at a real juvenile delinquent event during this period was "the fish." As Lewis Yablonsky describes in *The Violent Gang*, "In its extreme form the couples did not move their feet at all, but merely stood in the same spot and undulated to the rock and roll music."[46] Posters for the film version of *Crime in the Streets*, in the theaters a year before *West Side Story* opened, advertised that the film gave insight into the "rock 'n roll generation." Robbins did not create rock dance numbers for his theatrical teenagers. What Bernstein and, presumably, his collaborators chose was the music of the heavily Jewish middle class, particularly the Latin dance music popular both in New York City and particularly in the Catskills summer resorts.[47]

In this way, *West Side Story* represented, more than anyone would have guessed, the split between youth and adult culture that it ostensibly deplored. The issues of authenticity identified by the street kids who were taken to see the work reflected the very real rift between the adults who created it and the youths it portrayed. As James Gilbert has pointed out, the parent-adolescent confrontation during this time period was symbolized by their radically *different* styles of music and dance.[48] In *West Side Story*, the kids dance to the same music as do the adult audience members—though (in the mambo contest) a wilder version of it. Instead of being their worst nightmare, these juvenile delinquents provide an alter ego, an escapism for the audience.

As this difference in musical styles and entertainment options between parents and their children and the inability to find a common ground for shared activities became more pronounced, so the world of the Broadway musical was nearing the end of its Golden Age. That the Youth Board kids had never been in a theater was not just a proof of their economic status: it was indicative of the changing culture, which was to focus more on film and television than on the particular dramaturgical norms of the live Broadway stage and of the musical. And, more importantly, youth would fasten on to rock and roll while jazz became increasingly the domain of the adult. By the 1960s, social awareness, cynicism, and a more postmodern outlook (*Cabaret, Company, Hair, Pippin*) attempted to address an audience that in many ways had already abandoned Broadway. The days of the optimistic musical were over, and by the late 1960s, *West Side Story* would have seemed tame in some ways. Ultimately, a central issue to juvenile delinquents was their inability to find a place within society, to assimilate or relate to it. They may have appeared cynical, but underneath they were frustrated hopers and passionate strivers, not the chilly nihilists that the popular press portrayed.

THE *COOL WORLD* TRAP

Proving Cheryl Crawford correct to a certain extent, *West Side Story* appeared just early enough to escape overexposure of the subject matter. Among the works coming out just after the musical was Warren Miller's best-selling novel *The Cool World* (eventually adapted to film). Published in 1959 and presumably picking up on the popularity of *West Side Story* and other juvenile delinquency works, *The Cool World* attempts a kind of street argot similar to that of Laurents, but it is more difficult to approach as the entire story is told in first-person slang narrative, with the odd spellings of a teenager who has only recently learned to read and write. The story takes the form of the memoirs of Duke Custis, a young African-American gang member in Harlem who rises to become the president of his gang, only to be arrested at the end after the murder of a Puerto Rican from a rival gang. In his new life he tends flowers and attends school in an unnamed upstate New York correctional facility, strikingly similar to the Highfields estate project that was one of the social-work solutions to youth criminality. Critical reflection after the fact congratulated *West Side Story*, in fact, for not having fallen into the *Cool World* trap, where the message was more obvious.[49] Miller's novel was soon adapted for the stage by the author and Robert Rossen and featured such future luminaries as Roscoe Lee Browne, James Earl Jones, Cicely Tyson, and Billy Dee Williams as the juvenile delinquent cast. The show ran one night in the Eugene O'Neill Theatre in 1960, the failure no doubt having as much to do with saturation of subject matter as the quality of the performance. The author was so disappointed with the flop that he divorced himself from future adaptations. A film version of 1964, produced by Frederick Wiseman and directed by Shirley Clarke, fared much better, fitting into a trend of documentary drama that would become popular in the years following. Although *The Cool World* obviously follows more closely the territory of *West Side Story* (whose protagonists don't darken the door of a high school) than *The Black-*

board Jungle, with gang rumbles, war council meetings, and an antagonistic view of Puerto Ricans, it also seemed to come a little too late in the game. *The Blackboard Jungle* at least had the box office draw of Poitier as the class leader who faces off against a new high school teacher in a tough, inner-city school.

WEST SIDE STORY SYNDROME

Ultimately, although *West Side Story* seemed to have raised a certain amount of consciousness about its subject, it may have done more harm than good. It was precisely this tameness, not the show's grittiness, which would eventually lead to *West Side Story*'s more lasting social import: as a work that eventually shed *less* light on its topic than more. An article in the *New York Times* several years after its premiere asked the important question "Was *West Side Story* Bad for East Harlem?"[50] And, in a leading story in the second section of the *New York Times*, hollow-eyed youths describe their lives as homeless junkies in a violent, tribal society, hiding behind bullet-ridden windows in slums. This article, appearing as late as 1978, is entitled "True Story of City Gang Life No Glittery *West Side Story*," suggesting that, over twenty years later, the musical still stands in the public minds as the symbol of gang life. The article relates the lives of two teenage sisters who are estranged over their love for rival gang members. Like Maria or Anita, one of the girls states, "But she's in love with that man in jail. And when you're in love, I guess you do anything." Amid street shootings and rumbles, the police attempt to keep the peace, but one says, "This is no *West Side Story*. This is the real thing."[51] The "glitter" of the musical has led to a sociological phenomenon called *West Side Story* Syndrome, in which the romanticization of gang life as portrayed in both the musical and film appeals to young people while diverting media and government attention away from the real problems of gang culture.[52] Feminist criminologist Meda Chesney-Lind coined the term *West Side Story* Syndrome as a kind of male-dominated ritualistic society that excludes women (except as sexual or entertainment objects). As she writes, "The criminological fascination with male deviance and crime—which I have flippantly dubbed the 'Westside Story Syndrome'—is not, as some might contend, simply a reflection of the American crime problem. I suspect that it is also explained by Margaret Mead's observation that whatever men do, even if it is dressing dolls for religious ceremonies, has higher status and is more highly rewarded than whatever women do. For this reason, fields focus on male activities and attributes wherever possible: to study them is to convey higher status to the researcher."[53] The very misogynist underpinnings of the juvenile delinquency literature, which blames the mother for leaving the home, have lived on in the treatment of the issue in sociology.[54] Even four decades later, a Top 40 song of the late 1990s by an ensemble featuring famous guitarist Carlos Santana reflects this perfectly, the chorus running: "Maria, Maria—she reminds me of a *West Side Story*/Growing up in Spanish Harlem/She's living the life just like a movie star."[55] Director Jerome Robbins remembers this about the original production:

> We were talking about revivals over the years; as a director I discovered something fascinating. At the time we did the show, the cast understood the material very, very well, deeply and organically. It was part of the times. In the recent revival—and I don't mean to cast any slurs upon it—I found that the cast had rather middle-class attitudes. It was hard for them to understand the street, the turf, the toughness, the necessity to own something, the struggle on the street. I felt I could never get out of them a real understanding of the material from either an acting or a dancing point of view. The original cast knew what it was about and could react to it.[56]

Comparing recorded versions of the "Jet Song" from the original cast album and Bernstein's own 1980s recording of *West Side Story*, this difference seems startlingly clear. Although the performances of opera singers Kiri Te Kanawa and José Carreras have been faulted as too operatic, Kurt Ollmann, who sings the part of Riff, has more the skills of a singing actor and could have rendered this part in a realistic style. Instead, it becomes lyrical and light operatic in tone. The almost dreamy delivery makes it seem as though Ollmann has no idea what the text he is intoning is really about. Staging *West Side Story* out of its original context will always be difficult due to the stylized street lingo, the now-dated dance styles, and the cultural and social habits of its characters. Updating it to reflect the street music and aesthetic styles of following decades would be difficult, as so much of its flavor comes from the "mambo craze" era in which it was created. But, if this work must be kept as an encapsulation of America in the 1950s to maintain dramatic veracity, we must also realize that it has become in many ways simply another version of *Romeo and Juliet*, that, in Robbins's "middle-class" way, the toughness of the street that was so much a part of its original milieu renders *West Side Story* perhaps more archetypal than real.

NOTES

1. "Landmark," 18; and Arthur Laurents, *Original Story By*, 349.

2. Leonard Bernstein Collection, writing series, box 75, folder 7, Library of Congress, Washington, DC. It was also printed in *Playbill* during the original run of the show, and was reprinted in Bernstein, *Findings*, 144–47.

3. "We" refers to Roger Stevens, who continued an affiliation with the show after Crawford bowed out. Crawford to Arthur Laurents, 15 June 1956. Cheryl Crawford Collection, "Series V: Unproduced Works," box 83, folder 4.

4. Quoted by Don Ross, "Hal Prince's Perfect Stage Record: Even His Look-Alike Is a Big Hit," *New York Herald Tribune*, July 6, 1958.

5. Arthur Laurents recalls, "I remember Jerry asking the most important question asked any time about anything in the theater: 'What is it about?' One of the reasons why he is the most brilliant of all choreographers is that he knows a dance has to be *about* something, not just an abstract dance. When it's *about* something, no one knows better how to make it dance and move the story." "Landmark," 15.

6. Quoted in Zadan, *Sondheim & Company*, 28.

7. Laurents, *Original Story By*, 347.

8. Jerome Robbins Archive, box 2, folder 15, New York Public Library Dance Division.

9. Bernstein Collection, date book series, box 322, folder 1.

10. Cheryl Crawford to Arthur Laurents, 20 July 1956, Crawford Collection, box 83, folder 4. Crawford expresses similar reservations to Roger Stevens in a letter dated July 10: "For your information, a friend in the picture business who has read WEST SIDE STORY told me today that a play called On The 7th Day by the author of Blackboard Jungle which Jose Quintero is supposed to direct in November is very close to the story of WEST SIDE. It's about New York Puerto Ricans and a sailor who falls in love with one of them. I am getting a lengthy synopsis." The play seems never to have been produced, at least not by Quintero or on Broadway.

11. Interview with juvenile delinquents taken to see a matinee of *West Side Story*, ca. 1958, tape, Harold Prince Archive, New York Public Library for the Performing Arts, Theatre Division.

12. Early studies on delinquency started appearing in the 1920s.

13. Richard E. Harris, *Delinquency in Our Democracy* (Los Angeles: Wetzel, 1954).

14. Arthur Miller, "The Bored and the Violent," 50–52.

15. Elliott H. Aubrey, *Pillars of Support* (Austin, TX: Hogg Foundation for Mental Hygiene, 1956), 4.

16. Ronald Steel, *New Light on Juvenile Delinquency* (New York: H. W. Wilson, 1967), 24.

17. Aubrey, *Pillars of Support*, 5.

18. Sheldon and Eleanor Glueck, *Delinquents in the Making: Paths to Prevention* (New York: Harper, 1952); Alfred J. Kahn, *For Children in Trouble: An Exploratory Study of Major Problems Facing New York City Services* (New York: Citizens' Committee for Children of New York City, Inc., 1957); and Bernard Lander, *Towards an Understanding of Juvenile Delinquency* (New York: Columbia, 1954).

19. Starke H. Hathaway and Elio D. Monachese, *Analyzing and Predicting Juvenile Delinquency with the MMPI* (Minneapolis: University of Minnesota Press, 1953).

20. Sheldon and Eleanor Glueck, *One Thousand Juvenile Delinquents* (Cambridge, MA: Harvard University Press, 1934).

21. Glueck and Glueck, *One Thousand*, 110.

22. Steel, *New Light on Juvenile Delinquency*, 17.

23. Lloyd W. McCorkle, Albert Elias, and F. Lovell Bixby, *The Highfields Story* (New York: Henry Holt, 1958).

24. Kate Friedlander, *The Psycho-Analytical Approach to Juvenile Delinquency: Theory, Case Studies, Treatment* (New York: International Universities Press, Inc., 1960).

25. Belton M. Fleisher, *The Economics of Delinquency* (Chicago: Quadrangle, 1966).

26. Arthur Laurents, interview with the author, June 3, 2008.

27. These sketches are housed in Sondheim's archive in Madison, Wisconsin. Mr. Sondheim respectfully requested that these sketches not be reproduced in this publication.

28. Even the authors were aware of this aspect of the British premiere, although they attributed it to a later time period (the 1980s). Bernstein: "My impression in London was that they were very understanding of the material, maybe they came to it later." Laurents: "They're having a social revolution in England now." "Landmark," 23.

29. Harold Conway, "This Knocks *My Fair Lady* for Six," *London Daily Sketch*, December 13, 1958.

30. Quoted in John M. Martin, *Juvenile Vandalism* (Springfield, IL: Charles C. Thomas, 1961), 124.

31. Jerome Robbins: "It was not only cast that way, the collaboration continued, because once we found the people we wanted, Arthur began to write a little for them and even shift lines around. The characters were formed during the rehearsal period with Arthur being there to see what could happen and what could not happen." "Landmark," 23–24.

32. "Landmark," 23–24.

33. Donald Hunsberger, interview by author. Hunsberger knew pit musicians playing for the Washington premiere.

34. "They're not people. What lasts in the theater is character, and there are no characters in *West Side* nor can there be. It's the shortest book on record, with the possible exception of *Follies*, in terms of how much gets accomplished with how little dialogue. It's more about techniques, not about people, and Arthur recognized that problem right away and instead of writing people he wrote one-dimensional characters for a melodrama, which is what it is." Stephen Sondheim, quoted in Zadan, *Sondheim & Company*, 28.

35. Arthur Laurents: "The day of our first run-through for an audience, they came out on stage in colors they had chosen for Jets and Sharks and their girls. They did it on their own, by themselves, and it was very, very touching." "Landmark," 23.

36. Marvin E. Wolfgang, "The Culture of Youth," Department of Sociology, University of Pennsylvania (Washington, DC: United States Department of Health, Education, and Welfare. Office of Juvenile Delinquency and Youth Development.

Supt. of Docs., 1967), 105, reprinted in Steel, *New Light on Juvenile Delinquency*, 101–13.

37. Wolfgang, "Culture of Youth," 109.

38. Joseph N. Sorrentino, *The Concrete Cradle* (Los Angeles: Wollstonecraft, 1975), 290.

39. Lawrence, *Dance with Demons*. Lawrence provides an argument throughout on the role of homosexuality in Robbins's life. Arthur Laurents in *Original Story By* details throughout his struggles with his identity as a gay man during this era.

40. Laurents, *Original Story By*, 302.

41. Andrea Most, "'You've Got to Be Carefully Taught': The Politics of Race in Rodgers and Hammerstein's *South Pacific*," *Theatre Journal* 52 (2000): 307–37; and Most, "Big Chief Izzy Horowitz."

42. John McClain, "'Story' Acts as J.D. Deterrent," *New York Journal-American*, November 2, 1958.

43. As far back as 1948, events such as the dance at the gym were seen as reformatory. "As boys and girls reach the middle and late teens, they must have a wholesome place to come together for dances, social activities, and refreshments, or they will find their own rendezvous in the false glamour of tavern dance halls and night spots. If we want to encourage a certain standard of sexual behaviour among the young, we must provide a favorable setting where adolescents of both sexes can play together and get to know one another under wholesome conditions." John R. Ellingston, *Protecting Our Children from Criminal Careers* (New York: Prentice Hall, 1948), 307.

44. Ellingston, *Protecting Our Children*, 307.

45. Harrison Salisbury, *The Shook-Up Generation* (New York: Harper and Row, 1958).

46. Yablonsky, *The Violent Gang*, 54. The fish led up to the more lascivious dance of "the twist."

47. The film *Dirty Dancing*, released in the 1980s, portrays this culture and the dance styles associated with it.

48. James Gilbert, *A Cycle of Outrage: America's Reaction to the Juvenile Delinquent in the 1950s* (New York: Oxford University Press, 1986), 15.

49. "Legit Followup: *West Side Story.* Winter Garden, NY," *Variety,* May 4, 1960.

50. John J. O'Connor, "Television: Was *West Side Story* Bad for East Harlem?" *New York Times,* April 2, 1972. After a television broadcast of the film version on NBC, grade five and six students in East Harlem's Public School 108 (mostly Puerto Rican and black) started packing toy guns and knives and engaged in schoolyard "rumbles." They also nicknamed the lunchtime street monitor "Officer Krupke." None of these behaviors were documented before the film aired.

51. Dena Kleiman, "True Story of City Gang Life No Glittery *West Side Story,*" *New York Times,* March 6, 1978, B1–8.

52. Paul M. Sharp and Barry W. Hancock, *Juvenile Delinquency: Historical, Theoretical, and Societal Reactions to Youth* (Englewood Cliffs, NJ: Prentice Hall, 1995), 161.

53. Meda Chesney-Lind, "Doing Feminist Criminology," *The Criminologist* 13, no. 4 (1988): 1.

54. *Reader's Digest* ran a column in March 1958 which was headed, "Nine Words That Can Stop Juvenile Delinquency: Put Father Back at the Head of the Family." Quoted in Bernice Miburn Moore, *Juvenile Delinquency: Research, Theory, and Comment* (Washington, DC: Association for Supervision and Curriculum Development, 1958), 3. Robert C. Hendrickson and Fred J. Cook go even farther in *Youth in Danger* (New York: Harcourt, Brace, 1956), 82: "You don't know how empty and cold a house may be when mother is not there to talk to you." They blame working women's selfish desires for mink coats and keeping up with the Joneses as the roots of delinquency.

55. W. Jean, J. Duplessis, C. Santana, K. Perazzo, R. Rekow. The song "Maria Maria" appears on Santana, *Supernatural,* BMG/Arista, B00000J7J4.

56. "Landmark," 23

FIGURE 7.1
Dan Reisinger, Israeli poster of *West Side Story*. Courtesy of the Billy Rose Theatre Division, New York Public Library for the Performing Arts, Astor, Lenox and Tilden Foundations.

From the West Side to the East Side

Reception and Revision

Splendid and Super-Modern Musical Drama.

—John Chapman, opening night review ("West Side Story a Brand New Hit," New York Daily News, September 27, 1957)

Although the material is horrifying, the workmanship is admirable.

—Brooks Atkinson, opening night review ("Theatre: The Jungles of the City," New York Times, September 27, 1957)

As exciting (and sordid) as a subway mugging with music.

—Frank Farrell, opening night review ("New York—Day by Day—Christmas for Kovacs," New York World-Telegram, September 27, 1957)

West Side Story has become a canonical musical, and the attendant mythology that accompanies canon formation often involves the idea that the chosen work follows an inevitable path to its creation, quickly becoming a classic. At the same time that the tortured road that *West Side Story* took to the stage disproves the former assumption, the idea that it instantly rocketed to success is also neither entirely correct nor does it do justice to the rich history that this work has woven since its premiere in 1957. Although many pronounced it a "hit" (and certainly part of its mythology surrounds this signal moment), the work was not as wildly popular as some musicals that came before or since. A close look at documents and reviews surrounding the original production will present somewhat mixed views of this work, not an immediate or universal beatification. This period in the reception history of the musical is more fraught and more fascinating than we might assume. In fact, its very identity as American seems to have created not only some of the coolness of the original response, but also the zeal with which some international markets embraced it. Perhaps even more importantly, *West Side Story* did not so much create a new direction within the genre of the musical as it constructed a new way in which American musical theater intersected with popular culture and classical art music. As Sondheim suggests in a conversation with Steven Swayne, "and, in fact, *West Side Story* hasn't influenced anything at all. Because it's, as far as I'm concerned, sui generis. I mean, name me a musical that's been influenced by *West Side Story*. I can't think of one." He goes on to say, "there are shows that are originals and there are shows that are dead ends in and of themselves, because they respond only to the requirements—as *West Side Story* does—of that particular story."[1] Whether or not we want to accept *West Side Story* as a "dead end," we certainly need to account (especially in light of Sondheim's assertion) for its considerable renown on an international scale and for the ways in which it continues to be remade to reflect changing tastes and perhaps changing uses of musical theater. Under these conditions, one has to ask why this musical has made such an impact so widely when more commercially successful ones have not. Certainly, the film version accounts for its wide dissemination, and no doubt the film's accolades (multiple Oscar wins, including Best Picture) explain why it came to the attention of an audience that perhaps otherwise had little or no awareness of the Broadway musical. However, the film recreates many aspects of the original version, and so the theatrical, musical, and cultural work it does is in many respects an extension of what the authors created for the stage.

Whatever artistic aspirations the original creators and even producers espoused, they all aimed for the common and universal objective of a Broadway show: commercial success. Although they all admittedly took on the project as a labor of love, their hope was also for a hit or at least a chance to break even on their substantial production costs. Obviously, then, the publicity material that accompanies any Broadway theater production is aimed to attract audiences, and so includes a certain amount of harmless hyperbole to boost ticket sales. However, a reading of how *West Side Story* was represented by its authors and the press shows how the roots of the Great American Musical were planted even before the work premiered and how this in turn factors into a more widespread aspiration toward "art" that characterizes this period in musical theater history.

"Here Comes the First Fall Musical"

—*headline*, Herald Tribune

Advance publicity for the piece contained the usual hype but also telling hints about the cultural climate into which it fell. Not all the coverage promoted the musical in glowing terms; in fact, little of it did, although it was not overtly negative either. In one newspaper photo, Robbins is described as "The Man with the Know How" as he directs three of his dancers (Carol Lawrence, Lee Becker, and Chita Rivera). The caption describes the women as appearing in "graceful positions dictated by the all-knowing Robbins."[2] The musical was presented equally cerebrally as "the product of the minds of Laurents, Bernstein and Sondheim."[3] The music was described somewhat differently, but also as highbrow: "Not aimed at general popularity" was one polite epithet. Bernstein was being hailed as a new conducting wunderkind, so his classical music credentials overshadowed his previous experiences *and successes* with musical theater. *West Side Story*, then, was prepared in the public mind as a difficult, angry, and experimental "think piece"—too arty and serious for general popularity. Investors in the show expected to lose all of their money, only backing it so that Hal Prince and his partner Robert Griffith would keep them in mind for future, presumably successful, projects (their investment, of course, eventually paid off at 640 percent within the first fifteen years).[4] The original investors' instincts were probably correct, judging by the difficultly and dissonance of the score compared to "normal" Broadway fare. It was not just the tragic story or the highbrow aspects of the piece deriving from its Shakespearean pedigree, but the fact that it adhered to none of the normal Broadway values, that made it dangerous. Nubile chorus girls, big production numbers, and a recognizable star were conspicuously absent. An article on the casting process reported that the creators were trawling the streets for untrained talent (although none of the living collaborators claims to remember anything about this part of the process), playing into the idea that the musical was so groundbreaking in its style and serious in its dramatic purpose that there was going to be little to entertain the average theatergoer.

Reviews were good, at least good enough to know that the creators had a relatively good critical success on their hands, but that did not turn instantly into great commercial success. Although initial reviews were generally good, the show wasn't hailed *universally* as a masterpiece. For many, the problem seemed to be the tragic plot, but for others, the music posed aesthetic confusion. People knew it was deep, but didn't know exactly how to respond. The *New York Post*'s Richard Watts Jr. described the score as "blithely unconcerned with tunes" and, although he found it admirable, it "was just a trifle too lacking in warmth."[5] A British reviewer was even more damning:

> It was written by the man whom "Time" called a "wonder child"—Leonard Bernstein, who has made his mark as a conductor, a composer, a pianist, a teacher of music, and an American phenomenon of the first order. Matters of taste obtrude here in a big way. I have heard one of the shrewdest judges of such things say that the music of "West Side Story" is repulsive: a less shrewd judge has said that there is no tune in the score that could be whistled by the traditional messenger boy.[6]

Indeed, the music—which has now become perhaps the best-loved aspect of the show—was summed up by Frank Farrell: "there is nothing to sing from it, powerfully little book and pitifully few laughs . . . it should have been half as long. Strictly for the arty set."[7] The relative lack of singability of the show seemed to be a general concern for its original detractors, but at least its incomprehensibility provided the outward appearance of a "deep" musical work. But the genre was also criticized. Howard Taubman, in an article entitled "A Foot in Each Camp," judged that the musical faltered between musical and opera, fulfilling the expectations of neither genre.[8]

The material accompanying the opening also established a tone that suggested a long and serious gestation period. Bernstein's "*West Side Story* Log," published in the original *Playbill* and reproduced in his book *Findings* some twenty-five years later, ostensibly presents the most intimate thoughts of the composer as he works on his great project. "Jerry R. called today with a noble idea: a modern version of *Romeo and Juliet* set in slums at the coincidence of Easter-Passover celebrations," reads the first entry, dated January 6, 1949. The "noble idea" progresses, but the jet-setting composer cannot keep up and thinks altruistically: "Maybe they can find the right composer who isn't always skipping off to conduct somewhere. It's not fair to them or to the work." The readers are on the edge of their seats until they discover, on September

6, 1955, that "Jerry loves our gang idea. A second solemn pact is sworn. Here
we go, God bless us!" On July 8, 1957, Bernstein writes this apologia for the
reader: "I can't believe it: forty kids are actually doing it up there on the
stage! Forty kids singing five-part counterpoint who never sang before—and
sounding like heaven. I guess we were right not to cast 'singers': anything that
sounded more professional would inevitably sound more experienced, then
the 'kid' quality would be gone. A perfect example of a disadvantage turned
into a virtue." Given that the audience for the first Broadway performances
knew little about the piece and could not have been prepared for some of the
innovations or complexities of the work, they could not fail to be influenced
as they read these words in *Playbill* just moments before the curtain went up.
With this discreet disclaimer, they would be perfectly ready to forgive the
forty kids for not being "singers" but still managing to sing five-part counterpoint, and believe that it must actually sound "like heaven" if the person who
is telling them this is the recently appointed principal conductor of the New
York Philharmonic. In the last entry, Bernstein delivers the final message,
that the premiere in Washington, DC, was a hit: "And I guess what made it
come out right is that we all really *collaborated*; we were all writing the *same*
show. Even the producers were after the same goals we had in mind. Not
even a whisper about a happy ending was heard. A rare thing on Broadway.
I am proud and honored to be part of it." The audience, primed for a tragic
ending and complicated music, moved by the description of the long and
selfless collaborative process, and cheering for the forty kids, could not help
but be swayed by the young composer's outpouring of emotion and be ready
to give this tragic, epic musical their full attention. Bernstein's diary entries,
so personal but also so authoritative, did far more than the usual marketing
strategies could have achieved. Too bad they weren't actually real.[9]

For although certainly Bernstein kept date books, the "log" is in fact a
creative fabrication after the fact. The published diary entry for November
14, 1955, indicates that "a young lyricist named Stephen Sondheim came
and sang us some of his songs today." In fact, according to Bernstein's date
book, the two had already been working together by then. Bernstein's papers
include numerous drafts and rewrites of the supposed *West Side Story* log.
Loosely based on the general order of events, it is an invented and highly
romanticized piece of fiction made to sound like glimpses into a composer's
personal journal. A diary entry dated September 18, 1957, reminds Bernstein to "Write Playbill Piece (570 words)."[10] Bernstein's tack was clearly

publicity-oriented, and he certainly cannot be faulted for that. But that he reprinted it twenty-five years later not only in *Findings* but as the first item to appear in the liner notes of his own definitive operatic version of the same year (describing it as "Entries from 1949 to 1957, Published in 1957")[11] suggests that Bernstein had no desire to disabuse his readers of the notion that it represented excerpts from an actual diary, even that long after the fact.

Clearly, Bernstein's apologia was understandable considering the advance coverage the piece had garnered. Even with it, the audience reaction was confused. As Sondheim recalls:

> No, for the first half hour the audience was pretty dead, they'd heard this was a work of art—capital W, capital A—so they sat there like children in church until "America." At that point they realized this was a musical, and they were supposed to be having a good time. From then on it went very well.[12]

Although not all critics appreciated the music, all could agree that the show was somehow a departure from Broadway norms. Early reviews commented on how groundbreaking it appeared in comparison with previous offerings of the genre. "It bears no relation to any other musical ever done before, neither in concept nor execution. It is in a real sense an experiment, but a wondrously complete and detailed one," wrote Whitney Bolton in the *New York Morning Telegraph*.[13] Bernstein remembers that it was theatrical elements that seemed to garner the most praise.

> What I remember best from opening night was the set change from the quintet, which drew prolonged applause, into the remarkable rumble set that Jerry mentioned. The quintet applause was just beginning to dip as the set changed before your eyes. The whole wave rose again until it doubled the preceding applause. For me, this was one of the most magical moments in the theater. That's where I had the sense that we had a hit.[14]

"B'Way Goes to the White House"

—headline, Journal American

The work's status as a hit certainly remained fresh in the minds of the creators when they reminisced about the work at the Dramatists Guild Symposium (again, twenty-five years after its premiere), but it was more popular in the tryout city of Washington than it ever was in New York City. No doubt the work's message, very clear but also not overtly political, would have appealed to the numerous diplomats who saw the show and were more aware than perhaps even the New York audiences of the particular social problems the work so eloquently addressed. As Bernstein recalls,

> It was an incredible night. It was August in Washington—horribly hot—and none of us knew whether anyone would listen to the show, or look at it, or stay in the theater. We'd had a lot of insults, a lot of warnings: "You're crazy," "Give it up," and so forth. At intermission I remember Justice Felix Frankfurter, the most distinguished man in Washington, in a wheelchair, in tears. And this was only intermission. It was an incredible hello, because we didn't know whether the show was even all right, let alone something special and deeply moving.[15]

During the lead-up to the Washington opening, Bernstein confided to his wife,

> Well, look-a me. Back to the nation's capitol, & right on the verge. This is Thurs. We open Mon. Everyone's coming, my dear, even Nixon and 35 admirals. Senators abounding, & big Washington-hostessy type party afterwards in Lennuht's honor. See what you miss by going away. Then next Sunday, which is my birthday, there is the Jewish version—a big party for me, but admission is one Israel bond. All helps the show. We have a 75 Thurs. advance, & the town is buzzing. Not bad.[16]

At the opening, Bernstein also credited some of the success to the audience in attendance, which he describes as "the Senate practically in toto." He goes on:

> I've just lunched at the White House . . . Invited by Sherman Adams & the whole gang. Again—you should have been there! What a beautiful place—such credenzas, such breakfronts. I really felt "in." Adams & Rabb & Gen. Snyder—all were talking of nothing but West Side Story—I think the whole government is based on it. Jim Hagerty (Ike's press secretary) turns out to be a fan of music! It's all so crazy and unexpected. Even Adams turns out to be an amateur musician![17]

Although certainly the Washington reception helped to establish the credentials of the show, it would turn out to create some of *West Side Story*'s early political problems. Perhaps capitalizing on the initial popularity in Washington, Robert Griffith and Harold Prince organized a "command performance" for President Eisenhower in May of 1958, part of a formal state dinner honoring the Supreme Court. Larry Kert and Carol Lawrence, reprising their roles as Tony and Maria, performed "Tonight" and were featured as the opening number at the White House gala (cast members from *My Fair Lady* and *New Girl in Town* also performed). The producers held a press conference in Washington to promote the event, but were not anticipating the negative reaction both in Washington and New York. Apparently the Broadway audiences were not advised in advance that they were seeing understudies as a result of the Washington performance, and both producers and performers were naturally seen as abandoning their "real" paying audience. Columns in all the major New York and Washington papers covered the event, most deploring (as Richard L. Coe did in the *Washington Post* in a column entitled "What's in a Promise?") the insult to New York audiences.[18] Whatever offense may have been taken, the producers probably felt the risk was worth it considering the larger project they had afoot: to keep the Broadway musical and the East Coast on par politically with the more dominant West Coast's genre of film. It also set the stage to take *West Side Story* farther east than they could have imagined: to the Soviet Union.

VEST SIDESKAYA ISTORIA

Falling as it did at the height of the cold war period, there were reasons for the work to attempt to both bridge a gap between Soviet and American culture and to become a part of the competitive spirit that informed relations between the two countries on both political and artistic fronts. That Robbins's choreography shows influences from Anthony Tudor's ballet choreography for Prokofiev's *Romeo and Juliet* is as much Robbins's challenge to the hegemony of Russian ballet as it is a general zeitgeist artistic influence. Even Bernstein, whose music was criticized as sounding like Prokofiev by Broadway producer George Abbott, must have felt that his *Romeo and Juliet* (as balletic as it was) would be compared with Prokofiev's popular score. Bernstein and Robbins, at least, had something to gain by putting their new, integrated, modern work up against the best that Russia had to offer. And it would not take long for it to happen. Only a few days after the White House gala, *Time* magazine carried a story about Soviet dancers who were touring the United

States and their visit to a performance of *West Side Story*.[19] The ensemble was
the acclaimed Moiseyev Dance Company, established by ex–Bolshoi ballet
master Igor Moiseyev in the mid-1930s and featuring a repertoire that mixed
ballet and folk dance styles. By the mid-1950s, the group started touring internationally, and made an incredible impact in the United States, where their
Metropolitan Opera House debut garnered a twenty-five-minute ovation.
Part of a U.S.-Soviet cultural exchange during the spring of 1958, they even
appeared on *The Ed Sullivan Show*, which featured an entire hour devoted to
the group.[20] Clearly impressed by *West Side Story*, the company returned to
the Soviet Union to praise its considerable artistic and social innovations. In a
three-and-a-half-hour talk entitled "The Cultural Life of America," Moiseyev
reported to a large gathering of musicians, dancers, actors, and writers on the
cultural riches of the United States, particularly the dynamism of live theater.
Although Moiseyev felt that both *My Fair Lady* and *West Side Story* were
works that should be brought to Moscow, he lauded *West Side*, specifically
the contributions of Bernstein and Laurents.[21] Perhaps inadvertently entering
into the debate over who should have won the most important Tony awards
(*West Side Story* lost to *The Music Man* in the key categories), Moiseyev
criticized the contemporaneous Meredith Willson musical as "lacking in
message" and did not include it on works recommended for Soviet audiences.

On April 29, 1959, just a few months after this report, the Bolshoi Ballet
visited New York on a similar tour, and the dancers were offered free tickets
by Griffith and Prince to the new musical they had heard so much about back
home. This time the press was ready, taking pictures of Carol Lawrence and
other cast members as they studied Russian-language recordings in preparation for their meeting with the Bolshoi dancers. As predicted, the Russians
(130 dancers in all saw the show) were impressed by the musical, particularly
the amount of dance involved. In a strange mixture of competition and
cultural exchange, dancers from *West Side Story* attempted to teach Bolshoi
women how to "mambo," and Victor Smirnoff from the Russian troupe el-
evated Carol Lawrence into a balletic lift backstage.[22]

Harold Prince, who was trying to put together a European tour for the
work after its London premiere, quickly seized on the opportunity to bring
West Side Story to Russian audiences. Initial talks with the State Department (within a month of the Bolshoi visit) were discouraging. Prince would
need their imprimatur, under the conditions of the 1958 cultural exchange

agreement, to mount the production in exchange with a Soviet work. There were two problems: the Soviet authorities were predicted not to support jazz music, even if in the form of the Broadway musical, and the United States government felt that displaying the scourge of juvenile delinquency in their cities was not the image of American society that they wanted portrayed to the Russians. Prince flew to Moscow in July to negotiate both the European tour and the possibility of taking *West Side Story* behind the Iron Curtain. Max Franks, an expatriate living in Moscow, wrote to the drama editor of the *New York Times* arguing a case for presenting the show there.

> Every Russian theatregoer and intellectual is painfully aware of the awkward striving of the contemporary Soviet arts for the successful use of modern social problems in their literature and on their stages. This ambition has not been realized, not for lack of talent and not for lack of contemporary problems, but because meaningful and yet sanctioned conflicts for public display are difficult to contrive here. The impression that *West Side Story* would make on an art community so frustrated is incalculable but enticing.[23]

Franks asks that if modern American musical theater, especially a show that expresses such "Americana," cannot be shown off, what was the point of cultural exchange in the first place? Although Prince felt that the work would go over well in the Soviet Union (considering that they had their own juvenile delinquency problems), he agreed to abide by the State Department's wishes.[24]

On September 1, 1959, Harold Prince was surprised to read a report in the *New York Times* that a dispatch had arrived from Gennady Osipov, chief of the theatrical section of the Ministry of Culture, announcing that *West Side Story* would be produced later in that season in Moscow. The previous May an unsanctioned version of *My Fair Lady* was staged in the Soviet Union, primarily because there were no copyright agreements between the two countries. Prince was quick to write to Osipov to inquire as to what "usual capitalistic gratuities" would be offered.[25] The end result was that the show was staged without most music and dancing, emphasizing the race conflict. Considering the brevity of Laurents's book, it must have made for a very strange performance indeed.[26] In fact, it would not be until the film version came out a few years later that Russian audiences had any idea as to what the show was really like.[27] *West Side Story* continued to be staged illegally through 1964, along with *My Fair Lady*, which meant that the Soviet authorities did not pay royal-ties on either work.[28]

The Moiseyev and Bolshoi accolades did more than just create a context for international attention. They also seem to have boosted ticket sales in New York. Once box office returns started to slow in the fall, the producers decided to close and take it on the road. Having enjoyed a good run, *West Side Story* might well have wound up its career at this point and we might not know it so well today. Then, late in 1958, a second thing happened to change *West Side Story*'s career—the London West End premiere.

"LIKE A SHARK WAS LET LOOSE IN AN AQUARIUM": PANDEMONIUM ON THE WEST END

The British love affair with American musical comedy was not a new phe-nomenon. The postwar London production of *Oklahoma!* was a major turn-ing point for the art form there. But the response to *West Side Story* would prove even bigger. As early as March 1958 (only six months after *West Side Story* opened on Broadway), London papers were reporting the incredible black-market popularity of the show among the society set. Specifically, it was the music (brought to the British through the Broadway original cast recording) that was hooking audiences long before the show opened there. Kenneth Allsop, in an article entitled "Their Jet Song Will Get You," predicted that *West Side Story* would become the next West End rage. Significantly, his article was not on theater or dance, but was a record column.[29] Bootleg cop-ies of the LP cast recording were selling for £5, the equivalent of about $70 in today's currency (a standard new-release classical LP sold for approximately £1.75 in 1958). It was all the rage at London society parties, with "Gee, Officer Krupke!" the most popular number from the score. Before the show opened, before the British even knew what it was about or what the choreography and sets were like (a large part of the appeal for American audiences), the show was promising to rival the popularity of even *My Fair Lady*, which up until then had been enjoying the same kind of "scalper" success. Tickets for *My Fair Lady* were selling for the equivalent in today's currency of approximately $600 a pair. *West Side Story* was predicted to top this, and the show wasn't to open for another nine months. The work was prepared in the public mind quite differently than by the preopening coverage in New York papers, and quite aggressively. The *London Sunday Times* sent one of its most prominent journalists, Kenneth Pearson, to the United States to interview the creators. His column, grandly entitled "The Birth of a Musical," ran once a week starting November 2, strategically placing the final installment the Sunday after previews opened in Manchester (November 16) and before London's December premiere. The article rehashed the entire creative process behind the show, something not even covered by American papers.

Pearson's narrative tended toward the starstruck. Recalling that the impetus for *West Side Story* came from Montgomery Clift's appeal to Robbins as to how to portray the character of Romeo, the author writes:

> A man may reject many things during the course of his life, but he will find it difficult to discard a creative idea. Like the grain of sand in an oyster will both irritate and stimulate until talent gives it the lustre of a pearl. Robbins had a grain of sand. He leant back, closed his eyes and tried to imagine a Romeo set against the contemporary scene.[30]

This romanticized view of the creative process gives way later to a description of the authors themselves, portrayed almost like supermen.

> Despite outward appearances of humility, any artist of worth is an egocentric. He must have a confidence in his view of life which would make lesser men tremble. Laurents, Bernstein and Robbins were no different. As they drew together it was like the approaching points of an arc lamp. The sparks began to leap the gap before solid contact was ever made.[31]

Bernstein especially was depicted like a movie star.

> His scores for ballet and orchestra were a source of joy; they showed a capacity for deep and continuous thinking where others were content to freewheel. His public *persona* was gratifying. He was warm, kind and considerate. Dark, strong-featured and youthful in appearance, he was the idol of all New York matrons.[32]

Everything about the conception and genesis of the work was glamorized (Laurents and Bernstein met in Beverly Hills where "Lauren Bacall lay in the sun not far away") and portrayed the creators as artists separated from the madding crowd of ordinary people. Laurents had built a "lonely house on the Atlantic shore of Long Island. It was a hideaway, a refuge from the frantic haste of New York . . . Here, in the autumn of 1955, Laurents shut himself away, behind the dunes and the long, windswept grass. Across the beach lights burned long into the night."[33] Robbins, similarly, "Worked throughout the day in his house on the East Side. His study contained a white iron bed and a score of ballet designs, souvenirs of a lifetime. Here he spent hours in thought, the door closed, the telephone cut off. He paced the room, resenting his close confinement."[34] Robbins's depiction, like that of a wild animal, is echoed in the way each author was painted. All were described in somewhat exotic terms, Bernstein "dark," Laurents with "an Indian head," and Sondheim with "heavy-lidded eyes."

Exclusive previews like this were not the only press *West Side Story* enjoyed. The famous union concessions granted to *West Side Story* also prepared it as a major, exotic event. Citing the popularity of the musical through illegal recordings, Edward Goring announced *West Side Story*'s eclipse of *My Fair Lady* three months before the musical had even opened in a *London Daily Mail* article entitled, "The Show That Knocks 'MFL' for Six." He reports on the startling concessions by British Equity to drop their ban on all-American casts, something that hadn't happened for British productions of American shows since *Oklahoma!* in 1947. He quotes Harold Prince as saying, "If Equity had refused to allow this we would not bring the show here. It is so American that it must be done by an all-American cast."[35] The producers argued that the show was so modern and advanced in the American dance idiom that if the choreography were not pulled off exactly as conceived, the show would suffer. Even in the United States, the audition process had been grueling. How much harder would it be with non-Americans? Even British theater professionals who had seen the work in the United States appeared before the Equity Board as witnesses.[36] It was no wonder that, with this preparation, London audiences voraciously consumed *West Side Story*. The particularly American quality became a prominent theme in coverage of the show. An opening-night review by John Thompson in the *London Daily News* included a small map of Manhattan so that Londoners could see where the West Side really was.[37]

Although the article is headed, "The *West Side Story* the Public Knows— The LP Record," worries of the producers that advance familiarity with the music would create a stale audience proved unfounded. The opening was unbelievable. Anthony Carthew wrote, "It was as if someone had let loose a shark in an aquarium when 'West Side Story' arrived at Her Majesty's Theatre in London last night."[38] Other reviews describe the opening in similarly visceral terms: "With a punch like a knuckle-duster Broadway's Teddy Boy musical West Side Story last night knocked spots off My Fair Lady as the first night of 1958," wrote Edward Goring, following up his earlier prediction.[39] "It struck London last night like a flash of lightning set to music," wrote Cecil Wilson. "Electrifying is not a word that crops up more than once in 10 years, if that, in this writer's vocabulary," wrote another.[40]

All of London society was there: actor, playwright, and songwriter Noël Coward, ballerina Margot Fonteyn, Sandy Wilson, and Duncan Sandys. Coward even went backstage to congratulate the cast, a rare and honored event. Twelve curtain calls followed a performance that had been stopped a full five times by audience frenzy. The first showstopper was, not surprisingly, "America," which received cheers for its satirization of American society. Princess Margaret, who at that time was the party girl of London society, saw the show several times, including at a preopening fundraiser. Already a fan after having listened to the musical for a year before the premiere, she even went backstage to shake hands with the entire cast. The princess saw it multiple times over the next three years. She returned one night to ask the stage manager if she could come in the back way and avoid the royal entrance. "I hope you don't mind," she said, "I've brought my sister."[41]

It wasn't just a social event, though—Londoners saw it as a turning point in musical theater, "the show which marks the beginning of a new era in musicals," as one critic described it.[42] The imprimatur of Margot Fonteyn seemed to establish the work as a serious ballet. A few days before the premiere, an article by Peter Brinson brought the cachet of an American ballet choreographer to the mix, quoting a conversation he had the previous summer with Agnes de Mille: "West Side Story is a point of departure," she had confided to the author after the work's American premiere. "After this we shall move into a more fluid, mobile theater. The strength of West Side Story lies not in individuals but in its group anger, group clashes, group emotions."[43] Not just fueling the publicity fire already raging before its London opening, the article described West Side Story as the culmination of a movement begun by Fred Astaire's use of dance, growing out of and advancing plot. "West Side Story completes the process," writes Brinson. "Dancer and singer alike unite to become the actor-singer-dancer, a total artist whose role is so conceived that dancing (whether 'dancing' or just 'moving') is inseparable from singing and acting. At the top the choreographer and director become one."[44] Indeed, a photo accompanying this article highlights the more balletic aspects of the "dream sequence" (the same term, of course, for de Mille's ballet in *Oklahoma!*), as did much of the press coverage.[45] New genre classifications such as *dansical* were coined to describe it.[46] As one critic wrote:

> The musical comedy has grown up! *West Side Story* is no mutation freak. It isn't just marvelous music, superb dancing, better singing, and better acting than we're used to. It is *different*. So different and so *much* better that there will be no going back to sentimental flimsiness. The usual musical's anaemic, happy-ever-after plot will be as impossible now as women's magazine stories after *War and Peace*. See it. See it if you have to queue up in the street for tickets. See it if you have to book seats a year ahead. See it and you'll see what watery gruel other musicals have been.[47]

Called things such as "the most remarkable, most dynamic musical ever seen on a London stage,"[48] *West Side Story*, as predicted, sounded the death knell to the reigning monarch of the West End, *My Fair Lady*. A surprising number of reviews set up this particular dichotomy. In a roundtable discussion in the *Evening Standard* appropriately entitled "*West Side Story* Defeats *My Fair Lady*," critics voted on the top musicals of the year. British conductor Malcolm Sargent, one of the panelists, attributed *West Side Story*'s popularity to the fact that it was louder than *My Fair Lady* (perhaps this was the beginning of fully amplified musicals). But another panelist, film producer Michael Balcon, declared, "I say that *West Side Story* is not only the best musical, I say it is also one of the finest pieces of theater I have ever seen in my life."[49] Sargent was not the only detractor, of course, but even lukewarm reviews took a pre-emptive stance. Harold Hobson's blaring title "A Warning from Noel" opens with an account of the reviewer's conversation with Noël Coward (described in the article as "the most comprehensive theatrical genius of our time") after the opening-night performance. Coward was still in his seat after the rest of the audience had left, clearly overwhelmed by *West Side Story*. "That was great theatre we've had tonight, wasn't it?" he intoned. When Hobson expressed his dissent, Coward seemed incredulous but pleaded, "Harold, do be careful, please, please be careful."[50] In the rest of the review, Hobson criticizes aspects of the production from within the couched terms that Coward requested. Such dissention, however, was rare. Kenneth Pearson perhaps sums up best how the British saw the piece. "It was as if over here, Benjamin Britten had written the score, Kingsley Amis the book, and both had been inspired by one of our best choreographers."[51] Perhaps part of the show's ballet success had to do with the fact that Bernstein had conducted his own *Fancy Free* at Covent Garden in 1946, with Jerome Robbins dancing. The audience was already primed for the work of these two artists, as exotic as they may have seemed to some.

The collaborators also realized that the work's London reception had something to do with the subject matter. Although Bernstein mused, "My impression in London was that they were very understanding of the material or maybe they came to it later," Arthur Laurents felt that England's social revolution was the basis for their interest.[52] Indeed, the social message was picked up on quickly by most reviewers. An article by Gerard Fay from Manchester, England, traces the development of American musical theater as one increasingly concerned with messages and cites Blitzstein's *Cradle Will Rock* and *No For an Answer* as well as political implications of *Pajama Game*.[53] Fay seemed to take more to the piece even than Americans, claiming that, when he saw it in New York City, he enjoyed it more than the rest of the audience seemed to, which he attributed to the fact that Americans might find the work a little too close to home. Consider the juvenile delinquents who were taken to *West Side Story* and their surprise that the audience did not share their enthusiasm for the message of the show. Fay claims that New York City has always looked for easily definable scapegoats, and traces the history of African-American and Puerto Rican issues formerly raised by Irish immigration. That the ethnic and political history of New York City takes precedence over the review of the musical itself suggests that the British were as interested in *West Side Story*'s subject matter as its drama.

"America Must Be Proud of Boys Like Those"

—New York World-Telegram *reopening night review*

Reports of the sensational London debut appeared in *Variety* within a few days in December of 1958, just months after the other significant event that no doubt changed *West Side Story*'s history—Leonard Bernstein's appointment as music director of the New York Philharmonic.[54] The show, which was selling on twofers (which are "two for the price of one" tickets) to ensure full houses in New York, started to sell out and continued to do so until the show's scheduled closing in the spring. A tour was already booked, but plans were quickly made to allow for a reopening in New York City. Once a theater was secured, the "revival," as it was called, but really the continuation of *West Side Story* (especially since it included most of the original principals), opened on Broadway. Part of the audience draw was to see Bernstein himself, now the music director (not just one of two principal conductors) of the New York Philharmonic. Apparently there was either some intentional misleading or perhaps miscommunication: instead of conducting the entire score, as originally publicized, Bernstein led only the opening, and the rest of the show would be conducted by musical director Joseph Lewis. Bernstein arrived in a chauffeur-driven Lincoln Continental, sporting black tie and evening cape. After continuing through the foyer of the theater instead of the stage entrance, Bernstein gave the audience what they clearly wanted.

> Just as the houselights dimmed, and with a hush of expectancy the audience awaited the appearance of Mr. Bernstein to conduct the overture. A lone spotlight picked him out as he made his way through the pit to the podium. The silence was broken by long, loud applause, which he had to cut short before he could start the overture in what must surely be its most brilliant direction and performance. The prolonged applause and shouted bravoes at the end went on for some time before the curtain could be raised and Mr. Bernstein could turn over the baton to conductor Joseph Lewis.[55]

When Bernstein appeared in the pit, the cheers and applause were described by critic Brooks Atkinson as "like Old Home week at Yankee Stadium."[56] The postshow party was held at the Roseland dance club, featuring everyone who was anyone and a cha-cha contest (Bernstein won). It was like London all over again. Suddenly *all* the reviews were favorable. Suddenly everyone had *always* considered *West Side Story* the Great American Musical. This was definitely the impression the producers desired. The morning after the Roseland party, Roger Stevens complained to Harold Prince about the expense involved in the "opening night" of a show that he spent more than three thousand dollars to fete at its premiere two years earlier (with an extensive guest list) at the Ambassador Ballroom.[57] Prince responded, "But actually, it did exactly what we intended. We've gotten a lot of press coverage, and we succeeded in giving the show the atmosphere of an opening night rather than a return engagement. I'm sure that is valuable. Bear in mind that the press people who covered the show were informed of the intended festivities at Roseland, and we believe this helped induce them to return."[58] Indeed, major critics who had attended the premiere returned and rereviewed the work. Canonization of *West Side Story* had begun.

There was another reason, perhaps, that *West Side Story* planned a triumphant return at this point: the visit of the Russian ballet troupe. Robert Saffron, in his review of the revival, starts out his commentary not about the show itself, but about the Moiseyev dancers who had recently seen the show and complained that it was too suggestive. "Whatever our shortcomings in missiles, we have progressed a long way from Mother Russia's prudery in the arts. What they labeled suggestive is a realism—compounded of throbbing sensuality, explosive joy and brutishness—rarely achieved in the music-drama."[59]

"When a Hit Becomes a Headache"

—Sunday News *headline*

West Side Story's triumphant return would be short-lived. Within months, the show was in trouble, partly the result of union unrest. A strike in the summer of 1960 (resulting in theater owners charging the producers for the cost of musicians) caused a loss of five thousand dollars in just one week (in 1960s currency) and by October grosses were dropping. By November, the authors were waiving royalties, and Prince reported to investors, "business is a see-saw."[60] The Alvin Theatre was needed for *Wildcat* (a Lucille Ball vehicle by Cy Coleman, N. Richard Nash, and Carolyn Leigh), and the producers were not able to find another theater in time.[61] They obtained permission from Actors' Equity to suspend the show for a period of two to five weeks, ready to make a move if another theater became available. However, the producers seemed none too eager for that to happen. As they wrote to investors on December 5, 1960, "There isn't any real money left in the show, but we hate to close it. However, if we don't get to reopen, we can't complain after almost three and a half years."[62] The *New York Herald Tribune* reported the December closing as a financial rather than an artistic decision. Columnist Stuart Little blamed "rule book negativism" on the part of two theatrical unions, the Association of Theatrical Press Agents and Managers (ATPAM) and the Associated Federation of Musicians (AFM). The producers requested, on short notice, that the unions be approached to sanction employment on a half-week basis for the week before Christmas to ensure an economical reopening. "We believe in West Side Story and we're perfectly willing to run the show indefinitely if it just breaks even. And it's certainly not an easy show to run," stated Prince. Although Prince complained that failing returns meant that a meager profit had to be shared between producers and investors, Milton Weintraub of the ATPAM cited reports in Variety the previous day that as of November the investors had made 230 percent profit on their original $300,000 investment.[63] Although West Side Story's Broadway stage life was coming to a close, it was about to be remade in a new genre. On July 17, 1958, Seven Arts Productions confirmed that they had completed negotiations to purchase screen rights for West Side Story, a deal that would provide the original creators three hundred and $50,000 plus an additional percentage of profits on the film.[64] Obviously not imagining how popular West Side Story would become, they bought the play Two for the Seesaw at the same time for almost twice that. The rest is history.

Although the film version of West Side Story was vital in disseminating the work to a larger audience, the European tour that encompassed Israel and Western Europe did much to promote the work even before the film was in the theaters. In New York, the film version sold advance tickets totaling $420,000, leaving it poised to be the largest-grossing film of its time. When it opened to general accolades and won numerous Academy Awards, it continued to garner substantial public interest, playing for years on reserved-seating tickets. One Paris house ran it for three years. The New York Times reported that the theater manager was on hand to welcome the one-millionth customer, and one Parisian had seen the film sixty-four times at that point. At the Rivoli Theatre in New York City it ran for two and a half years, although, in a bizarre "life imitates art" moment, the theater coffers were robbed by hoodlums while the film ran upstairs.[65]

The major changes to the film version were the sanitation and addition of some dialogue (one of the Jets deplores that Tony has been corrupted by the "youth board"—no doubt an update to play up the juvenile delinquency angle) and the reordering of numbers—particularly the "Cool" ballet and "Krupke." However, with Jerome Robbins actively involved in the initial part of the production, much of the musical's original style and tone were maintained, as well as his choreography.[66] Part of what the film achieved was to permanently "fix" the work in a particular time and place, much more so than the changeable medium of live theater (with each new production employing different designers, directors, and cast), and to establish it in the minds of many as the "original" *West Side Story*. Indeed, by the time *West Side Story* went into revivals, audiences had so identified the work from its film version that it was seen as the authentic version that could not be adulterated.

"WEST SIDE OF JAPAN"
Of all the countries in which the filmed *West Side Story* found a loyal following, Japan provided perhaps the most curious attitudes toward the work. As it was extremely popular with teenagers (who made up most of the film's audiences), law enforcement took this opportunity to use the work as a deterrent for juvenile delinquency. Next to poster advertisements for the movie was printed a newly composed poem entitled "West Side of Japan." A literal translation reads:

> Fairies in red tight-pants and blue pirate-striped jackets!
> They swagger on the street of morality with non-gravity!
> They streak on the short cut to the sexual reaction!
> Now, let me tell you whose energies are spent in wrong way,
> The right way to the right mind.
> Go straight into the new light with big courage.[67]

In Japan, the film had become so wildly popular that it had run in movie houses for three years, and it was considered normal to have seen it five or six times. No doubt attempting to capitalize on this commercial and artistic success, an American cast was sent over and rehearsed for two months in preparation for performances at the Nissei theater in Tokyo in the summer of 1965. Even Robbins flew over to spend two weeks to get the cast into top form. Despite the expensive ticket prices (seats were reported to cost the equivalent of a week's salary), the show was sold out nine months in advance. American musicals were so popular in general in the Japanese market that translated versions of *My Fair Lady*, *The Sound of Music*, and *Annie Get Your Gun* (among others) had recently been mounted there with great success.

Memories of the London premiere must have flooded the minds of the promoters. What they had not counted on, however, was that whereas the Londoners knew the music from recordings, the Japanese knew the work from
the film version. The audience's reaction to the staged version was disbelief.
"This couldn't be the complete cast," one complained. "In the movie there
were many more dancers. And why was my favorite number, 'Cool,' played
in front of a drop of a drug store instead of in a large empty garage?" Others
complained that the costumes were not authentically Puerto Rican (despite
the fact that no doubt a very small segment of the Japanese teenage population had ever, to use Sondheim's phrase, "met a Puerto Rican").[68] Clearly the
staged version was not authentic enough to be "real" for these audiences, yet
the production ultimately was a commercial success. Indeed, the *New York
Sunday News* reported in 1979 that, since its opening, there had never been a
time when a stage production of *West Side Story* was not running somewhere
in the world.[69]

"The Composer's Final Intentions"

—program note, West Side Story *full score*

In 1984, near the end of Bernstein's compositional life, the composer recorded his own "definitive" version of two of his theater works, *West Side
Story* and *Candide*. Both featured opera singers instead of theater singers, and
both were followed by publications of the works in full score. Bernstein often
recalled in his later years that he wished he had spent more time composing.
Indeed, decisions as to how much time and energy he could spend on performing, conducting, and composition haunted him throughout his career.
With a reasonable number of musical works, both from art and popular music traditions, under his belt, it is interesting that he chose *West Side Story* as
one to revisit and, further, attempt to immortalize with a definitive full score
and recording. Certainly, it was his most famous and most commercially successful work. However, despite his feelings before the Washington opening,
that his "best" music had been cut down by the collaborative process, he did
not reinstate any of the more extended or operatic versions of many of the
numbers even when he had the opera singers to do so. The recording, featuring a handpicked orchestra and stars Kiri Te Kanawa and José Carreras, was
released on the Deutsche Grammophon label, attempting to fix it for all time

as one of the "classics," a canonization that, in part due to the imprimatur of the Deutsche Grammophon label, made it part of the classical music repertoire. Even a documentary on the making of the *West Side Story* recording was released, to further heighten the sense of urgency and historical import of the recording. And yet, when asked how his new recording differed from versions of the past, Bernstein says:

> There are two big fiddles in the new recording. One is, I'm conducting the score for the first time ever, and the performers are all opera singers. I've always toyed with this idea. It can't be done on the stage, obviously. There is that built-in collision between dance and singing performance in the work. We were very, very lucky with this show, because in every production we've always found people against all odds, who formed casts and could do all the different things they had to do. But there is an ideal way of hearing "One Hand, One Heart," for example. I've always kept it in the back of my mind, feeling that maybe some day I could hear that song sung the way I've always wanted it to be sung, which is quite slow with real operatic voice control and quality. In some ways it's come true on this record, in which I also have a hand-picked orchestra and a fabulous cast.[70]

The "big fiddles" (in the sense of "fiddling with") to which Bernstein refers do not seem particularly big—they are more related to interpretive issues, but are certainly not changes to the musical numbers or even the orchestration. For Bernstein, as for the rest of the world, the film version had become so standardized that the "final intentions" had less to do with the original collaborative process than with the culture's collaborative remaking of the work after its premiere. As Charles Harmon explains in the editor's note to Bernstein's full score, it represents "its original orchestration, practicable for theatrical production, with all underscoring and scene change music intact."[71] Although certainly the publication of a Broadway musical in full score was a signal moment, Bernstein's "original" and "definitive" intentions turn out to be simply the musical as it was written. That Bernstein had to defend his own composition against the film version suggests that even he had lost ownership of it by that time.

AMERIKA: WEST SIDE STORY IN THE TWENTY-FIRST CENTURY

The borrowings, influences, and parodies of *West Side Story* are so numerous and so pervasive that they defy presentation, let alone classification. Ev-

erything from marching-band arrangements, cartoon adaptations, as in the
"West Side Pigeons," to the myriad recordings discussed earlier in this study,
show how pervasive and penetrating has been the musical's influence in many
aspects of American and international culture. To pick one or even a number
of appropriations or reflections out of this dizzying plethora of examples
would give an unbalanced view of *West Side Story*'s influence. However, one
example leads us back to the world of classical art music, not the destination
we would imagine the musical to travel to in musical time and space. As late
as 2001, Canadian composer Chris Paul Harman won the Jules Léger Prize for
New Chamber Music for a work entitled *Amerika*, based on the melodies of
West Side Story. Drawn from the largest pool of entrants to date (122 works
by 89 composers), this national competition resulted in a public concert,
wide publicity, and a radio broadcast on both French and English Canadian
Broadcasting Centre networks. The work was first presented by New Music
Concerts in Toronto, Ontario, conducted by Canadian composer Robert Ait-
ken (who, incidentally, was at the MacDowell Colony with Bernstein in the
late 1960s). Harman describes the genesis of the work:

> When AMERIKA was commissioned by New Music Concerts, it was originally
> to be on a concert called "All Canadian, Eh," so I decided to look for material
> that was decidedly non-Canadian. I had previously been thinking about using
> material from West Side Story as the basis for a piece anyway, as there was
> some technical impetus for using this material. Bernstein's melodies transpose
> in ways that give them a free atonal structure, which with a few more simple
> steps could be quite easily serialized. Having done this, I found it interesting to
> maintain some of the gestures and feelings of the original music after restruc-
> turing the pitch material.[72]

Harman's maintenance of the "gestures and feelings" of the work reflects
not only the original musical but its reception history. As Harman explains,
"The title of course comes from the song whose lyrics feature 'I want to live
in America.' This irony is further encapsulated in the title, whose spelling
with a 'k' is used by the Japanese, the Dutch, and others."[73] Considering that
Harman was born in 1970, almost a decade after the film version of *West Side
Story* was released, the choice of this work over the entire corpus of works
that might easily be seen as "Americana" seems telling. Indeed, Harman's approach reflects the fractured existence that was discussed in the opening pages

of this study. The form of *Amerika* is a series of short musical movements, interspersed with rests from two to seven seconds long. Harman explains, "I like to think of it more like a comic book, where the action takes place within little boxes."[74] He goes on to say:

> I think that this was because I wanted to suggest some of the programmatic elements of the source material (from Bernstein's West Side Story), while treating them in a non-contextual way. I wasn't trying to build a line or a bridge between these different impressions, but wanted to take these elements, which are somewhat popular, romanticized, even schmaltzy, and treat them in a very abstract way.

Described in this way, Harman's approach to the work treats *West Side Story* less as one autonomous musical creation that is alluded to by a later composer, but almost as an entire genre, whose associations and "programmatic elements" are so widely understood and internalized in the culture (even Canadian classical music culture, as it turns out), that they need to be abstracted in order to allow Harman's own compositional space to unfold. Harman's work not only memorializes *West Side Story*, it also evinces a kind of personal ownership over the original material. "As the work progresses," he says, "the identity of the source material is very subtly hinted at, but is never allowed to be released from its context of abstraction."[75] The fact that Harman does not allow the material to be "released" (except at brief moments when Bernstein's score becomes more apparent; the section in example 7.1 foregrounds the melody of "America," the song after which the work was named), yet it is still recognizable to the audience, suggests a deeper intimacy with *West Side Story* than we would imagine four decades after it left the stage.

That this work won a major contemporary competition prize suggests that the subject material has achieved a level of status within art music that Bernstein would not have imagined even twenty years earlier, when he recorded his own final version. Not long after, the *West Side Story Suite*, for violin and orchestra, was recorded and also filmed featuring internationally recognized Joshua Bell as soloist. An adaptation by composer William David Brohn, this work falls quite nicely into the genre of one-movement fantasy pieces for soloist and orchestra, a standard of the nineteenth-century romantic repertoire (Sarasate's *Carmen Fantasy* springs to mind) meant to showcase the violinist's

EXAMPLE 7.1
Chris Paul Harman, *Amerika*, 2001. Courtesy of Chris Paul Harman.

virtuosity against the backdrop of well-loved operatic arias. A beautiful, moving, and elegant work, it transmutes Bernstein's original score into a version less heavy than the *Symphonic Dances* and more allusive than a texted work, and is clearly intended as another way in which the musical repenetrates the classical canon. Bell is pictured on the cover in a black leather jacket, twenty-first-century cool for a twentieth-century classic. The composer's classical composition *Serenade* is paired with the work, along with other (non-texted) theater music by Bernstein. At the time of this writing, Amazon's sales gambit of listing "customers who bought this also bought" shows that patrons exclusively have paired the work with other Joshua Bell recordings, suggesting that it is not Broadway enthusiasts or Bernstein aficionados who are interested in this work, but those who value the classical violin repertoire.

Although *West Side Story* may not, as Agnes de Mille predicted, have started a new, more fluid direction in musical theater, it has also defied Stephen Sondheim's assertion that it was a "dead end." And, unlike Broadway musicals such as *A Chorus Line*, which were wildly successful within the first few years of their premieres, it has continued to be a part of the standard repertoire of American musical theater beyond the initial decade which produced it and whose musical and theatrical styles it represents. Even if it has failed to become a duplicable (or even applicable) theatrical model, *West Side Story* has outlived (and, as we have seen, rebelled against) its own original context, becoming in the process a part of musical consciousness both in America and abroad. The making of the work into a Great American Musical cannot be attributed solely to its creators or publicists, or to those anxious to establish a canon within the repertoire it represents. *West Side*'s stories have continued to be told because American culture still struggles with the artistic, social, and aesthetic issues it raised in the twentieth century. In all likelihood, this has accounted for its prevalence almost fifty years after it should have become hopelessly dated.

At the time of this writing, only two of the authors, Arthur Laurents and Stephen Sondheim, are living. Laurents's recent autobiography, *Original Story By*, and his *Mainly on Directing*, and two recent books on Sondheim (*Sondheim on Music: Minor Details and Major Decisions* by Mark Horowitz and *Sondheim: A Biography* by Meryle Secrest)[76] suggest that the eras these two artists represent are coming to a close, as well. Almost fifty years after the work premiered on Broadway, *West Side Story* seems as prevalent in both theatrical

and musical contexts as in its early history. In its international market pen-
etration, ubiquitous representation in incredibly diverse venues (even recent
paeans to Michael Jackson mention *West Side*'s influence on his dance chore-
ographies), and its iconic status by any measure imaginable, this musical continues to outlive its original material. Although the attraction of the tragic and
timeless story and the quality of the music can explain some of this appeal, it
seems that the ways in which its indigenous and international cultures have
perceived its Americanness are perhaps the key to its success. Not the brave,
green pioneering spirit of *Oklahoma!*, nor the Midwest hometown earnestness
of *The Music Man*, nor the existential Manhattan angst of *A Chorus Line*, nor
the national pastime of *Damn Yankees*, nor the historical panoply of *Love Life*
have taken on the same role as an expression of the American as has *West Side
Story*. That it was about Puerto Rican and immigrant juvenile delinquents in
New York in the 1950s, a constituency that under most circumstances would
never have seen or heard this work, remains a deeply ironic but fascinating
idea about who we think we are.

NOTES

1. Stephen Sondheim, interview by Steven Swayne, in "Hearing Sondheim's
Voices" (PhD diss., University of California, Berkeley, 1999), 346–47.

2. Clearly the photo was staged for publicity, as Anybodys never dances with Maria
or Anita in the show, much less in "graceful positions."

3. John McClain, "Griffith and Prince Steal Early Lead," *New York Journal-
American*, July 14, 1957, 17.

4. *Variety*, February 16, 1972.

5. Richard Watts Jr., "Two on the Aisle," *New York Post*, September 27, 1957.

6. Gerard Fay, "A Musical with a Message: *West Side Story* Sets a Pattern,"
Manchester Guardian.

7. Frank Farrell, *New York Telegram*.

8. Harold Taubman, "A Foot in Each Camp," *New York Times*, October 13, 1957.

9. One of the first "myths" of *West Side Story* that Arthur Laurents wanted to
disabuse me of in our interview was the veracity of the oft-cited "*West Side Story*
Log." Interview with the author, June 3, 2008. The first author to discover that

this log was created after the fact was Humphrey Burton in his biography *Leonard Bernstein*, 270 and passim.

10. Leonard Bernstein Collection, date book series, box 322, folder 1, Library of Congress, Washington, DC.

11. Leonard Bernstein, "Excerpts from a *West Side Story* Log," in *Findings*, 144; and also reprinted in *Leonard Bernstein Conducts "West Side Story,"* with Israel Philharmonic Orchestra, 1985 by Deutsche Grammophon, 415 253-1.

12. "Landmark," 23.

13. Whitney Bolton, "Stage Review: *West Side Story* Bold, Enchanting," *New York Morning Telegraph*, September 28, 1957.

14. "Landmark," 21.

15. "Landmark," 22.

16. Leonard Bernstein to Felicia Bernstein, 15 August 1957, Bernstein Collection, box 5, folder 33.

17. Leonard Bernstein to Felicia Bernstein, 23 August 1957, Bernstein Collection, box 5, folder 33.

18. Richard L. Coe, "One on the Aisle: What's in a Promise?" *Washington Post and Times Herald*, May 1958, A14; Jim O'Conor, "B'Way Goes to the White House," *New York Journal American*, May 9, 1958, 17; "It's Understudy Night," *New York Daily News*, May 9, 1958, 58; Marie McNair, "Curtain Falls to Music of the Stars," *Washington Post*, May 9, 1958; Tom Donnelly, "One Night Stand at the White House," *Washington Daily News*, May 9, 1958, 33; "For Supreme Court Stars Entertain at White House," *Washington Evening Star*, May 9, 1958, B1–5.

19. "Music," *Time*, May 12, 1958, 50.

20. The episode aired on national television on June 29, 1958.

21. Dana Adams Schmidt, "Moiseyev Glows in Report on U.S.," *New York Times*, January 19, 1959.

22. Stuart W. Little, "Theater News: Half of Bolshoi Dancers Attend *West Side Story*," *New York Herald Tribune*, April 30, 1959; Edith Evans Asbury, "*West Side Story* Plays Host to Frolicsome Bolshoi Dancers," *New York Times*, May 1, 1959; "Bolshoi Applauds *West Side Story*," *New York Post*, April 30, 1959.

23. Max Franks, "Drama Mailbag: An American in Moscow Explains Why *West Side Story* Should Go There," *New York Times*, September 13, 1959.

24. The tensions and connections between East and West during the cold war period as they relate to the Broadway musical deserve a much longer discussion than can be afforded in the present study.

25. Louis Calta, "Producers Pleased at Plans in Soviet to Stage U.S. Show," *New York Times*, September 4, 1959.

26. "Russians to Stage *West Side Story*," *New York Times*, December 4, 1959; "Music and Dancing to Be Dropped, Leaving Stark Play on Delinquency," *New York Times*, December 12, 1959.

27. "'Vest Sideskaya Istoria' Puzzles, Thrills Moscow," *New York Herald Tribune*, June 25, 1965.

28. "WSS Is Staged in Soviet," *New York Times*, December 31, 1964.

29. Kenneth Allsop, "Kenneth Allsop's Record Column: Their Jet Song Will Get You," *London Daily Mail*, March 1, 1958, 8. Allsop describes the cast album as "electrifying" and "lyrical."

30. Kenneth Pearson, "The Birth of a Musical," *London Sunday Times*, November 2, 1958, 8.

31. Pearson, "The Birth of a Musical," 8.

32. Pearson, "The Birth of a Musical," 8.

33. Pearson, "The Birth of a Musical," 8.

34. Kenneth Pearson, "Six Lonely Men," *London Sunday Times*, November 16, 1958, 8.

35. Edward Goring, "The Show That Knocks 'MFL' for Six," *London Daily Mail*, September 27, 1958, 3.

36. British Equity allowed the exemption on the condition that English dancers were kept on payroll and trained so that they could start replacing the American cast after about a year. John McClain, "Yanks Dance into London," *New York Journal-American*, October 24, 1958, 25.

37. John Thompson, "Welcoming the Most Fantastic Opening Forty Minutes Ever to Hit the London Theatre: Enter the 'Dansical' New Hit Show Era!" *Express Photo News/Daily Express*, December 13, 1958.

38. Anthony Carthew, "London Cheers New Star Chita as *West Side Story* Wows 'Em," *London Daily Herald*, December 13, 1958.

39. Edward Goring, "They Rose, Roared, Clapped, Cheered," *London Daily Mail*, December 14, 1958.

40. Alan Dent, "Broadway's Version of 'Romeo' is Electrifying," *London News Chronicle*, December 13, 1958.

41. Leonard Lyons, "The Lyons Den," *New York Post*, January 26, 1961, 23. Also William Hickey, "West End Story Princess," *London Daily Express*, December 12, 1958.

42. Carthew, "London Cheers New Star."

43. Peter Brinson, "The New Kind of Dancer," *London Sunday Times*, December 7, 1958.

44. Brinson, "The New Kind of Dancer."

45. W. A. Darlington, "Gang 'Romeo' Musical in Ballet Terms," *London Telegraph*, December 13, 1958; and "The Dancing and the Music," *London Observer*, December 14, 1958, describe it as "dance-drama."

46. Thompson, "Welcoming."

47. "The Theatre: A Musical That Makes the Others Look Pale," *London Sunday Express*, January 12, 1959.

48. Harold Conway, "This Knocks *My Fair Lady* for Six!" *London Daily Sketch*, December 13, 1958. It is interesting that Conway uses the same verbiage as Edward Goring.

49. "Evening Standard Drama Awards: *West Side Story* Defeats *My Fair Lady*," *London Evening Standard*, January 12, 1959, 5.

50. Harold Hobson, "Theatre: A Warning from Noel," *Sunday Times*, December 13, 1958. Humphrey Burton recalls that Hobson's pan of *Candide* caused an angry reaction which resulted in Bernstein's public attack of Hobson on live British television. See Humphrey Burton, "Bernstein and the British: A Tempestuous Affair," *BBC Music Magazine*, May 1994, 20.

51. Kenneth Pearson, "Plays and Players: 'West Side' Goes East," *London Sunday Times*, 1958.

52. "Landmark," 23.

53. Gerard Fay, "A Musical with a Message," *Manchester Guardian*, December 12, 1958, 8.

54. "*West Side Story* Wows West End; Top Musical Sensation Since *Okla*," *Variety*, December 17, 1958.

55. Alice Griffin, "Opening Night Glamour at *West Side Story*," *The Theatre*, June 1960, 26–27.

56. Brooks Atkinson, "Theatre: Musical is Back," *New York Times*, April 28, 1960.

57. James J. Marooney of NBC's *Today* show to Roger Stevens, 25 September 1957, on the network's coverage of the opening night party, Roger Stevens Collection, box 43, folder 3, Library of Congress.

58. Harold Prince to Roger Stevens, 28 April 1960, Stevens Collection, box 43, folder 1.

59. Robert Saffron, "At Winter Garden: *West Side Story* Again on Broadway," *New York World-Telegram*, April 28, 1960.

60. Harold Prince and Robert Griffith to *West Side Story* investors, 7 November 1960, Stevens Collection, box 43, folder 1.

61. Described by John McClain as "a new champion in the nothing sweepstakes," *Wildcat* was neither a commercial nor critical success and closed the following June.

62. Harold Prince and Robert Griffith to *West Side Story* investors, 5 December 1960, Stevens Collection, box 43, folder 1.

63. Stuart Little, "Theater News," *New York Herald Tribune*, December 15, 1960.

64. Thomas M. Pryor, "*West Side Story* Sought for Film; Seven Arts Near Completion of Deal for Stage Musical—Madison Ave. Chided," *New York Times*, July 17, 1958.

65. "16,000 Stolen during Running of Gang Movie," *New York Herald Tribune*, February 16, 1962.

66. Robbins, difficult to work with at the best of times, was fired partway through production. Although the film version of *West Side Story* deserves a full-length examination of its own, the present study will consider it at least as a further extension of the revision and reception that the work went through during its

initial incarnation. For a discussion of changes made to the film version, see Nigel Simeone, *Leonard Bernstein: "West Side Story"* (Aldershot: Ashgate, 2009).

67. "Osaka Cops Adopt *West Side Story* to Hit Own Punks," *Variety*, March 28, 1962.

68. John Paul, "*West Side Story* in Japan," *Dance Magazine*, April 1965, 35–38.

69. *New York Sunday News*, December 2, 1979, 118.

70. "Landmark," 23.

71. Charles Harmon, "Editor's Note," in *West Side Story* (New York: Amberson/ Boosey & Hawkes, 1994).

72. Interview by Paul Steenhuisen in October 2001, "Composer to Composer," *The Whole Note*, November 1–December 7, 2001.

73. Chris Paul Harman, program note, *Amerika*, New Music Concerts, May 26, 2001.

74. Chris Paul Harman in "Composer to Composer," interview by Paul Steenhuisen in October 2001, *The Whole Note*, November 1–December 7, 2001.

75. Harman, program note.

76. Mark Eden Horowitz, *Sondheim on Music: Minor Details and Major Decisions* (Lanham, MD: Scarecrow Press, 2003); and Secrest, *Stephen Sondheim*.

8

"Finale"

Opening night of *West Side Story* in December of 2008 would have seemed a strange sight indeed to the play's original audience. An automatic ticket reader now greeted attendees to the intensely turquoise lobby of the National Theatre in Washington, and Arthur Laurents's more racy and in-your-face directorial style would have left a late 1950s audience even more astonished than they were when they first saw this work, over fifty years ago. One thing that had not changed was the musical's lasting influence. Bernstein's son Alexander greeted the audience and talked about the work's profound influence on both his family and American musical theater. December 15, 2008, was declared "West Side Story Day" in DC. The curtain warmer and the branded products for sale (now hoodies and wool caps, the uniform of contemporary would-be gang members) are similar in design to the logos produced for the movie version, now also over forty years old. The addition of a child singing "Somewhere" (instead of an offstage woman's voice) was now reminiscent of Bernstein's *Mass*, another product of Bernstein's interest in music for the common man that seemed to feel right for this new, updated production. Although the addition of Spanish dialogue and lyrics was the most remarkable remake of the show, so many of the images and associations we have with *West Side Story* have been added back into the original. Laurents himself wandered through the house at intermission, recognized by almost none of the audience members, and memories of that first night in Washington in

August of 1957 must have been in his mind as he took the pulse of the night's full and enthusiastic crowd. Laurents's remake, inspired by his beloved and recently departed partner Tom Hatcher, sings with the ethos of a new century, a new revivication of a more authentic Hispanic voice in a post–*In the Heights* world. Sondheim has agreed (perhaps with relief, considering his aversion to his own lyrics) to have "I Feel Pretty" translated into Spanish by Lin-Manuel Miranda, composer of the successful musical about another Manhattan locale, Washington Heights. After the DC previews, Laurents decided to drop the subtitles, which have been projected onto screens on either side of the stage. In his memoir of the production, *Mainly on Directing*, the playwright reports that audiences were even more engaged than when they (presumably) had a better understanding of what was being communicated in that song and in other Spanish-language-dominated scenes. Was this due to the power of the dramaturgy, the music, or both? Does *West Side Story* transcend language entirely, now that it is so well known that audiences do not even need to understand some of the lines? Certainly for Laurents, this is the feeling, if not the exact letter, of what the original should have been.

Between *West Side Story*'s genesis as a tragedy on Catholic and Jewish tensions and its eventual canonization as a "great" Latin-tinged Broadway musical stand a great many collaborative decisions and compromises, between creators and performers but also involving audiences. The very rich source material from which Bernstein took his musical inspiration and influences shows not just one composer's search for an appropriate sound and style; it addresses much deeper issues of "originality" and the autonomous artwork than are normally raised by the already collaborative nature of the Broadway musical. That Bernstein's score has remained popular and, ultimately, "singable," fifty years after its premiere, shows how far tastes and attitudes (accepting of darker subject matter, as evidenced in musicals such as Sondheim's *Passion*) have changed over the last several decades. Indeed, Stravinsky's *Rite of Spring* can hardly still be considered shocking, especially after generations of composers' styles have echoed it. Similarly, the "modern" aspects of *West Side Story*'s subject matter and score have become tame by today's standards, no longer making audiences or critics feel that they have experienced a "subway mugging set to music."

The musical's treatment of "Hispanicism," both musically and culturally, also now seems quite dated, and it will be interesting to follow the reception of this aspect of the musical in our postmodern and politically correct culture. It seems difficult to imagine an audience's acceptance of this kind of ethnic stereotyping were the musical written in 2007, not 1957. Indeed, Harold Prince's production of *Show Boat* (also canonic and, of course, much older) was picketed in tryouts in Toronto in the early 1990s because of its perceived blatant racism. Although *West Side Story* comes from a much later generation, it may simply take longer for audiences to react in the same way, and it is unclear whether Laurents's updated version will remove completely any perceived ethnic stereotyping in the work. Considering also that *Show Boat* (like *West Side Story*) was considered a highly sensitive plea for tolerance and understanding, it is interesting that it eventually came to stand for that which it most greatly opposed.

In a similar vein, the treatment of female characters now seems a little dated, as the continual domination of female stars (Bernadette Peters, Sarah Brightman, Bebe Neuwirth) in musical theater has reversed the "nonstar" objectives of *West Side Story*'s creators. Indeed, the new style of musical theater that Agnes de Mille predicted would follow from *West Side Story* has not entirely come to pass, or at least not in the straight line of development that she (and certain theater critics) predicted. As for the conflation of the ethnic "other" with female characters, this seems to be palatable today only in musicals whose plots take place in an earlier historical time period (*Miss Saigon*, the animated *Pocahontas*, and Elton John's *Aida*, for instance). The collection of Disney musicals appearing over the last decade prominently feature strong female characters (Belle in *Beauty and the Beast*) and characters such as Maureen in *Rent* make Anybodys look very old-fashioned by comparison.

Even if *West Side Story*'s social message seems to be as relevant to today's America as it was in 1957, the treatment of the subject matter (again, considered deeply sensitive by most in its time) would probably be too unrealistic and stylized to make the same impact today. And, although Arthur Laurents felt that *West Side Story*'s message was the most important and enduring aspect of the musical, one wonders how much more cultural work could have been done if the protagonists had been white and African-American, instead of white and Puerto Rican. Certainly, this would have been considered even more highly controversial than the tensions that were portrayed in *West Side Story*, but such a treatment might have focused the work more on specific legislative issues regarding civil rights in America than on the more general issues of universal tolerance in a postwar environment.

As late as 2003, a number of musicals playing on Broadway showed a strong bond with their ancestor, *West Side Story*. The Greg Kotis and Mark Hollmann musical *Urinetown*, which sends up a number of Broadway musicals as part of its allusive language, references Robbins's finger-snapping choreography of "Cool" and an updated "Rumble" as part of its fin de siècle black comedy. *Hairspray*, which won the Tony Award for Best Musical, depicts a teenage romance between star-crossed lovers (both fat/thin and black/white) set against a midcentury period backdrop. Like *West Side Story*, much of the music of these teenagers has more to do with the tastes of its middle-aged audience (in this case, 1970s and 1980s pop) than with the tastes of the protagonists whose struggle it ostensibly portrays (the same could be said of *Mamma Mia*, a musical set to the music of ABBA, a group whose popularity surged in the 1970s, or *Movin' Out*, which capitalizes on the mostly decades-old songs of a graying Billy Joel). *Gypsy*, in a revival directed by Sam Mendes, brought back the collaborative work of Arthur Laurents, Jerome Robbins, and Stephen Sondheim from the early post–*West Side Story* era, although Arthur Laurents was to revive it only a few years later. Although Sondheim seems quick to dismiss the impact of *West Side Story*, its success paved the way for this, and his subsequent musicals. Yet another recent recording of *West Side Story* in a more operatic guise (featuring renowned lyric soprano Barbara Bonney, Michael Ball, the Royal Philharmonic Orchestra, and conductor Barry Wordsworth), released on MVC Records, attests to the longevity of Bernstein's score but also to the continuing transformation from a "great musical" into a "great opera." It is difficult to predict how *West Side Story* will be remembered or portrayed in the coming decades, as we move farther and farther from the mambo craze of the mid-1950s. It seems, however, that, although the characters, situations, and musical styles of *West Side Story* have become increasingly dated, its influence has become permanent. Indeed, one short-lived musical, Paul Simon's 1998 *The Capeman* (based on his best-selling CD of songs about gang warfare between Puerto Ricans and "whites" in 1959 New York City) seems quite directly indebted to *West Side Story*. There is even a number in which Sal (like Tony) is cajoled by Hernandez (like Riff) into joining with the gang to protect "the neighborhood." More generally, one might argue that the trend toward highly integrated (in the music/dance/theater/spectacle sense) musicals or serious subjects, beginning with some biblical ones (*Godspell, Jesus Christ Superstar*) and moving on to *Les Misérables, Phantom of the Opera*, and the recent Disney vehicles such as *The Lion King*, had inspiration or encouragement from what the *West Side Story* creative team accomplished—often with more modest means—in the late 1950s.

As I conclude the current study, Bernstein's description of his own score as "one piece, not many" reflects my impression that this is "many perspectives, not one." Although many more studies could be written on any of the perspectives I have presented here, some intriguing issues suggest new avenues for scholarship. Although this book addresses aspects of international reception that are the direct result of the film version, it does not specifically discuss the film. There are two reasons for this: the film shows a fairly substantial departure in the ordering of numbers from the stage musical, reflecting in some ways Robbins's rethinking of the structure and ordering of numbers, and thereby becoming much more his vision (along with that of codirector Robert Wise) than the vision of his original collaborators. Secondly, the film version is in and of itself a topic that should be discussed in a separate and lengthy study, and perhaps fits more into the purview of film scholarship than musicology.

Although gender is discussed in this study in terms of the portrayal of female characters, an equal treatment of male (and specifically gay male) identity in the work would yield interesting insights into the gender politics of the 1950s. Writers on gay male life at midcentury (specifically Charles Kaiser's *The Gay Metropolis: 1940–1996*)[1] and biographers of all the collaborators have singled out the importance of sexual identity for the authors during this period, and there seems little question that the "Somewhere" the musical seeks includes a place for gay identity in the 1950s. D. A. Miller's *Place for Us*, a study of gay men and the Broadway musical, uses, not insignificantly, a line from "Somewhere" as its title.[2]

Along with the more overt Puerto Rican stereotyping in this work, the conflation of African-American identity with Hispanic, both musically and in the treatment of prejudice issues in *West Side Story*, invites further study. The kind of integration of European classical material with African-American elements that Bernstein lays out in great detail in his 1939 Harvard bachelor's thesis, "The Absorption of Race Elements into American Music," suggests that Bernstein's absorption of the Hispanic could be read as a stand-in for the African-American. Considering the racial tensions in the United States in the late 1950s and 1960s, it seems plausible that the creators simply could not address these issues as openly as they might have liked. A promoter who was considering the work for a West Coast audience wrote to Cheryl Crawford in a way that hits on the issue.

> I read "West Side Story" over the weekend. Since you asked for a quick answer, I am giving it to you so that you won't be held up in any other potential plans. I thought the writing very powerful and I could feel a lot of Jerry's collaborative touch in the stagecraft. The combination of Bernstein, Laurents and Robbins certainly seems "right" for this project.
>
> I realize that the construction will be subject to many changes in the rewriting but even anticipating them I have one deep reservation which is applicable to your interests as well as my own regarding the suitability of premiering this work in our Season. As you know, our Los Angeles Auditorium presents certain censorship problems because of the Church ownership. While we don't have to be Pollyanna in our attitudes, we do have to be damned careful about the language we use. Where a show has been first presented in New York and accepted there, it is not too much of a problem to make the few changes necessary for the piece to be palatable to the Church authorities, and such changes have never yet hurt any show that we've played because the basic values in the show were already established and the objectionable matter was not vital to success. But when you're doing a new show, to have to censor it before it is really born, may tend to destroy indigenous characters. For example, "Porgy and Bess" could never have been premiered in this Auditorium. The same applies to many other shows that we've played very successfully later in their careers. I also have some doubts as to whether this kind of "sterner stuff" theatrically, works as well outside of New York except in the customary tryout cities. I do not disparage the intelligence or the tastes of our audiences out here, but I have leaned to lighter fare where original presentations are concerned.[3]

This letter, from Edwin Lester, general director of the Los Angeles Civic Light Opera Association, suggests—without daring to state it—that it was not just the more "stern" aspects of juvenile delinquency that would offend his audience, but the interracial ones. Indeed, at the time that *West Side Story* was so wildly popular in London, stage plays which addressed white-black relationships were also running quite successfully. Although works such as *The Cool World* portrayed a specifically African-American gang life, *West Side*

Story almost seems tame, a kind of toned-down "white" version for a middle-class audience in America. During this time period, African-American film versions of works in the classical tradition (*Carmen Jones* and—in the mid-1960s—*Black Orpheus*) suggest that these two cultural worlds were so far apart that they would not have been believable (nor, arguably, palatable) to American audiences if presented as the "warring factions" of *West Side Story*. And yet, in the same way that rock and roll was the "real" music of teenagers during this time period, it was not so much the Puerto Rican problem, but the much more serious white/African-American dichotomy, that the work more obliquely addressed.

There are other aspects of 1950s culture which *West Side Story* seems connected to; specifically, the idea of "cool" as it relates to not only race relations but to the emotional aesthetic of this era. Arthur Laurents claims that the word was used as a result of the musical and its popularity. Peter J. Stearns's *American Cool: Constructing a 20th Century Emotional Style* suggests that Laurents's idea was not unique but did indeed play into a larger attempt for Americans to forge a particular psychological identity.[4] But we must ask ourselves, since the original "Dance at the Gym" scene included an "atom bomb" mambo, whether politics of the cold war played more important a role than has been suggested in this study. Was the irrational and pointless competition between the Jets and the Sharks seen as a kind of metaphor for other, large-scale tensions, most notably—as Ralph Locke has suggested—the one between the West and the USSR?[5]

Although this study refers directly and alludes to cut numbers from the score, a more detailed study of Bernstein's sketch material and the compositional process (including Bernstein's relationship with orchestrators Irwin Kostal and Sid Ramin, largely responsible for the "sound" of *West Side Story*) would provide a deeper understanding of the work and also reveal it as much more "fiddled with" (to use Bernstein's term) than we might think. Although there were fewer changes during the rehearsal process than many musicals endure, *West Side Story* did undergo a number of substantial changes early on in its history. Specifically, the transition from a more operatic work (although "operatic" qualities have always been attributed to it, even in its final version) to a stage work suggests that *West Side Story* was in fact more integrated and organic than the musical we know. Although audiences and critics alike have learned *West Side Story* in its final version, a new version that incorporates

Bernstein's more operatic portions might well reveal to us a work that we find even more compelling than the musical in its final form. A concert at the Library of Congress just a few years ago of "cut numbers" and different versions of some of the songs suggests that audiences and scholars are ready and eager to hear these different musical "stories."

But for all its seeming longevity, something is happening to *West Side Story*. In the summer of 1999 I saw two professional productions. One was in London, England, at the Prince of Wales Theatre, the other at the Stratford Festival in Ontario, Canada. Both touted "authenticity" to the original in their promotional material, as a selling point but also as evidence of the artistic superiority of their production over others. For the most part, "authenticity" meant a dogged adhesion to Robbins's original choreography and more or less faithful reading of the music. Of course, these two performances could not have been more different. The London production, directed by Arthur Laurents, infused the characters with more passion, something he would continue and expand on in his recent Broadway revival, but the actors seemed less confident in delivering the piece, as though they were mounting a museum piece that they were afraid to alter.[6]

The production at Stratford departed more strongly from the original, with chain-link fences moving around on wheels, creative staging, a black Anita (lending a harder edge to the racial implications of the story), and a starker ending: whereas usually the rival gangs experience a momentary understanding as a result of the tragedy, here both groups maintained their hatred and moved off in separate directions. Instead of having Maria proudly follow the funeral cortege, director Kelly Robinson had the abandoned Maria kneel over Tony's body as the curtain descended to the strains of the "Somewhere" motive. There was in fact no actual curtain, but a huge scrim painted like a brick wall, which descended and also encroached from each side so that all that was left at the end was a tiny window in which the two figures remained. I thought this was tremendous, but because a new act of interpretation had been performed upon the piece. And I realized that this was unusual. However, marring the quality of this otherwise good production was the performance of soprano Ma-Anne Dionisio in the role of Maria, just off her recent success in the wildly popular Toronto production of *Miss Saigon*. Miss Dionisio seemed to fight her way through Bernstein's score, creating more than a few touchy moments, but no one seemed to mind this. In fact, it seemed that a good part of the audience was there expressly to see her. This, for them, was just another version of the *Saigon* story, with different music, and, of course, without the ubiquitous helicopter. Here the audience had remade it, inauthentically, into the star vehicle that it was never meant to be.

One of the best, most satisfying productions of *West Side Story*, with vocal talent, acting ability, good dancing, a competent orchestra, creative lighting, and astonishingly good set design, was at the Pittsford-Mendon High School in Rochester, New York, which I attended. Tickets were three dollars. The students performed with vitality and an innate understanding of the piece, not just of the problems of its teenage protagonists. Perhaps these performers were young enough that they could let go of any preconceptions as to how it should look or sound. In that way, it was the most authentic in its essence. I thought back on reports from the 1950s of the initial auditions for *West Side Story*. The creators considered trying out hundreds of high school students and talented street kids for the roles, and I realized that this production was close to what Jerome Robbins really envisioned. In 2009, the Stratford Festival mounted a second, new production of the work, directed by Gary Griffin, which *Toronto Star* theater critic Richard Ouzounian has called "the best production of a musical in Stratford's long and distinguished list of triumphs, but it may well be one of the best productions of a musical I've seen anywhere in the world in 55 years of theatregoing."[7] Citing the adaptation of Robbins's choreography for a thrust stage, and particularly the performance of actor Paul Nolan as Tony, Ouzounian summarizes the production as "perfection." As an audience member who has seen many productions of this musical, I was also astonished by this production, particularly the emphasis on Laurents's text. Griffin wanted the actors to focus on the text in the same way they would were they acting in a Shakespeare play, and the deliveries of lines were so nuanced and powerful that they brought a new appreciation of Laurents's stagecraft. Paul Nolan was the standout performer, and no doubt the best Tony I have ever seen. When asked how he saw the work, from an actor's perspective, he remarked, "It is a masterpiece. It is almost perfect."[8]

The wild success that has been enjoyed by this production and Laurents's own on Broadway, concurrently, suggests that whatever aspects of the work may have been a part of 1950s culture, the underlying values and the quality of the music, choreography, lyrics, and book will continue to keep this work in the repertoire for many years to come and have transcended their original context. The work of the present study has not been to review the musical's history dispassionately or to valorize it, but instead to show that artistic works of great quality, like this one, are rich particularly as a result of their formative processes and the many layers of nuance, meaning, and connection that they form within themselves and with the culture that surrounds them. The interstices that these stories have revealed and discussed tempt us away from simple acceptance of *West Side* as a "masterpiece" and instead ask us to consider the broader and deeper implications of this and other musicals. As scholarship continues to expand and embrace the musical, and new productions revisit this work, many more of *West Side*'s stories will be told by the many collaborators who have made and continue to make it one of the greatest achievements of the American musical theater.

NOTES

1. Charles Kaiser, *The Gay Metropolis, 1940–1996* (Boston: Houghton Mifflin, 1997).

2. D. A. Miller, *Place for Us.*

3. Edwin Lester, general director of Los Angeles Civic Light Opera Association to Cheryl Crawford, 6 December 1956, Cheryl Crawford Collection, "Series V: Unproduced Works," box 83, folder 4, New York Public Library for the Performing Arts.

4. Peter J. Stearns, *American Cool: Constructing a Twentieth-Century Emotional Style* (New York: New York University Press, 1994).

5. Ralph P. Locke, "The Border Territory Between Classical and Broadway."

6. The authenticity of the production seemed particularly marred by the performers' New York accents, which resembled more closely the inflections of Scotland. One line was delivered sounding like "Get off me turf!"

7. Richard Ouzounian, "This Story Achieves Greatness," *Toronto Star*, June 8, 2009.

8. Paul Nolan, interview with author, August 21, 2009.

A

Lyrics to Select Songs

"I Feel Pretty"
Act 2, scene 1

I feel pretty,
Oh, so pretty,
I feel pretty, and witty, and bright,
And I pity
Any girl who isn't me tonight.

I feel charming,
Oh, so charming—
It's alarming how charming I feel,
And so pretty
That I hardly can believe I'm real.

See the pretty girl in that mirror there;
Who can that attractive girl be?
Such a pretty face,
Such a pretty dress,
Such a pretty smile,
Such a pretty me!

I feel stunning
And entrancing—
Feel like running and dancing for joy,
For I'm loved
By a pretty wonderful boy!

(Rosalia and Consuelo)
Have you met my good friend Maria,
The craziest girl on the block?
You'll know her the minute you see her—
She's the one who is in an advanced state of shock.

She thinks she's in love.
She thinks she's in Spain.
She isn't in love,
She's merely insane.

It must be the heat
Or some rare disease
Or too much to eat,
Or maybe it's fleas.

Keep away from her—
Send for Chino!
This is not the Mar-
Ia we know!

Modest and pure,
Polite and refined,
Well-bred and mature
And out of her mind!

(Maria)
I feel pretty,
Oh, so pretty,
That the city should give me its key.
A committee
Should be organized to honor me.

I feel dizzy,
I feel sunny,
I feel fizzy and funny and fine,
And so pretty,
Miss America can just resign!
See the pretty girl in that mirror there:

(Rosalia and Consuelo)
What mirror where?

(Maria)
Who can that attractive girl be?

(Rosalia and Consuelo)
Which? What? Where? Whom?

(Maria)
Such a pretty face,
Such a pretty dress,
Such a pretty smile,
Such a pretty me!

(All)
I feel stunning
And entrancing—
Feel like running and dancing for joy,
For I'm loved
By a pretty wonderful boy!

"Something's Coming"
Act 1, scene 2

Who knows?
(Music starts as he sings)
Could be! . . .
Who knows? . . .
There's something due any day;
I will know right away
Soon as it shows.

It may come cannonballin' down through the sky,
Gleam in its eye,
Bright as a rose!
Who knows? . . .
It's only just out of reach,
Down the block, on a beach,
Under a tree.
I got a feeling there's a miracle due,
Gonna come true,
Coming to me!

Could it be? Yes, it could.
Something's coming, something good,
If I can wait!
Something's coming, I don't know what it is
But it is
Gonna be great!

With a click, with a shock,
Phone'll jingle, door'll knock,
Open the latch!
Something's coming, don't know when, but it's soon—
Catch the moon,
One-handed catch!

Around the corner,
Or whistling down the river,
Come on—deliver
To me!

Will it be? Yes, it will.
Maybe just by holding still
It'll be there!
Come on, something, come on in, don't be shy,
Meet a guy,
Pull up a chair!

The air is humming,

And something great is coming!
Who knows?
It's only just out of reach,
Down the block, on a beach . . .
Maybe tonight . . .

Officer Krupke
Act 2, number 14

ACTION: Dear kindly Sergeant Krupke,
                      You gotta understand,
                      It's just our bringin' upke
                      That gets us out of hand.
                      Our mothers all are junkies,
                      Our fathers all are drunks.
                      Golly Moses,
                      Natcherly we're punks.

TUTTI: Gee, Officer Krupke, we're very upset;
                      We never had the love that ev'ry child oughta get.
                      We ain't no delinquents,
                      We're misunderstood.
                      Deep down inside us there is good!
                      There is good!
                      There is good, there is good, there is untapped good.
                      Like inside, the worst of us is good!

SKIT 1
SNOWBOY: (imitating Krupke) That's a touching good story.
ACTION: Lemme tell it to the world!
SNOWBOY: (shoving him) Just tell it to the judge.
ACTION: (to Diesel) Dear kindly judge your honor,
                      My parents treat me rough.
                      With all their marijuana,
                      They won't give me a puff.
                      They didn't wanna have me,
                      But somehow I was had.
                      Leapin' lizards,
                      That's why I'm so bad!

DIESEL:	(imitating Judge) Right! Officer Krupke, you're really a square; This boy don't need a judge, he needs an analyst's care! It's just his neurosis that oughta be curbed. He's psychologically disturbed! I'm disturbed! We're disturbed, we're disturbed, we're the most disturbed, Like we're psychologically disturbed.
SKIT 2 DIESEL:	(imitating Judge) In the opinion of this court, this child is depraved on account he ain't had a normal home.
ACTION:	Hey, I'm depraved on account I'm deprived!
DIESEL:	So take him to a headshrinker
ACTION:	(to A-Rab) My father is a bastard, My ma's an SOB My grandpa's always plastered, My grandma pushes tea. My sister wears a mustache, My brother wears a dress. Goodness gracious, That's why I'm a mess!
A-RAB:	(imitating psychiatrist) Yes! Officer Krupke, you're really a slob, This boy don't need a doctor, just a good honest job. Society's played him a terrible trick, And sociologically he's sick!
ACTION:	I am sick!
TUTTI:	We are sick, we are sick, we are sick, sick, sick, Like we're sociologically sick!
SKIT 3: A-RAB:	(imitating psychiatrist) In my opinion, this child don't need to have his head shrunk at all. Juvenile delinquency is purely a social disease!

ACTION:	Hey, I got a social disease
ARAB:	So take him to a social worker!
ACTION:	(to Baby John) Dear kindly social worker,
	They say go earn a buck,
	Like be a soda jerker,
	Which means like be a schmuck.
	It's not I'm antisocial,
	I'm only antiwork.
	Glory osky,
	that's why I'm a jerk!
BABY JOHN:	(imitating female social worker) Eek!
	Officer Krupke, you've done it again.
	This boy don't need a job, he needs a year in the pen.
	It ain't just a question of misunderstood;
	Deep down inside him, he's no good.
ACTION:	I'm no good!
TUTTI:	We're no good, we're no good, we're no earthly good,
	Like the best of us is no damn good!
JUDGE:	The trouble is he's crazy.
PSYCH.:	The trouble is he drinks.
SOCIAL WORKER:	The trouble is he's lazy.
JUDGE:	The trouble is he stinks.
PSYCH:	The trouble is he's growing.
SOCIAL WORKER:	The trouble is he's grown.
TUTTI:	Krupke, we got troubles of our own!
	Gee, Officer Krupke, we're down on our knees,
	'Cause no one wants a fellow with a social disease.
	Gee, Officer Krupke, What are we to do?
	Gee, Officer Krupke, krup you!

Chronology

1944 Leonard Bernstein and Jerome Robbins premiere *Fancy Free* ballet, American Ballet Theatre. Bernstein, Robbins, Betty Comden, and Adolph Green premiere *On the Town*, Adelphi Theatre.

1949 Robbins choreographs *The Guests*, a ballet about star-crossed lovers. Montgomery Clift consults Robbins about portraying Romeo for an *Omnibus* telecast. (Actor Kevin McCarthy was playing Romeo in an *Omnibus* telecast, and apparently worked with Clift on his interpretation. Presumably Clift at the same time consulted Robbins on the characterization.) Robbins approaches Bernstein and Laurents about a possible musical based on *Romeo and Juliet*.

1955 **Summer:** Laurents and Bernstein approach Robbins about *Serenade*, a work about homosexual identity; when discussing the *Romeo* project, they glance at a *Los Angeles Times* story and change the locale to the West Side of Manhattan and the rival gangs to so-called Americans and Puerto Ricans. **October:** Laurents meets young lyricist Stephen Sondheim at a party and brings him on board; work begins in earnest.

1956 **July:** Cheryl Crawford and Roger Stevens sign contract to produce.

1957 **April:** Backers' meetings prove unsuccessful and Cheryl Crawford backs out. **May:** Casting takes place, now with producers Robert Griffiths and Harold Prince. **June:** Casting complete. **July:** In production, change of name from *Gangway!* to *West Side Story.* **August:** Opens to previews in the National Theatre, Washington, DC. **September:** Opens Broadway, Winter Garden Theatre.

1958 **April:** Loses Best Musical to *The Music Man* at Tony Awards, wins for choreography and scenic design. **May:** Command performance by principals at White House irks New York fans, receives substantial press coverage. **November:** British production opens Manchester, England. **December:** British production opens, West End, London.

1959 **January:** Wins *Evening Standard* Theatre Award, London. **April:** Notable cold war commentary appears in press as Bolshoi Ballet dancers attend production in New York. **June:** U.S. nine-month tour begins.

1960 **April:** Reopens in New York as first revival, Winter Garden Theatre.

1961 **January:** International nine-month tour begins, with the show visiting seven countries. **October:** Film version opens.

1962 **April:** Film wins ten Oscars, including Best Picture and Best Directing. **May:** *Stan Kenton's "West Side Story"* wins Grammy for Best Jazz Recording by a Large Group.

1964 **April:** City Center production, New York, showcasing Debbie Allen.

1980 **February:** New York revival, Minskoff Theatre.

1984 Bernstein's recording with Kiri Te Kanawa and José Carreras released.

1985 Recording wins Grammy for Best Musical Show Album.

1996 *Songs of West Side Story*, in which most numbers of the show are covered by famous pop artists, released by RCA Victor.

2008 **December:** Previews of Laurents's revival, National Theatre, Washington, DC.

2009 **March:** Laurents's revival opens New York, Palace Theatre. **June:** Karen Olivo (as Anita) wins Tony Award for Best Performance by a Featured Actress in a Musical.

C

Cast and Crew of Various Productions, Including Award Nominations and Wins

1957–1959 PRODUCTION

Cast

Tony: Larry Kert
Maria: Carol Lawrence
Bernardo: Ken Le Roy
Anita: Chita Rivera
Riff: Mickey Calin
Anybodys: Lee Becker

Crew

Producers: Robert E. Griffith and Harold S. Prince
Musical Director: Max Goberman
Director: Jerome Robbins
Choreographers: Jerome Robbins and Peter Gennaro
Set Design: Oliver Smith
Costume Design: Irene Sharaff
Lighting Design: Jean Rosenthal
Sound Design: Sound Associates, Inc.
Production Stage Manager: Ruth Mitchell
Stage Manager: Harry Howell

Award Nominations

1958 Tony Award Best Musical

1958 Tony Award Best Featured Actress in a Musical (Carol Lawrence)

1958 Tony Award Best Costume Design (Irene Sharaff)

1958 Tony Award Best Conductor and Musical Director (Max Goberman)

Awards Won

1958 Tony Award Best Scenic Design (Oliver Smith)

1958 Tony Award Best Choreography (Jerome Robbins)

1960 PRODUCTION

Cast

Tony: Larry Kert

Maria: Carol Lawrence

Bernardo: George Marcy

Anita: Allyn Ann McLerie

Riff: Thomas Hasson

Anybodys: Pat Birch

Crew

Producers: Robert E. Griffith and Harold S. Prince

Musical Director: Joseph Lewis

Director: Jerome Robbins

Choreographers: Jerome Robbins and Peter Gennaro

Set Design: Oliver Smith

Costume Design: Irene Sharaff

Lighting Design: Jean Rosenthal

Production Stage Manager: Joe Calvan

Stage Manager: Ross Hertz

Award Nominations

None

Awards Won

None

1964 PRODUCTION

Cast
Tony: Don McKay
Maria: Julia Migenes
Bernardo: Jay Norman
Anita: Luba Lisa
Riff: James Moore
Anybodys: Erin Martin

Crew
Producers: New York City Center Light Opera Company
Musical Director: Charles Jaffe
Director: Gerald Freedman
Choreographers: Tom Abbott and Peter Gennaro
Set Design: Peter Wolf
Costume Design: Irene Sharaff
Lighting Design: Jean Rosenthal
Production Stage Manager: Herman Shapiro
Stage Manager: Lo Hardin

Award Nominations
1964 Tony Award Best Conductor and Musical Director (Charles Jaffe)
1964 Tony Award Best Producer (Musical)

Awards Won
None

1980 PRODUCTION

Cast
Tony: Ken Marshall
Maria: Jossie de Guzman
Bernardo: Héctor Jaime Mercado
Anita: Debbie Allen
Riff: James J. Mellon
Anybodys: Missy Whitchurch

Crew

Producers: Gladys Rackmil, The John F. Kennedy Center for the Performing Arts, and James M. Nederlander, in association with Zev Bufman

Associate Producers: Allan Tessler, Steven Jacobson, and Stewart F. Lane

Musical Directors: John DeMain and Donald Jennings

Directors: Jerome Robbins and Gerald Freedman

Choreographers: Jerome Robbins and Peter Gennaro

Set Design: Oliver Smith

Costume Design: Irene Sharaff

Lighting Design: Jean Rosenthal

Sound Design: Jack Mann

Production Stage Manager: Jack Horrigan

Stage Manager: Brenna Krupa

Award Nominations

1980 Tony Award Best Featured Actress in a Musical (Debbie Allen)

1980 Tony Award Best Featured Actress in a Musical (Jossie de Guzman)

1980 Tony Award Reproduction (Play or Musical)

Awards Won

1980 Drama Desk Award Outstanding Featured Actress in a Musical (Debbie Allen)

2009 PRODUCTION

Cast

Tony: Matt Cavenaugh

Maria: Josefina Scaglione

Bernardo: George Akram

Anita: Karen Olivo

Riff: Cody Green

Anybodys: Tro Shaw

Crew

Producers: Kevin McCollum, James L. Nederlander, Jeffrey Seller, Terry Allen Kramer, Sander Jacobs, Roy Furman/Jill Furman Willis, Freddy DeMann, Robyn Goodman/Walt Grossman, Hal Luftig, Roy Miller, The Weinstein

Company, and Broadway Across America (John Gore, CEO; Thomas B. Mc-
Grath, chairman; Beth Williams, COO and head of production)
Associate Producer: LAMS Entertainment
Musical Director: Patrick Vaccariello
Director: Arthur Laurents
Choreographers: Joey McKneely, based on a conception by Jerome Robbins
Set Design: James Youmans
Costume Design: David C. Woolard
Lighting: Howell Binkley
Sound Design: Dan Moses Schreier
Production Stage Manager: Joshua Halperin
Stage Manager: Lisa Dawn Cave

Award Nominations
2009 Tony Award Best Revival of a Musical
2009 Tony Award Best Actress in a Musical (Josefina Scaglione)
2009 Tony Award Best Lighting Design in a Musical (Howell Binkley)
2009 Drama Desk Award Outstanding Revival of a Musical
2009 Drama Desk Award Outstanding Featured Actress in a Musical (Karen
Olivo)

Awards Won
2009 Tony Award Best Featured Actress in a Musical (Karen Olivo)
2009 Theatre World Award (Josefina Scaglione)

Discography of Complete Show Recordings

West Side Story: 1957 Original Broadway Cast (remastered). Carol Lawrence, Larry Kert, Chita Rivera, and Art Smith. 1998 by Sony (also Columbia Broadway Masterworks). B000056TB2.

Green, Johnny, dir. *1965 Original Motion Picture Soundtrack* (remastered 2004). *West Side Story* Orchestra, George Chakiris, Marni Nixon, Betty Wand, Tucker Smith, Natalie Wood, Jimmy Bryant, and Russ Tamblyn. 2004 by Sony (also Columbia Broadway Masterworks). B00023GGK8. 1992 by Sony. B0000027WF.

Bernstein, Leonard, David Stahl, dirs. *West Side Story: 1985 Studio Cast Recording*. José Carreras, Kiri Te Kanawa, Tatiana Troyanos, Kurt Ollman, and Marilyn Horne. 1991, 1998 by Deutsche Gramophon. B000009ON5 (also 2007 in special edition, B000TP5T6Q).

Edwards, John Owen, dir. *West Side Story: 1997 Studio Cast Recording*. National Symphony Orchestra, Irwin Kostal, Sid Ramin, Julie Paton, Paul Manuel, Tinuke Qlafimihan, Nicholas Warnford, and Nick Ferranti. 1997 by Jay Records. B000005BHB.

Schermerhorn, Kenneth, dir. *West Side Story: The Original Score*. Nashville Symphony Orchestra, Morrison, Eldred, Cooke, Dean, and San Giovanni. 2002 by Naxos American. B00006LI1Z.

Wordsworth, Barry, dir. *West Side Story: Cast Recording.* Royal Philharmonic Orchestra, Michael Ball, Lindsay Benson, Barbara Bonney, Mary Carewe, and Michael Dore. 2003 by Warner Classics. B00009RAG4.

Westernra, Hayley, Vittorio Grigolo, and Connie Fisher. *West Side Story: 50th Anniversary Cast Recording.* 2007 by Decca. B000UNMUCS.

West Side Story: The New Broadway Cast Recording. Josefina Scaglione, Matt Cavenaugh, and Karen Olivo. 2009 by Sony Classics. B0021X5158.

Bibliography

SPECIAL COLLECTIONS AND ARCHIVES

Leonard Bernstein Collection. Library of Congress Music Division, Washington, DC.

Cheryl Crawford Collection. New York Public Library Theatre Division, New York.

Harold Prince Collection, New York Public Library Theatre Division, New York.

Jerome Robbins Collection. New York Public Library Dance Division, New York.

Stephen Sondheim Collection. State Historical Society of Wisconsin, Madison, Wisconsin.

Roger Stevens Collection. Library of Congress, Music Division, Washington, DC.

NEWSPAPERS

London Daily Herald

London Daily Mail

London Daily Sketch

London Evening Standard

London News Chronicle

London Observer

London Sunday Times

Manchester Guardian

New York Daily News

New York Herald Tribune

New York Journal American

New York Morning Telegraph

New York Post

New York Sunday News

New York Times

New York World Telegram

Newark Sun News

Variety

Wall Street Journal

Washington Daily News

Washington Evening Star

Washington Post and Times Herald

BOOKS, ARTICLES, THESES, AND DISSERTATIONS

Adams, Michael Charles. "The Lyrics of Stephen Sondheim: Form and Function." PhD diss., Northwestern University, 1980.

Albright, Daniel. *Berlioz's Semi-Operas: "Roméo et Juliette" and "La damnation de Faust."* Rochester, NY: University of Rochester Press, 2001.

Altman, Rick. *Genre, The Musical: A Reader.* London: Routledge and Kegan Paul, 1981.

Álvarez, José Hernández. "The Movement and Settlement of Puerto Rican Migrants within the United States, 1950–1960." *International Migration Review* 2, no. 2 (1968): 40–51.

Amberg, George. *Ballet in America: The Emergence of an American Art.* New York: Mentor, 1951.

Ames, Evelyn Perkins. *A Wind from the West: Bernstein and the New York Philharmonic Abroad.* Boston: Houghton Mifflin, 1970.

Andre, Don Alan. "Leonard Bernstein's *Mass* as Social and Political Commentary on the Sixties." Doctor of Music diss., University of Washington, 1979.

Au, Susan. *Ballet and Modern Dance.* London: Thames and Hudson, 1988.

Aubrey, Elliott H. *Pillars of Support.* Austin: Hogg Foundation for Mental Hygiene, 1956.

L'Avant-Scène. "Broadway: Republic of the Spectacle." Special issue, *Avant-Scène,* 1987.

Babbitt, Milton. "Who Cares If You Listen?" *High Fidelity,* February 1958, 38–40.

Bailey, Robert, ed., *Prelude and Transfiguration from "Tristan und Isolde."* New York: Norton, 1985.

Banfield, Stephen. *Sondheim's Broadway Musicals.* Ann Arbor: University of Michigan Press, 1993.

Bellman, Jonathan, ed. *The Exotic in Western Music.* Boston: Northeastern University Press, 1998.

Bergeron, Katherine, and Philip V. Bohlman, eds. *Disciplining Music: Musicology and Its Canons.* Chicago: University of Chicago Press, 1992.

Berle, Beatrice Bishop. *80 Puerto Rican Families in New York City: Health and Disease Studied in Context.* New York: Columbia University Press, 1958.

Bernstein, Burton. *Family Matters: Sam, Jennie and the Kids.* New York: Summit, 1982.

Bernstein, Leonard. *Findings.* New York: Simon and Schuster, 1982.

———. *The Infinite Variety of Music.* New York: Simon and Schuster, 1966.

———. Interview by Susan Lacy, date unknown. *Reaching for the Note.* DVD. Directed by Susan Lacy. New York: Winstar, 1998.

———. *The Joy of Music.* New York: Simon and Schuster, 1959.

———. *Latin American Fiesta*. Recording notes. Reissued as Sony Classical SMK 60571.

———. *Leonard Bernstein's Young People's Concerts*. Edited by Jack Gottlieb. New York: Anchor, 1992 (originally published 1962 and 1970 by Simon and Schuster).

———. "Speaking of Music." *Atlantic*, December 1957), 104–6.

———. *The Unanswered Question: Six Talks at Harvard*. Cambridge, MA: Harvard University Press, 1976.

———. *The Unanswered Question*. VHS. New Jersey: Kultur, 1992.

Bernstein, Leonard, and Gene Krupa. "Has Jazz Influenced the Symphony?" *Esquire*, February 1947, 47, 152–53.

Bernstein, Leonard, and Terence McNally, Arthur Laurents, Jerome Robbins, and Stephen Sondheim. "Dramatists Guild Round Table Series, Landmark Symposium: *West Side Story*," *Dramatists Guild Quarterly* (1985): 11–25.

Block, Geoffrey. "The Broadway Canon from *Show Boat* to *West Side Story* and the European Operatic Ideal." *Journal of Musicology* 11 (1993): 525–44.

———. "Frank Loesser's Sketchbooks for *The Most Happy Fella*." *Musical Quarterly* 73 (1989): 60–78.

———. "*West Side Story*: The Very Model of a Major (Canonic) Modern Musical." In *Enchanted Evenings: The Broadway Musical from "Show Boat" to Sondheim*. Oxford: Oxford University Press, 1997.

Boelzner, David E. "The Symphonies of Leonard Bernstein: An Analysis of Motivic Character and Form." Master's thesis, University of North Carolina, 1978.

Bonds, Mark Evan. *A History of Music in Western Culture*. Upper Saddle River, NJ: Prentice Hall, 2003.

Bordman, Gerald. *American Musical Comedy: From "Adonis" to "Dreamgirls."* New York: Oxford University Press, 1982.

———. *American Musical Theatre: A Chronicle*. New York: Oxford University Press, 1978.

Boroff, Edith. "Origin of the Species: Conflicting View of American Musical Theater History." *American Music* 2, no. 4 (Winter 1984): 101–11.

Brett, Philip, Elizabeth Wood, and Gary C. Thomas, eds. *Queering the Pitch: The New Gay and Lesbian Musicology*. New York: Routledge, 1994.

Briggs, John. *Leonard Bernstein: The Man, His Work, and His World*. Cleveland, OH: World Publishing, 1961.

Brodkin, Karen. *How Jews Became White Folks and What That Says about Race in America*. New Brunswick, NJ: Rutgers University Press, 1998.

Burkholder, Peter J., Donald J. Grout, and Claude Palisca. *A History of Western Music*. 8th ed. New York: W. W. Norton, 2009.

Burma, John H. *Spanish-Speaking Groups in the United States*. Duke University Press Sociological Series 9. Durham, NC: Duke University Press, 1954.

Burton, Humphrey. "Bernstein and the British: A Tempestuous Affair." *BBC Music Magazine*, May 1994, 20.

———. "Bernstein's *West Side Story*: A Session Report." *Gramophone*, April 1985, 1195–96.

———. *Leonard Bernstein*. New York: Doubleday, 1994.

Burton, William Westbrook. "Bernstein on Broadway: Carol Lawrence on *West Side Story*." In *Conversations about Bernstein*, by William Westbrook Burton, 167–89. New York: Oxford University Press, 1995.

Carcaterra, Lorenzo. *Sleepers*. New York: Ballantine, 1995.

Cardona, Luis A. *The Coming of the Puerto Ricans*. Washington, DC: Unidos, 1974.

Carter, Tim. *"Oklahoma!" The Making of an American Musical*. New Haven, CT: Yale University Press, 2007.

Castiglione, Enrico. *A Life for Music: Conversations with Leonard Bernstein*. Translated by Eva Reisinger. Berlin: Henschel, 1993.

Challender, James Winston. "The Function of the Choreographer in the Development of the Conceptual Musical: An Examination of the Work of Jerome Robbins, Bob Fosse, and Michael Bennett on Broadway between 1944 and 1984." PhD diss., Florida State University, 1986.

Chapin, Schuyler. *Leonard Bernstein: Notes from a Friend*. New York: Walker, 1992.

———. "Leonard Bernstein: The Television Journey." *Television Quarterly* 25, no. 2 (1991): 13–19.

Chase, Gilbert. *The American Composer Speaks: A Historical Anthology, 1770–1965.* Baton Rouge: Louisiana State University Press, 1966.

———. *America's Music, from the Pilgrims to the Present.* 3rd rev. ed. Urbana: University of Illinois Press, 1987.

———. *The Music of Spain.* 2nd rev. ed. New York: Dover, 1959.

———. "Towards a Total Music Theatre." *Arts in Society* 6, no. 1 (1969): 26–29.

Chenault, Lawrence. *The Puerto Rican Migrant in New York City.* New York: Columbia University Press, 1938.

Chesney-Lind, Meda. "Doing Feminist Criminology." *The Criminologist* 13, no. 4 (1988): 1–17.

Ciccone, Kathleen. *A Study of the Development of Dance in the American Musical Theater.* Master's thesis, University of Colorado at Boulder, 1980.

Citron, Marcia J. *Gender and the Musical Canon.* Cambridge: Cambridge University Press, 1993.

Citron, Stephen. *The Musical from the Inside Out.* Chicago: Ivan R. Dee, 1992.

Clum, John M. *Something for the Boys.* New York: St. Martin's Press, 1999.

Cocchi, Jeanette Frances. "Lehman Engel's Criteria for Libretti as Applied to Four Musical Adaptations of Shakespeare's Plays on the Broadway Stage." PhD diss., New York University, 1983.

Cone, Molly. *Leonard Bernstein.* New York: Crowell, 1970.

Conrad, Jon Alan. "Bernstein, Leonard," "Candide," "A Quiet Place," and "West Side Story." In *New Grove Dictionary of American Music,* edited by H. Wiley Hitchcock and Stanley Sadie. New York: Macmillan, 1986.

———. "Bernstein on Disc II: The Composer." *Opera Quarterly* 9, no. 1 (Fall 1992): 1–23.

———. "*Candide*: The Most Confused of All Possible Worlds." *Opus* 3, no. 1 (1986): 23–25, 62.

———. "Glitter and Be Gay." *Musical Times* 136 (1995): 346–47.

———. "Style and Structure in Published Songs by George Gershwin, Published 1924–1938." PhD diss., Indiana University, 1985.

Copland, Aaron, and Vivian Perlis. *Copland: 1900 through 1942.* London: Faber and Faber, 1984.

Cottle, William Andrew, Sr. "Social Commentary in Vocal Music in the Twentieth Century as Evidenced by Leonard Bernstein's *Mass.*" Doctor of Arts diss., University of Northern Colorado, 1978.

Crawford, Cheryl. *One Naked Individual: My Fifty Years in the Theatre.* Indianapolis: Bobbs Merrill, 1977.

Crawford, Richard. *America's Musical Life: A History.* New York: Norton, 2001.

Dame, Robert G. "The Integration of Dance as a Dramatic Element in Broadway Musical Theatre." Master's thesis, University of Nevada–Las Vegas, 1995.

Deimler, Kathryn Mary George. "Quartal Harmony: An Analysis of Twelve Piano Compositions by Twentieth-Century Composers." PhD diss., New York University, 1981.

Dennhardt, Gregory. "The Director-Choreographer in the American Musical Theatre." PhD diss., Urbana: University of Illinois, 1978.

Diamond, David. Interview with the author, tape. July 14, 2002. Rochester, New York.

Dizikes, John. *Opera in America: A Cultural History.* New Haven, CT: Yale University Press, 1993.

Drabkin, William. "Stephen Sondheim." In *New Grove Dictionary of Music and Musicians.* Vol. 17. New York: Macmillan, 1980.

Druxman, Michael. *The Musical: From Broadway to Hollywood.* New York: Barnes, 1980.

Duany, Jorge. "Popular Music in Puerto Rico: Toward an Anthropology of *Salsa.*" *Latin American Music Review* 5, no. 2 (1984): 186–216.

Dubner, Stephen J. "The Pop Perfectionist." *New York Times Magazine,* November 9, 1997, 43.

Dusella, Reinhold, and Helmut Loos, eds. *Leonard Bernstein: Der Komponist.* Bonn: Boosey and Hawkes, 1989.

Ellingston, John R. *Protecting Our Children from Criminal Careers.* New York: Prentice Hall, 1948.

Engel, Lehman. *The American Musical Theater: A Consideration.* New York: Macmillan, 1975.

———. *The Making of a Musical.* New York: Macmillan, 1977.

———. *Words with Music: The Broadway Musical Libretto.* New York: Schirmer Books, 1981.

Evett, Robert. "Music: Bernstein's *Romeo and Juliet.*" *New Republic,* September 9, 1957, 21.

Ewen, David. *Leonard Bernstein.* London: W. H. Allen, 1967.

———. *New Complete Book of the American Musical Theatre.* New York: Holt, Rinehart and Winston, 1970.

———. *The Story of America's Musical Theater.* Rev. ed. Philadelphia: Chilton, 1968.

Ferracuti, Franco, Simon Dinitz, and Esperanza Acosta de Brenes. *Delinquents and Nondelinquents in the Puerto Rican Slum Culture.* Columbus: Ohio State University Press, 1975.

Fifield, Christopher. "Appreciation: Leonard Bernstein." *Musical Times* 132, no. 1775 (January 1991): 706.

Fitzpatrick, Joseph. *Puerto Rican Americans: The Meaning of Migration to the Mainland.* Englewood Cliffs, NJ: Prentice Hall, 1971.

Fleisher, Belton M. *The Economics of Delinquency.* Chicago: Quadrangle, 1966.

Fluegel, Jane. *Bernstein Remembered.* New York: Carroll and Graf, 1991.

Forte, Allen. *The American Popular Ballad of the Golden Era, 1924–1950.* Princeton, NJ: Princeton University Press, 1995.

Fraser, Barbara Means. "The Dream Shattered: America's Seventies Musicals." *Journal of American Culture* 13, no. 3 (1989): 31–37.

———. "A Structural Analysis of the American Musical Theatre between 1955 and 1965: A Cultural Perspective." PhD diss., University of Oregon, 1982.

Freddie Sateriale's Big Band, *Broadway Latin American Party: Cha chas, Merengues and Mambos,* Newark: Pirouette Records, 1956.

Freedland, Michael. *Leonard Bernstein.* London: Harrap, 1987.

Friedlander, Kate. *The Psycho-Analytical Approach to Juvenile Delinquency: Theory, Case Studies, Treatment.* New York: International Universities Press, Inc., 1960.

Gänzl, Kurt. *The Encyclopedia of the Musical Theatre.* 2 vols. American ed. New York: Schirmer Books, 1994.

Gänzl, Kurt, and Andrew Lamb. *Gänzl's Book of the Musical Theatre.* London: Bodley Head, 1988.

Garebian, Keith. *The Making of "West Side Story."* Toronto: ECW Press, 1995.

Gilbert, James. *A Cycle of Outrage: America's Reaction to the Juvenile Delinquent in the 1950s.* New York: Oxford University Press, 1986.

Glasser, Ruth. *My Music Is My Flag: Puerto Rican Musicians and Their New York Communities, 1917–1940.* Berkeley: University of California Press, 1995.

Glazer, Nathan. *Beyond the Melting Pot: The Negroes, Puerto Ricans, Jews, Italians, and Irish of New York City.* Cambridge, MA: MIT Press, 1963.

Glueck, Sheldon, and Eleanor Glueck. *Delinquents in the Making: Paths to Prevention.* New York: Harper, 1952.

———. *One Thousand Juvenile Delinquents.* Cambridge, MA: Harvard University Press, 1934.

Gordon, Eric. *Mark the Music: The Life and Work of Marc Blitzstein.* New York: St. Martin's Press, 1989.

Gordon, Joanne. *Art Isn't Easy: The Theatre of Stephen Sondheim.* New York: Da Capo, 1992.

Gottfried, Martin. *Broadway Musicals.* New York: H. N. Abrams, 1979.

———. *Opening Nights: Theater Criticism of the Sixties.* New York: Putnam, 1969.

Gottlieb, Jack. *Bernstein on Broadway.* New York: Schirmer, 1981.

———, ed. *Leonard Bernstein: A Complete Catalog of His Works: Celebrating His 70th Birthday.* New York: Jalni, 1988.

———. "The Music of Leonard Bernstein: A Study of Melodic Manipulations." Doctor of Music diss., University of Illinois at Urbana-Champaign, 1964.

———. "Symbols of Faith in the Music of Leonard Bernstein." *Musical Quarterly* 66 (1980): 287–95.

Gottfried, Martin. *Broadway Musicals*. New York: H. N. Abrams, 1979.

———. *Opening Nights: Theater Criticism of the Sixties*. New York: Putnam, 1969.

Gradante, William. "Seis." In *New Grove Dictionary of Music and Musicians*. London: Macmillan, 2001.

Gradenwitz, Peter. *Leonard Bernstein: The Infinite Variety of a Musician*. New York: Oswald Wolff Books, 1987.

Grant, Mark. *The Rise and Fall of the Broadway Musical*. Boston: Northeastern University Press, 2004.

Grauch, Arlene Evangelista. "A Comparison of Four Stage and Motion Picture Production Costumes Designed by Irene Sharaff." PhD diss., University of Michigan, 1988.

Green, Stanley. *Broadway Musicals, Show by Show*. Milwaukee, WI: H. Leonard Books, 1985.

———. *Encyclopedia of the Musical Film*. New York: Oxford University Press, 1988.

———. *Encyclopedia of the Musical Theatre*. New York: Dodd, Mead, 1976.

———. "*Oklahoma!* Its Origins and Influence." *American Music* 2, no. 4 (Winter 1984): 88–94.

———. *The World of Musical Comedy: The Story of the American Musical Stage*. New York: Da Capo, 1984.

Grismer, Kay L. "Cheryl Crawford Presents . . . A History of Her Broadway Musical Productions, 1936–1949." PhD diss., Wayne State University, 1993.

Gruen, John. *Bernstein: Complete Works for Solo Piano*. Recording notes. Pro Arte PAD 109, 1983.

———. *The Private World of Leonard Bernstein*. New York: Viking Press, 1968.

Gruver, Bert. *The Stage Manager's Handbook*. 1952. Revised by Frank Hamilton. New York: Drama Book Publishers, 1972.

Guernsey, Otis L. *Broadway Song and Story: Playwrights/Lyricists/Composers Discuss Their Hits*. New York: Dodd, Mead, 1985.

———, ed. *Playwrights, Lyricists, Composers on Theater*. New York: Dodd, Mead, 1974.

Guest, Ann Hutchinson. "The Golden Age of the Broadway Musical: A Personal Reminiscence." *Dance Chronicle* 16, no. 3 (1993): 323–71.

Handlin, Oscar. *The Newcomers: Negroes and Puerto Ricans in a Changing Metropolis.* Cambridge, MA: Harvard University Press, 1959.

Hapgood, Robert. "*West Side Story* and the Modern Appeal of *Romeo and Juliet.*" In *Deutsche Shaekspeare-Gesellschaft West Jahrbuch 1972,* 99–112. Heidelberg: Quelle and Meyer, 1972.

Harman, Chris Paul. *Amerika.* Program Note. New Music Concerts, May 26, 2001.

———. "Composer to Composer." Interview by Paul Steenhuisen in October 2001. *The Whole Note,* November 1–December 7, 2001.

Harmon, Charles. "Editor's Note." In *West Side Story.* New York: Amberson/Boosey and Hawkes, 1994.

Harper, Richard C. *The Course of the Melting Pot Idea to 1910.* New York: Arno Press, 1980.

Harris, Conwell Ray, Jr. "Unifying Techniques in the *Anniversaries* of Leonard Bernstein." Doctor of Music diss., Louisiana State University and Agricultural and Mechanical College, 1993.

Harris, Richard E. *Delinquency in Our Democracy.* Los Angeles: Wetzel, 1954.

Hathaway, Starke H., and Elio D. Monachese. *Analyzing and Predicting Juvenile Delinquency with the MMPI.* Minneapolis: University of Minnesota Press, 1953.

Hendrickson, Robert C., and Fred J. Cook. *Youth in Danger.* New York: Harcourt, Brace, 1956.

Herbert, Peggy Stewart. "A Comparison of Gounod's Opera *Roméo et Juliette* and Bernstein's *West Side Story.*" Master's thesis, Maryville College, 1981.

Heyl, Alice von. "Die *West Side Story* im Musikunterricht." *Musik und Bildung* 20, no. 2 (February 1988): 110–16.

Hiemenz, J. "Bernstein Conducts *West Side Story.*" *Musical America* 107, no. 2 (1987): 27–28.

Hirsch, Foster. *Harold Prince and the American Musical Theatre.* Cambridge: Cambridge University Press, 1989.

Hirst, David. "The American Musical and the American Dream: From *Show Boat* to Sondheim." *New Theatre Quarterly* 1, no. 1 (1982): 24–38.

Hischak, Thomas. *American Musical Theatre Song Encyclopedia.* Westport, CT: Greenwood Press, 1995.

———. *Stage It with Music: An Encyclopedic Guide to the American Musical Theatre.* Westport, CT: Greenwood Press, 1993.

———. *Word Crazy: Broadway Lyricists from Cohan to Sondheim.* New York: Praeger, 1991.

Hollis, Alpert. *Broadway! 125 Years of Musical Theatre.* New York: Little, Brown, 1991.

———. *The Life and Times of "Porgy and Bess": The Story of an American Classic.* New York: Knopf, 1990.

Horowitz, Joseph. "Professor Lenny—Leonard Bernstein's Young People's Concerts." *New York Review of Books* 40, no. 11 (June 10, 1993): 39–44.

———. *Understanding Toscanini: How He Became an American Culture-God and Helped Create a New Audience for Old Music.* Berkeley: University of California Press, 1987.

Horowitz, Mark Eden. *Sondheim on Music: Minor Details and Major Decisions.* Lanham, MD: Scarecrow Press, 2003.

Huber, Eugene R. "Stephen Sondheim and Harold Prince: Collaborative Contributions to the Development of the Modern Concept Musical, 1970–1981." PhD diss., New York University, 1990.

Huck, William. "Review: *Bernstein: A Biography* by Joan Peyser." *Opera Quarterly* 5, no. 4 (1987–1988): 95–99.

Hummel, David. *The Collector's Guide to the American Musical Theatre.* Metuchen, NJ: Scarecrow Press, 1984.

Ilson, Carol. "Harold Prince, Producer/Director." PhD diss., City University of New York, 1985.

Jackson, Gertrude. "*West Side Story*: Thema, Grundhaltung, und Aussage." *Maske und Kothurn* 16, no. 1 (1970): 97–101.

Jackson, Richard. "Leonard Bernstein." In *New Grove Dictionary of Music and Musicians*. Vol. 2. New York: Macmillan, 1980.

Johnson, John Andrew. "Gershwin's 'American Folk Opera': The Genesis, Style, and Reception of *Porgy and Bess*." PhD diss., Harvard University, 1996.

Juvenile delinquents from the University Settlement House, interview, ca. 1958. Tape, Harold Prince Collection, New York Public Library Theatre Division, New York.

Kahn, Alfred J. *For Children in Trouble: An Exploratory Study of Major Problems Facing New York City Services*. New York: Citizens' Committee for Children of New York City, Inc., 1957.

Kaiser, Charles. *The Gay Metropolis, 1940–1996*. Boston: Houghton Mifflin, 1997.

Keiler, Allan. "Bernstein's *The Unanswered Question* and the Problem of Musical Competence." *Musical Quarterly* 64 (1978): 195–222.

Kerman, Joseph. "A Few Canonic Variations." *Critical Inquiry* 10 (1983): 107–26.

———. *Opera as Drama*. New York: Knopf, 1956.

Kilroy, David Michael. "Kurt Weill on Broadway: The Postwar Years (1945–1950)." PhD diss., Harvard University, 1992.

Kimball, Robert. "The Road to *Oklahoma!*" *Opera News* 58, no. 1 (July 1993): 12–16, 18–19.

Kimball, Robert, and Tommy Krasker, eds. *Catalog of the American Musical: Musicals of Irving Berlin, George and Ira Gershwin, Cole Porter, Richard Rodgers, and Lorenz Hart*. Washington, DC: National Institute for Opera and Music Theater, 1988.

Kirle, Bruce. *Unfinished Showbusiness: Broadway Musicals as Works-in-Process*. Carbondale, IL: Southern Illinois University Press, 2005.

Kislan, Richard. *Hoofing on Broadway: A History of Show Dancing*. New York: Prentice Hall, 1987.

———. *The Musical: A Look at the American Musical Theater*. Englewood Cliffs, NJ: Prentice Hall, 1980.

Knapp, Raymond. *The American Musical and the Formation of National Identity*. Princeton, NJ: Princeton University Press, 2005.

Koch, Gerhard. "Europa ich komme! Portrait des Komponisten, Dirigenten und Showstars Leonard Bernstein." *Musik und Medezin* 1 (1979): 40–44.

Koestenbaum, Wayne. *The Queen's Throat: Opera, Homosexuality and the Mystery of Desire.* New York: Poseidon Press, 1993.

Korrol, Virginia E. Sánchez. *From Colonia to Community: The History of Puerto Ricans in New York City, 1917–1948.* Westport, CT: Greenwood Press, 1983.

Kowalke, Kim H. "Kurt Weill, Modernism, and Popular Culture." *Modernism/ Modernity* 2 (1995): 27–69.

Krummel, D. W. *Bibliographical Handbook of American Music.* Urbana: University of Illinois Press, 1987.

Kvaraceus, William C. *Juvenile Delinquency.* What Research Says to the Teacher 15. Washington, DC: Department of Classroom Teachers, American Research Association, 1958.

Laird, Paul R. "The Best of All Possible Legacies: A Critical Look at Bernstein, His Eclecticism, and *Candide*." *Ars Musica Denver* 4, no. 1 (Fall 1991): 30–39.

Lander, Bernard. *Towards an Understanding of Juvenile Delinquency.* New York: Columbia, 1954.

Laurents, Arthur. *Mainly on Directing: "Gypsy," "West Side Story," and Other Musicals.* New York: Knopf, 2009.

———. *Original Story By: A Memoir of Broadway and Hollywood.* New York: Applause, 2000.

Lawrence, Carol. *Carol Lawrence: The Backstage Story.* New York: McGraw-Hill, 1990.

Lawrence, Greg. *Dance with Demons: The Life of Jerome Robbins.* New York: G. P. Putnam, 2001.

Ledbetter, Steven, ed. *Sennets and Tuckets: A Bernstein Celebration.* Boston: BSO Association, 1988.

Lee, George Shelby. "*Romeo and Juliet* and *West Side Story*: A Comparative Study." Master's thesis, Arkansas State University, 1967.

Leemann, Sergio. *Robert Wise on His Films: From Editing Room to Director's Chair.* Los Angeles: Silman-James Press, 1995.

Lehan, Carole Marie. *The Dialectical Lyrics of Stephen Sondheim in Selected Musicals.* Master's thesis, University of Maryland at College Park, 1990.

Lehman, Ernest. *West Side Story: Screenplay.* Photocopy of typed film script. Burbank, CA: Screenplay Library Services, 1960.

Lewis, Oscar. *La Vida: A Puerto Rican Family in the Culture of Poverty—San Juan and New York.* New York: Random House, 1966.

Livermore, Ann. *A Short History of Spanish Music.* London: Duckworth, 1972.

Locke, Ralph P. "The Border Territory between Classical and Broadway: A Voyage around and about *Four Saints in Three Acts* and *West Side Story*," In *Liber Amirorum Isabelle Cazeaux: Symbols, Parallels and Discoveries in Her Honor*, edited by Paul-André Bempéchat, 179–226. Hillsdale, NY: Pendragon Press, 2005.

———. "Constructing the Oriental 'Other': Saint–Säens's *Samson et Dalila*." *Cambridge Opera Journal* 3, no. 3 (1991): 261–302.

———. "Reflections on Orientalism in Opera and Musical Theater." *Opera Quarterly* 10, no. 1 (1993): 48–64.

Lockett, Edward B. *The Puerto Rico Problem.* New York: Exposition Press, 1964.

LoMonaco, Martha Schmoyer. "Broadway in the Poconos: The Taniment Playhouse, 1921–1960." PhD diss., New York University, 1988.

Long, Robert Emmet. *Broadway: The Golden Years: Jerome Robbins and the Great Choreographer-Directors.* New York: Continuum, 2001.

Loza, Steven. *Tito Puente and the Making of Latin Music.* Urbana: University of Illinois Press, 1999.

Luther, Sigrid. "The *Anniversaries for Solo Piano* by Leonard Bernstein." Doctor of Music diss., Louisiana State University, 1986.

Malzberg, Benjamin. *Mental Disease among the Puerto Rican Population of New York State, 1960–1961.* Albany, NY: Research Foundation for Mental Hygiene, 1965.

Mandelbaum, Ken. *Not Since "Carrie": Forty Years of Broadway Musical Flops.* New York: St. Martin's Press, 1991.

Maney, Ruth. "*West Side Story*: Its Predecessors and Importance in American Musical Theatre History." Master's thesis, Southern Illinois University, Carbondale, 1993.

Martin, John M. *Juvenile Vandalism*. Springfield, IL: Charles C. Thomas, 1961.

Marvin, William. "Simulating Counterpoint in Broadway Musicals: The Quodlibet as Compositional Procedure." Paper read at the Joint Meeting of the American Musicological Society and Society for Music Theory, Columbus, OH, 2002.

Mata, Homero Leonel. "The Non-Verbal Communication of Bernardo in *West Side Story*." Master's thesis, San Diego State University, 1987.

McCall, Sarah B. "The Musical Fallout of Political Activism: Government Investigations of Musicians in the United States, 1930–1960." PhD diss., University of North Texas, 1993.

mcclung, bruce d. "American Dreams: Analyzing Moss Hart, Ira Gershwin, and Kurt Weill's *Lady in the Dark*." PhD diss., University of Rochester, 1994.

———. *"Lady in the Dark": Biography of a Musical*. New York: Oxford University Press, 2007.

McCorkle, Lloyd W., Albert Elias, and F. Lovell Bixby. *The Highfields Story*. New York: Henry Holt, 1958.

McGovern, Dennis, and Deborah Grace Winer. *Sing Out Louise! 150 Stars of the Musical Theatre Remember 50 Years on Broadway*. New York: Schirmer, 1993.

McMillin, Scott. *The Musical as Drama: A Study of the Principles and Conventions behind Musical Shows from Kern to Sondheim*. Princeton, NJ: Princeton University Press, 2006.

Medved, Harry, and Michael Medved. *The Golden Turkey Awards: Nominees and Winners, the Worst Achievements in Hollywood History*. New York: Perigee, 1980.

———. *The Hollywood Hall of Shame: The Most Expensive Flops in Movie History*. New York: Perigee, 1984.

Miller, Arthur. "The Bored and the Violent." *Harper's*, November 1962, 50–52.

Miller, D. A. *Place for Us: Essay on the Broadway Musical*. Cambridge, MA: Harvard University Press, 1998.

Miller, Raphael Francis. "The Contributions of Selected Broadway Musical Theatre Choreographers: Connolly, Rasch, Balanchine, Holm, and Alton." PhD diss., University of Oregon, 1984.

Mills, C. Wright. *New York's Newest Migrants*. New York: Harper, 1950.

Moore, Bernice Miburn. *Juvenile Delinquency: Research, Theory, and Comment.* Washington, DC: Association for Supervision and Curriculum Development, 1958.

Moore, James Walter. "A Study of Tonality in Selected Works by Leonard Bernstein." PhD diss., Florida State University, 1984.

Moore, Kenneth J. "The Mixing and Miking of Broadway: Changing Values of a Sound/Music Aesthetic." In *To the Four Corners: A Festschrift in Honor of Rose Brandel*, edited by Ellen C. Leichtman, 169–88. Warren, MI: Harmonie Park Press, 1994.

Moore, MacDonald Smith. *Yankee Blues: Musical Culture and American Identity.* Bloomington: Indiana University Press, 1985.

Mordden, Ethan. *Better Foot Forward: The History of the American Musical Theatre.* New York: Grossman Publishing, 1976.

——. *Broadway Babies: The People Who Made the American Musical.* New York: Oxford University Press, 1983.

Most, Andrea. "'Big Chief Izzy Horowitz': Theatricality and Jewish Identity in the Wild West." *American Jewish History* 87, no. 4 (1999): 314–41.

——. "'We Know We Belong to the Land': Jews and the American Musical Theater." PhD diss., Brandeis University, 2001.

——. "'You've Got to Be Carefully Taught': The Politics of Race in Rodgers and Hammerstein's *South Pacific.*" *Theatre Journal* 52 (2000): 307–37.

Nevares, Dora, Marvin E. Wolfgang, and Paul E. Tracy. *Delinquency in Puerto Rico: The 1970 Birth Cohort Study.* New York: Greenwood Press, 1990.

New York Board of Education. *The Puerto Rican Study, 1953–1957; A Report on the Education and Adjustment of Puerto Rican Pupils in the Public Schools of the City of New York.* New York: New York Board of Education, 1958.

New York University Graduate School of Public Administration and Social Service, *The Impact of Puerto Rican Migration on Governmental Services in New York City.* New York: New York University Press, 1957.

Office of the Coordinator of Spanish-American Catholic Action at the Chancery Office of the New York Archdiocese. Conference on the Spiritual Care of Puerto Rican Migrants, San Juan, Puerto Rico, April 11–16, 1955.

Orgass, S. "Der Teil als Ganzes/das Ganze als Teil: *West Side Story.*" *Musik und Bildung* 26 (May–June 1994): 26–31.

Owen, Heidi. "Broadway Opera and Opera on Broadway: 1934–1958." PhD diss., University of Rochester, in progress.

Padilla, Elena. *Up From Puerto Rico.* New York: Columbia University Press, 1958.

Page, Christopher Jarrett. "Leonard Bernstein and the Resurrection of Gustav Mahler." PhD diss., University of California at Los Angeles, 2000.

Pahlen, Kurt, ed. *Leonard Bernstein: "West Side Story."* Mainz, Germany: Schott, 2002.

Pan American Union. *Music of Latin America.* Washington, DC: General Secretariat of the Organization of American States, 1963.

Parakilas, James. "How Spain Got a Soul." In *The Exotic in Western Music,* edited by Jonathan Bellman, 137–193. Boston: Northeastern University Press, 1998.

Paul, John. "*West Side Story* in Japan." *Dance Magazine,* April 1965, 35–38.

Peyser, Joan. *Bernstein: A Biography.* New York: Beech Tree Books, 1987.

Powell, Jenifer Harrison. "Unity and Tragedy in the Libretto and Score of Leonard Bernstein's *West Side Story.*" Master's thesis, Southern Methodist University, 1994.

Prado, Perez. *Mambos for Piano.* New York: Southern Music Publishing Company, 1955.

Prince, Harold. *Contradictions: Notes on Twenty-Six Years in the Theatre.* New York: Dodd, 1974.

Rand, Christopher. *The Puerto Ricans.* New York: Oxford University Press, 1958.

Reidy, John P., and Norman Richards. *People of Destiny: Leonard Bernstein.* Chicago: Children's Press, 1967.

Rittwagen, Marjorie. *Sins of Their Fathers.* Boston: Houghton Mifflin, 1958.

Roberts, John Storm. *The Latin Tinge.* Oxford: Oxford University Press, 1979.

Robinson, Alice M. *Betty Comden and Adolph Green: A Bio-Bibliography.* Westport, CT: Greenwood Press, 1994.

Rockwell, John. *All-American Music: Composition in the Late Twentieth Century.* New York: Alfred A. Knopf, 1983.

Rodgers, Richard. *Musical Stages: An Autobiography.* New York: Random House, 1975.

Rorem, Ned. "Leonard Bernstein: An Appreciation." *Tempo* 175 (December 1990): 6–9.

Rosenberg, Bernard, and Ernest Harburg. *The Broadway Musical: Collaboration in Commerce and Art.* New York: New York University Press, 1993.

Rozen, Brian D. "Leonard Bernstein's Educational Legacy." *Education Digest* 57 (December 1991): 70–71.

Salisbury, Harrison. *The Shook-Up Generation.* New York: Harper and Row, 1958.

Schiff, David. "Re-hearing Bernstein." *Atlantic,* June 1993, 55–58.

Schlundt, Christena L. *Dance in the Musical Theatre: A Guide.* New York: Garland, 1989.

Schoettler, Eugenia Volz. "From a Chorus Line to *A Chorus Line*: The Emergence of Dance in the American Musical Theatre." PhD diss., Kent State University, 1979.

Schubert, Gisela. "Leonard Bernstein." In *Die Musik in Geschichte und Gegenwart.* Kassel: Bärenreiter, 1994: 688–710.

Schuller, Gunther. "Afro-Cuban Jazz." In *New Grove Dictionary of Jazz.* Vol. 1. London: Macmillan, 1988.

Secrest, Meryle. *Leonard Bernstein: A Life.* New York: Alfred A. Knopf, 1994.

———. *Stephen Sondheim: A Life.* New York: Alfred A. Knopf, 1998.

Senior, Clarence. *The Puerto Ricans: Strangers—Then Neighbors.* New York: Random House, 1966, reprinted 1968 and 1969.

Sharp, Paul M., and Barry W. Hancock. *Juvenile Delinquency: Historical, Theoretical, and Societal Reactions to Youth.* Englewood Cliffs, NJ: Prentice Hall, 1995.

Sheng, Bright. "Leonard Bernstein: Portrait of the Artist by a Young Man." *Ear* 14, no. 8 (November 1989): 34–38.

Shulman, Irving. *West Side Story.* New York: Simon and Schuster, 1961.

Simas, Rick. *The Musicals No One Came to See: A Guidebook to Four Decades of Musical Comedy Casualties on Broadway, Off-Broadway, and in Out-of-Town Tryout, 1943–1983.* New York: Garland, 1987.

Simeone, Nigel. *Leonard Bernstein: "West Side Story."* Aldershot, UK: Ashgate, 2009.

Snyder, Linda June. "Leonard Bernstein's Works for the Musical Theatre: How the Music Functions Dramatically." Doctor of Music diss., University of Illinois at Urbana-Champaign, 1982.

Solie, Ruth, ed. *Musicology and Difference: Gender and Sexuality in Musical Scholarship.* Berkeley: University of California Press, 1993.

Sondheim, Stephen. "Theatre Lyrics." In *Playwrights, Lyricists, Composers on Theater,* edited by Otis L. Guernsey. New York: Dodd, Mead, 1964.

Sorrentino, Joseph N. *The Concrete Cradle.* Los Angeles: Wollstonecraft, 1975.

Spurrier, James Joseph. "The Integration of Music and Lyrics with the Book in the American Musical." PhD diss., Southern Illinois University, Carbondale, 1979.

Stearns, David Patrick. "Something's Coming! (Behind the Scenes of Recording Sessions for Bernstein's *West Side Story*)." *Opera News,* April 13, 1985, 10–13.

Stearns, Peter J. *American Cool: Constructing a Twentieth-Century Emotional Style.* New York: New York University Press, 1994.

Steel, Ronald. *New Light on Juvenile Delinquency.* New York: H. W. Wilson, 1967.

Stempel, Larry. "The Musical Play Expands." *American Music* 10, no. 2 (1992): 136–69.

Steyn, Mark. *Stephen Sondheim.* London: Josef Weinberger and Music Theatre International of New York, 1993.

Stoop, Norma McLain. "Tony & Larry & Bobby & Larry." *After Dark,* June 1971, 40–43.

Subotnik, Rose Rosengard. *Deconstructive Variations: Music and Reason in Western Society.* Minneapolis: University of Minnesota, 1996.

Summers, Louis Jeriel, Jr. "The Rise of the Director/Choreographer in the American Musical Theatre." PhD diss., University of Missouri–Columbia, 1976.

Suskin, Steven. *Opening Night on Broadway: A Critical Quotebook of the Golden Era of the Musical Theatre.* New York: Schirmer, 1990.

———. *Show Tunes, 1905–1991: The Songs, Shows and Careers of Broadway's Major Composers.* New York: Limelight, 1992.

Swain, Joseph Peter. *The Broadway Musical: A Critical and Musical Survey.* New York: Oxford University Press, 1990.

Swayne, Steven. "Hearing Sondheim's Voices." PhD diss., University of California, Berkeley, 1999.

———. "Sondheim: An American Composer Only a British Musicologist Can Love?" *Indiana Theory Review* 21 (2000): 231–52.

Teachout, Terry. "Reviews: Bernstein Triumphs in a Miscast *West Side Story.*" *Hi Fidelity/Musical America* 35, no. 11 (1985): 54.

Thomas, Naomi. "Bernstein's *Unanswered Question*: A Journey from Deep Linguistic Structure to the Metaphysics of Music." Master's thesis, Florida Atlantic University, 2004.

Thomas, Piri. *Down These Mean Streets.* New York: Knopf, 1967.

———. *Memoirs of Bernardo Vega: A Contribution to the History of the Puerto Rican Community in New York.* New York: Monthly Review Press, 1984.

Thompson, Frank T. *Robert Wise: A Bio-Bibliography.* Westport, CT: Greenwood Press, 1995.

Thornhill, William Robert. "Kurt Weill's Street Scene." PhD diss., University of North Carolina at Chapel Hill, 1990.

Tischler, Barbara L. *An American Music: The Search for an American Musical Identity.* New York: Oxford University Press, 1986.

Torres, Andrés. *Between Melting Pot and Mosaic.* Philadelphia: Temple University Press, 1995.

Van Leer, David. "What Lola Got: Cultural Carelessness on Broadway." In *The Other Fifties: Interrogating Midcentury American Icons,* edited by Joel Freeman, 171–96. Urbana: University of Illinois Press, 1997.

Van Vechten, Carl. *The Music of Spain.* New York: Knopf, 1918.

Wakefield, Dan. *Island in the City: Puerto Ricans in New York.* New York: Corinth, 1959.

Walsh, David, and Len Platt. *Musical Theater and American Culture.* Westport, CT: Praeger, 2003.

Weber, J. F. *Leonard Bernstein.* Utica, NY: Weber, 1975.

Weber, William. "The History of Musical Canon." In *Rethinking Music*, edited by Nicholas Cook and Mark Everist, 336–55. New York: Oxford University Press, 2001.

Weber, Wolfgang. "*West Side Story*, 1981." *Österreichische Musikzeitschrift* 36, nos. 7–8 (July–August 1981): 376–79.

Wells, Elizabeth A. "*West Side Storie(s):* Perspectives on an American Musical." PhD diss., New York: University of Rochester, 2004.

Wentworth, Brenda Kathryn. "Six Designers Look at Costuming for the Broadway Stage: 1958–1970." PhD diss., University of Missouri–Columbia, 1990.

Wilder, Alec. *American Popular Song—The Great Innovators 1900–1950.* New York: Oxford University Press, 1972.

Williams, Mary E., ed. *Readings on "West Side Story."* Greenhaven Literary Companion to American Literature Series. San Diego: Greenhaven, 2001.

Wolf, Stacy. *A Problem Like Maria: Gender and Sexuality in the American Musical.* Ann Arbor: University of Michigan Press, 2002.

Wolfe, Tom. *Radical Chic and Mau–Mauing the Flak Catchers.* New York: Farrar, Straus and Giroux, 1970.

Yablonsky, Lewis. *The Violent Gang.* New York: Macmillan, 1963.

Zadan, Craig. *Sondheim & Company.* 2nd ed., updated. New York: Da Capo, 1994.

Zangwill, Israel. *The Melting Pot.* New York: Macmillan, 1909.

Index

About the Author

Elizabeth A. Wells earned her bachelor's degree in music from the University of Toronto, with a concentration in history and literature of music. She then pursued a career in public broadcasting, working as a music programmer and producer of classical music programs for CJRT-FM in Toronto. In 1993, she entered the graduate program in musicology at the Eastman School of Music. Her doctoral work has been supported by three major fellowships, including the AMS-50 dissertation fellowship, the Elsa T. Johnson dissertation prize, and the Presser Award.

She has read papers at meetings of Feminist Theory and Music, the American Musicological Society (AMS), and the International Musicological Society. She has twice won the "Best Student Paper" from the New York State/St. Lawrence chapter of the AMS. Her work has been published in *Cambridge Opera Journal* and the *Journal of the American Musicological Society* and she is frequently interviewed about her work on CBC Radio.

Dr. Wells is currently associate professor and head of music at Mount Allison University, New Brunswick, Canada. Before that she taught music history at Mansfield University in Pennsylvania, the State University of New York at Geneseo, and the Eastman School of Music. In 2008, she won the Tucker Teaching Award, Mount Allison's highest recognition of teaching excellence, the Association of Atlantic Universities' Distinguished Teacher Award, and the 3M National Teaching Fellowship, which recognizes teaching excellence and educational leadership across Canada. Her research interests include music history pedagogy and both British and American musical theater of the 1950s.